Public Ethics at the European Commission

Since the early 2000s, reforms in the area of public ethics have represented a significant part in the European Commission's efforts to improve its internal governance and democratic legitimacy, and address the crisis of public confidence in European integration.

This book comprises a study of ethics and public integrity issues in the administrative services of the European Commission. The author traces the reforms implemented in this area since the early 2000s, and asks whether and how they have shaped Commission officials' thinking about appropriate behaviour in public office. Based on in-depth interviews and the use of vignettes, the book reveals that the influence of ethics regulations is subtle and full of contradictions: while a heightened awareness and discussion of ethical issues exists in the Commission nowadays, the topic is nonetheless often considered as a matter of "common sense". This book breaks new ground as the first analysis of ethics at the level of individual EU officials. It advances a new angle to the study of the Commission as an administrative actor, and sheds light on an important but under-researched component of its efforts to address criticism concerning democratic legitimacy. In the field of administrative ethics, the book tackles research gaps regarding the practice and impact of ethics policies within public organizations.

This text will be of key interest to scholars, students and practitioners of EU Studies/Politics, institutional reform, administrative ethics, and more broadly European governance and public policy.

Andreea Năstase is Assistant Professor in European Public Policy at Maastricht University, the Netherlands. She holds a PhD from the Central European University, Budapest.

Routledge Studies on Government and the European Union
Edited by Andy Smith,
University of Bordeaux, France

1   **The European Council and European Governance**
    The commanding heights of the EU
    Edited by François Foret and Yann-Sven Rittelmeyer

2   **The EU's Government of Industries**
    Markets, institutions and politics
    Edited by Andy Smith and Bernard Jullien

3   **Policy change in the Area of Freedom, Security and Justice**
    How EU institutions matter
    Edited by Florian Trauner and Ariadna Ripoll Servent

4   **The Mechanisms of Institutional Conflict in the European Union**
    Ludvig Norman

5   **Public Ethics at the European Commission**
    Politics, reform and individual views
    Andreea Năstase

Public Ethics at the European Commission

Politics, reform and individual views

Andreea Năstase

LONDON AND NEW YORK

First published 2017
by Routledge
2 Park Square, Milton Park, Abingdon, Oxon OX14 4RN

and by Routledge
711 Third Avenue, New York, NY 10017

Routledge is an imprint of the Taylor & Francis Group, an informa business

© 2017 Andreea Năstase

The right of Andreea Năstase to be identified as author of this work has been asserted by her in accordance with sections 77 and 78 of the Copyright, Designs and Patents Act 1988.

All rights reserved. No part of this book may be reprinted or reproduced or utilised in any form or by any electronic, mechanical, or other means, now known or hereafter invented, including photocopying and recording, or in any information storage or retrieval system, without permission in writing from the publishers.

Trademark notice: Product or corporate names may be trademarks or registered trademarks, and are used only for identification and explanation without intent to infringe.

British Library Cataloguing in Publication Data
A catalogue record for this book is available from the British Library

Library of Congress Cataloging-in-Publication Data
Names: Nastase, Andreea, author.
Title: Public ethics at the European Commission : politics, reform and individual views / Andreea Nastase.
Description: Abingdon, Oxon ; New York, NY : Routledge, 2017. | Series: Routledge studies on government and the European Union ; 5 | Includes bibliographical references and index.
Identifiers: LCCN 2016015213 | ISBN 9781138203785 (hardback) | ISBN 9781315470573 (ebook)
Subjects: LCSH: European Commission—Ethics. | European Commission—Officials and employees. | Political ethics—European Union countries.
Classification: LCC JN33.5 .N374 2017 | DDC 172/.4094—dc23
LC record available at https://lccn.loc.gov/2016015213

ISBN: 978-1-138-20378-5 (hbk)
ISBN: 978-1-315-47057-3 (ebk)

Typeset in Times New Roman
by Apex CoVantage, LLC

Printed and bound in Great Britain by
TJ International Ltd, Padstow, Cornwall

To my family

To my parents

Contents

List of illustrations ix
Acknowledgements x
List of abbreviations xii

Introduction 1

*Ethics management and corruption worldwide 3
Central concepts, limitations and some finer points 5
The analytical contribution of this book 7
The European Commission as a case study in ethics
   management 10
Research approach 11
Plan of the book 13*

1 Public ethics, socialization and the organizational profile of the European Commission 15

*1.1 A conceptual framework for addressing public ethics 15
1.2 Organizational socialization: learning ethics on the job 22
1.3 The officials of the European Commission and their organizational socialization 26
1.4 Conclusion 35*

2 Change, continuity and the politics of ethics reforms 39

*2.1 The compliance-integrity continuum 40
2.2 The development of ethics management in the European Commission services 41
2.3 The* Ethics Communication *and the delivery of change 49
2.4 Conclusion 59*

3 "You are the human face of the Commission": ethics translated in internal administrative practice — 62

　3.1 Ethics in internal communication: rules and the public image of the European Commission 63
　3.2 Ethics "hot spots" in the European Commission 67
　3.3 Conclusion 77

4 Individual views towards ethics in the European Commission — 80

　4.1 Methodological observations 80
　4.2 Individual positions on public ethics 83
　4.3 Ethics on the work-floor: commonalities, divergence and determinants 100
　4.4 Conclusion 110

5 Discussing "common sense": how ethics management shapes individual views towards ethics — 113

　5.1 Official communication and views from the work-floor 113
　5.2 Ethics as "common sense" 115
　5.3 Discussing ethics 118
　5.4 Conclusion 122

Conclusion — 125

Summary of findings 125
The limits of ethics management 129
The European Commission after ethics reforms 134
Outlook 137
Final remarks 140

References — 142
Index — 157

Illustrations

Figures

2.1	The compliance-integrity continuum	41
3.1	Types of ethics issues	68

Tables

1.1	Typology of integrity management instruments	21
1.2	Selected Directorate-Generals	33
4.1	Positions on freedom of expression	85
4.2	Positions on whistleblowing	90
4.3	Positions on meeting a lobbyist	95
4.4	Positions on the disclosure of information	98
4.5	Strict/flexible positions and nationality	103

Boxes

1.1	Values and ethical standards in the European Commission services	17
4.1	Vignette 1 "The Conference"	84
4.2	Vignette 2 "The Missing Files"	89
4.3	Vignette 3 "The Lobbyist"	93

Acknowledgements

Throughout this research project I received a great deal of intellectual and personal support, for which I express my deepest gratitude. First and foremost, I would like to thank Agnes Batory, who served as my PhD supervisor, and offered me outstanding guidance and continuous support over the years. Her feedback was always spot-on, constructive, and timely, and she allowed the intellectual space for my ideas to grow. I am also very grateful to Uwe Puetter for the thorough discussions and the input he has constantly provided, and to Nenad Dimitrijevic, whose observations have helped me navigate some thorny conceptual problems. I am forever indebted to the extraordinary people at the Department of Public Policy at the Central European University in Budapest, who have provided me with a nourishing intellectual home as a PhD student.

This project has been advanced in important ways through several research visits I undertook in Leuven, Maastricht, and Amsterdam. I owe my thanks for their hospitality and input to: Jeroen Maesschalck, Kim Loyens, Aneta Spendzharova, Thomas Conzelmann, Gjalt de Graaf, Annelies De Schrijver and Christoph Demmke. I am also very grateful to Sophie Vanhoonacker and Thomas Christiansen, who have supported this book from the beginning and provided valuable advice and encouragement through what has sometimes been a difficult process. I am furthermore grateful to the anonymous reviewer for very helpful and insightful comments, to Andy Smith, for his valuable and very timely help in putting the finishing touches on the manuscript, and to the editorial team at Routledge for their assistance. This book has benefited enormously from Michelle Cini's pioneering work on ethics in the European Commission. I thank Michelle for her constant support and for all our discussions, and especially for the first meeting in Bristol, which, to me, was very motivating and inspiring.

This book would not have been possible without the involvement of EU public officials. Although they must remain anonymous, I would like to thank all my interviewees for their time and openness, and for the many wonderful insights offered during our interviews. The time I spent walking the European quarter in Brussels was truly exceptional.

I am very grateful to all my friends and colleagues at the Central European University and the Faculty of Arts and Social Sciences at Maastricht University, who have made those past few years into a great experience. Special thanks is due to several people who have not only commented on my work, but also patiently supported me through the ups and downs of the research and writing process: Sara Svensson, Stefan Cibian, Elene Jibladze and Oana Lup. I am also much obliged to Teodora Danes and Adrien Elleboudt for their hospitality during my successive research trips to Brussels.

I would also like to express my gratitude for the financial and administrative assistance provided by the Central European University and the University of Maastricht.

Last but not least, I thank my family for their tremendous emotional support, patience, and faith in me.

Parts of this work have appeared previously as journal articles and are reproduced here with permission from Taylor & Francis Group. An early version of Chapter 2 has been published as Năstase, Andreea. 2013. "Managing Ethics in the European Commission Services." *Public Management Review* 15 (1): 63–81, and a small part of Chapter 1 has appeared previously in Năstase, Andreea. 2014. "Catering to Organizational Needs in Ethics Management: The Case of the European Commission." *International Journal of Public Administration* 37 (2): 93–105.

Abbreviations

AA	Appointing Authority
AD	Administrator
ALTER-EU	The Alliance for Lobbying Transparency and Ethics Regulation
AST	Assistant
AST/SC	Secretary/Clerk
CCP	Congé de convenance personnelle (leave on personal grounds)
CIE	Committee of Independent Experts
CPI	Corruption Perception Index
DG	Directorate-General
DG COMP	Directorate-General for Competition
DG ENV	Directorate-General for the Environment
DG HR	Directorate-General for Human Resources and Security
DG MARKT	Directorate-General for the Internal Market and Services
DG REGIO	Directorate-General for Regional Policy
DG TRADE	Directorate-General for Trade
ECHO	Directorate-General for Humanitarian Aid
EP	European Parliament
EPSO	European Personnel Selection Office
ETI	European Transparency Initiative
EU	European Union
IDOC	Investigation and Disciplinary Office of the European Commission
IT	information technology
MEP	Member of the European Parliament
NGO	non-governmental organization
NPM	New Public Management
OECD	Organisation for Economic Co-operation and Development
OLAF	The European Anti-Fraud Office
OS	organizational socialization
PSM	public service motivation
SG	Secretariat General
SNE	Seconded National Official
SR	Staff Regulations
TI	Transparency International

Introduction

During the past fifteen years, in the context of growing popular discontent and deteriorating legitimacy of the European Union, the European Commission has implemented substantial administrative reforms meant to improve its internal governance. Ensuring high standards of conduct for both Commissioners and staff members has been an important part of this effort. It came against accusations of blatant conflicts of interest and lobby capture, as well as juicy (and damaging) press scandals concerning the defrauding of the EU budget and officials treated to expensive gifts and free dinners in Brussels' top restaurants.

Many commentators trace the Commission's preoccupation with public ethics, and its administrative reform efforts more generally, to the dramatic resignation of the Santer Commission on March 15, 1999 (Cini 2004, 2007a, Kassim 2004, 2008, Ellinas and Suleiman 2008, Wille 2013). The resignation followed the scathing reports of the Committee of Independent Experts (CIE), which were commissioned by the European Parliament and exposed consistent evidence of fraud, mismanagement and nepotism in the Commission (CIE 1999a, 1999b). They concluded rather dramatically that "it is becoming difficult to find anyone [in the European Commission] who has even the slightest sense of responsibility" (CIE 1999a: 144). Predictably, the incoming Prodi Commission made it its business to clean up and modernize the organization. Commissioner Neil Kinnock was appointed to draft a reform program which was eventually fleshed out in 2000 as the *White Paper on Reforming the Commission* (also referred to as the White Paper, or the Kinnock reforms).

Although the Kinnock reforms did have a reactive quality, the evolution of the European Commission in later years has demonstrated its enduring concern with building systems and processes to uphold ethical behaviour. Kinnock's successor, Siim Kallas, continued the administrative reform with the well-publicized *European Transparency Initiative* (ETI), which contained, among others, measures to increase transparency in the use of EU funds and interest group activity, as well as rules and ethical standards for EU officials. The implementation of the ETI agenda continued during the second Barroso Commission, concomitantly with the introduction of amendments to the *Staff Regulations of Officials of the European Communities*, which strengthened conflict of interest prevention and the protection afforded to whistleblowers (i.e., insiders who report misbehaviour witnessed in their organizations). Finally, the current Commission, described by its president, Jean-Claude Juncker, as "the last chance Commission" to bring Europe closer to its citizens, has implemented within the first few months of its mandate obligations for Commissioners, their *cabinets*, and senior civil servants to make public on their respective web pages all meetings held with interest representatives.

The importance of the developments briefly sketched above should not be underestimated – they represent a part of the EU's prolonged bid to strengthen its democratic credentials and restore popular support for European integration. To elaborate, the European Commission – a remote, unelected executive body with far-reaching (and ever-growing) attributions – has been especially vulnerable to the accusations of "democratic deficit" that have plagued the EU since the early 1990s. Apart from successive treaty changes whereby external controls over the Commission were boosted (chiefly through the gradual empowerment of the European Parliament), the organization itself has also mounted a response to these legitimacy criticisms. The 2001 *White Paper on European Governance* bears mentioning here as a complex program meant to improve the quality of EU governance, by building a solid dialogue between the Commission and external stakeholders and boosting its openness, responsiveness and accountability across all tasks conferred on it by the treaties. The Kinnock reforms, mentioned above, targeted in turn the internal governance of the Commission, by aiming to create a "culture based on service" through far-reaching changes in the financial control and audit systems and personnel management and by rationalizing activity cycles within the Commission through the Strategic Planning and Programming System.

Ethics reforms should be understood as a part of these multilayered efforts at democratic legitimization. To be clear, ethics policies target the procedural or "throughput" legitimacy of public institutions, in other words what goes on within the "black box" of decision-making, between political input and policy output (on this point, see also Schmidt 2013: 6, Huberts 2014b: 269–271). They are predicated on the assumption that citizens' trust can be improved through the promotion of high behavioural standards among public office holders (Downe *et al.* 2013). Given that the Commission is already confronted with alarmingly low levels of citizen confidence,[1] it needs effective ethics policies and simply cannot afford the massive reputational damage (and subsequent loss of trust) inflicted by public scandals. It should be stressed that in this the stakes are particularly high for the Commission. While corruption scandals surely are damaging for any national-level executive, they represent a far greater threat for the Commission because its democratic legitimacy (and indeed that of the EU as a whole) is contested in ways that are unparallel at the national level. It is significant, thus, that while the Santer resignation remains the most traumatic scandal in the history of the organization, it is unfortunately not a singular occurrence. To give just one example that many readers will likely remember, in 2012 John Dalli, the Maltese Commissioner for Health and Consumer Policy, had to resign over improper dealings with tobacco lobbyists and suspicions of influence peddling. On a more general note, perceptions of corruption are currently widespread in the EU: a recent Eurobarometer has found that nearly 70 per cent of European citizens believe corruption is present in the European institutions (see TNS Opinion & Social 2014).

This book takes stock of the reforms implemented by the European Commission in the area of public ethics since the early 2000s. With a focus on the administrative levels of the organization, it asks whether – and how – such reforms have shaped Commission officials'[2] views regarding appropriate behaviour in public office. The investigation builds on the premise that such views are not static but can change and evolve over time – and, furthermore, that the organizational context is crucial to shaping this evolution. Two secondary questions are pursued as stepping stones: firstly, the book explores the body of institutional structures and procedures created by repeated waves of reforms, to show how the Commission defines and manages public ethics nowadays. Secondly, the book maps the views that Commission employees hold about public ethics, by analyzing their responses to three concrete scenarios depicting work-related ethical dilemmas. Based on this account, the influence of the ethics measures adopted at the Commission can be explored.

Ethics management and corruption worldwide

This book proposes an in-depth case study of the character and impact of public ethics reforms within one organization. However, the experience of the European Commission has a broader significance, since its engagement with such measures is aligned with a global trend towards "the institutionalization and formalization of public service ethics" (Lewis and Gilman 2005: 331). Since the mid-1970s, public organizations, first in the US and subsequently elsewhere in the world, have increasingly experimented with ethics policies. Covering a wide range of topics (dealings with lobbyists and members of the public, gifts and hospitality, ancillary activities and post-employment restrictions, whistleblowing – among others), they have now become standard practice. To give just one illustration, a survey conducted in 2000 revealed that all Member States of the Organisation for Economic Co-operation and Development (OECD) had adopted sets of values for public service (be it in the form of codes and/or legislation) and almost all provided communication and training activities on ethics issues. Requiring public servants to declare their personal financial interests was also commonplace, especially for elected officials and senior civil servants (OECD 2000). By 2009, most OECD countries (96.6 per cent) had in place procedures for public servants to report wrongdoing, and 86.2 per cent also had adopted specific protection measures for such individuals (OECD 2011). In the European Union, a 2007 survey found that "public service ethics is an issue that is taken seriously by every member state" (Moilanen and Salminen 2007: 30), although in terms of concrete measures countries found themselves at various stages of development. For instance, while most had in place value declarations or codes of conduct, and promoting ethics though human resource policies was common, only several Member States had established specialized agencies for dealing with ethics and integrity violations, or confidential integrity counsellors (Moilanen and Salminen 2007).

Ethics reforms have been introduced not only in national public administrations, but in international organizations as well, in keeping with a broader and generalized growth of internal oversight and accountability mechanisms in such bodies in the past fifteen years (see Klabbers 2013). The International Monetary Fund, for instance, has had a code of conduct for staff since 1998 and a distinct code of conduct for the members of its executive board since 2000; it established an Ethics Office and an internal independent Ombudsperson in 2000. Along very similar lines, the World Bank boasts a code of conduct entitled "Living Our Values" and has established an Office of Ethics and Business Conduct (which has run an Ethics Hotline since 2008). Symbolically, one of the Vice-Presidents of the Bank is charged with ensuring integrity. At the United Nations, an independent Ethics Office was set up in 2006, reporting directly to the Secretary-General. Significantly, like the European Commission, some international organizations have also turned to ethics reforms in the aftermath of corruption scandals. The UN Ethics Office, for instance, was established after it had been discovered that UN officials turned a blind eye to (and in some cases benefited from) the large-scale abuse of the Oil-for-Food Program, which had been launched in 1995 to allow Iraq to sell oil on the world market strictly to cover humanitarian needs – food, medicine and the like (Huberts *et al.* 2008: 241–242).

Finally, although the European Commission certainly remains a forerunner in what regards ethics reform, similar transformations have taken place in other European institutions as well. A 2007 study on conflict of interest regulation for high public office holders[3] found that the issue was covered to varying degrees in the Commission as well as the European Parliament, the European Court of Justice, the European Court of Auditors, the European Central Bank and the European Investment Bank (Demmke *et al.* 2007). A more recent and comprehensive assessment, which included all the institutions mentioned above (apart from the two banks), plus the European Council and Council of the European Union, the European Anti-Fraud Office, Europol, Eurojust, and the European Ombudsman, confirmed the existence of rules governing public actors' conduct across the board (TI-EU 2014).

The widespread popularity and use of ethics policies, as exemplified above, goes hand-in-hand with the global recognition of corruption as one of the most significant governance problems of today. Since the early 1990s, as the disastrous economic, social and political consequences of this phenomenon were being discerned, international anti-corruption regimes proliferated. Regional organizations such as the Council of Europe, the African Union, and the Organization of American States have all adopted anti-corruption conventions criminalizing certain acts, establishing preventive measures, and providing for international cooperation among signatory parties. On a global level, the OECD Anti-Bribery Convention was adopted in 1997, followed in 2003 by the UN Convention Against Corruption. Significantly, standards of conduct for public actors have represented an important plank in these codification processes, two illustrative examples being the UN-sponsored International Code of Conduct for Public Officials (1997) and the OECD Recommendation on Principles for Managing Ethics in the Public Service (1998). A multitude of non-governmental actors have also taken up the cause and contributed their part to this extensive web of conventions, monitoring arrangements and sanctions. The most notable is Transparency International (TI), the international NGO established in 1993 which describes itself as "the global coalition against corruption" and currently operates more than 100 national chapters (TI 2015a). At the level of policy practice, anti-corruption reforms became tightly bound to a relatively new agenda of major international donors and financial institutions to promote "good governance" in the recipient countries. As Huberts (2014a) notes, nowadays countries that seek financial assistance and developmental aid can expect to be regarded much less favourably if they don't commit to stamp out corruption. The EU itself has made wide use of anti-corruption conditionality not only in its external aid, but also in enlargement negotiations (most visibly with the accession of Romania and Bulgaria in 2007 and Croatia in 2013) and in the European Neighbourhood Policy.

With all this being said, it should be emphasized that public ethics has not exactly been discovered in the context of the global anti-corruption crusade: questions of right and wrong have always been linked to the exercise of power, simply because ethics is inextricably linked to choice. As Singer (1991: v) observes, "anyone who thinks about what he or she ought to do is, consciously or unconsciously, involved in ethics". What was new, however, was the idea that ethics could, and should, be *managed* "in the same breath and manner in which we talk about managing budgets, policies or people" Menzel (2001: 355). In other words, ethics came to be regarded not so much as an immutable characteristic of individuals in government, but as something that was amenable to manipulation through deliberate efforts, and therefore a domain of management in its own right. These ideas fit well not only with the general condemnation of corruption (as explained above), but also with certain trends in public administration reform. On the one hand, the boom of New Public Management (NPM) reforms in the 1980s and 1990s throughout the US, western Europe and the Commonwealth countries prompted fears that ethical standards in the public sector were failing as a result of introducing market-inspired practices. On the other hand, societal demands were changing, stressing more the need for forms of direct horizontal accountability of the administrator to the citizens. Instead of backtracking on these agendas, ethics management advocates found a solution in the design of ethics measures that would respond to the new challenges (Maesschalck 2004a: 468).

Central concepts, limitations and some finer points

Although the topic is expanded in Chapter 1, a brief explanation of the central concepts used in the book will be useful at this point. *Ethics* – or, rather, public ethics – is used here in a bounded sense, referring exclusively to appropriate behaviour in public office. It concerns the values which ground the operation of the public service: independence, objectivity, neutrality, loyalty, transparency etc. *Ethics management* is defined as "a systematic and conscious effort to promote organizational integrity" (Menzel 2005: 29). It is a regulatory exercise, as it represents purposeful action aimed at shaping individual conduct. Within organizations, such efforts are manifest in the creation of *ethics infrastructures*, or *ethics systems*, i.e., conglomerates of policy instruments, structures and processes (for instance, codes of conduct, conflict of interest policies, ethics training, integrity testing etc.) meant to sustain ethical conduct and prevent (and punish) integrity violations. Finally, I use the term *view* to describe – broadly speaking – what people think about ethics. In large part, the views explored here refer to judgements of acceptability regarding certain types of behaviour (i.e., what is ethical and what is not). But the term also covers related aspects, such as the justifications evoked in assessing acceptability, and opinions on what the "right" course of action would be.

A few observations are also in order as to the limits of this inquiry. First, the focus is on the administrative levels of the European Commission (i.e., the services), leaving aside the policy framework applicable to the College of Commissioners. Although there is a close relation of integrity (or lack thereof) between the political and administrative levels of an organization, the ethics of politicians and bureaucrats are substantively different, therefore requiring distinct management approaches (OECD 2009). This is indeed true of the Commission, which has two parallel systems in place, for Commissioners and officials, respectively (Cini 2007b: 138). In this analysis, I focus on the administrative level for two reasons. Firstly, the majority of ethics reforms in the Commission have been in this area. Secondly (and more importantly), officials in the administrative services spend most of their working lives in the Commission, and therefore it is with respect to this group that the influence of ethics management can be best assessed.

Furthermore, the research endeavour focuses strictly on EU officials' views and does not go further to make inferences about their actual behaviour. In the social sciences, the link between attitudes and behaviour is notably contested. Particularly in empirical ethics research, where actual behaviour is always difficult to investigate, there might be a temptation to use attitudes as proxies and predictors. This is not my purpose, although the book does include accounts of what officials report they *would* do when faced with certain ethics issues.

Finally, this book takes an empirical, not normative, perspective. As such, it does not go as far as making value judgements regarding Commission officials' views but is limited to a mapping exercise. Therefore, it is beyond my purpose to determine whether those who work for the Commission are ethical or not – rather, I simply explore their *interpretations* of ethical behaviour. By extension, the book does not offer a diagnosis of the ethical health of the Commission overall or the effectiveness of its ethics system. Admittedly, these points are perhaps the most obvious and significant, considering the themes treated here. Tackling them, however, would require the explicit adoption of normative criteria by which the ethical quality of the organization (and its employees) would be assessed, which would undercut a more open(-minded) exploratory exercise into how individuals understand and reason through ethics at work. Therefore, instead of offering a diagnostic, the book focuses on the element of process, and in doing so it seeks to improve our understanding of *how* ethics policies are enacted and how they are received by and influence the target group.

The analytical contribution of this book

Despite its importance as a policy issue, public ethics has rarely been mainstreamed in research on the European Commission (or other European institutions, for that matter). For example, monographs of the European civil service treat questions of ethics rather marginally, typically by discussing the controversial practices associated with Member States' influence on staffing policy of the Commission: the informal system of "national quotas"; the national flagging of key posts; the cabinets as national bastions; and the circumvention of official recruitment procedures by way of *parachutage, piston* etc. (see, for instance, Coombes 1970, Page 1997, Stevens and Stevens 2001, Spence and Stevens 2006). Likewise, the little anthropological research done on the Commission (e.g., Abéles *et al*. 1993, McDonald 1997, Shore 2000) discusses standards of behaviour only as they relate to the cultural aspects of life in the EU bureaucracy. Most commonly, analyses revolve around the role of diverging national traditions and the Commission's culture of informality. Shore's later work (2005, 2007) is somewhat of an exception, as it addresses head-on corruption in the EU civil service, in light of the dramatic events in 1999. The author concludes rather gravely that the "EU's technocratic elite appears to be transforming from a 'class in itself' to a 'class *for* itself' [...]. The danger for Europe is that this emerging elite ossifies into a self-serving caste, or European *'Nomenklatura'*" (Shore 2005: 150, emphasis in original).

Apart from this, there is also a small body of research (Dercks 2001, Cini 2004, 2007a, 2007b, 2008, 2010, Hine and McMahon 2004, Giusta 2006, Năstase 2013) which focuses specifically on public ethics in the European Commission, using a public management perspective. Michelle Cini's book (2007a) represents the most comprehensive study to date concerning the Commission's response to accusations regarding its ethical standards, after the Santer resignation in 1999. It demonstrates that the Commission emerged from the Kinnock reforms with many of the elements of an ethics infrastructure in place. The approach, however, has tended to be reactive, which largely explains the absence of systematic thinking on the issue and thus the "Commission itself not having a clear notion of where its ethics framework began and ended" (Cini 2007a: 213). Dercks (2001) and Hine and McMahon (2004) similarly find that following the Santer resignation, rules have been put in place. However, concerns linger as to whether the reform would succeed in reaching the organizational culture and aligning it with the new standards.

The present book contributes to this body of literature on ethics policy at the European Commission. It offers a chronological update – the coverage of existing contributions is largely limited to the Kinnock years,[4] whereas here the analysis extends to Siim Kallas' mandate as well (and, partially, to that of his successor). The update on policy framework is important, because during this time a major recalibration in the Commission's treatment of ethics (in the services) was attempted – therefore revisiting the conclusions of previous studies seems necessary. More significantly, however, the book takes further the ethics research agenda, as it shows how ethics reforms have played out in the internal life of the Commission. By exploring employees' views and interpretations of concrete ethics questions on the job, it breaks new ground as the first study of ethics at the level of individual Commission officials.

This being said, ethics reforms are part of a broader transformation process undergone by the European Commission since the early 2000s, and need to be understood in this context. On the one hand, they are but one component in a more consistent and vast effort of the Commission to modernize itself as a public bureaucracy. The changes operated during Neil Kinnock's mandate represent the largest reform program in the history of the organization – to paraphrase Kassim (2008), an impossible mission but one accomplished nonetheless. Unsurprisingly, they have attracted considerable scholarly attention (see Dimitrakopoulos 2004, Kassim 2004, 2008, Levy 2004, 2006, Balint *et al.* 2008, Bauer 2008, 2009, 2012, Ellinas and Suleiman 2008, Schön-Quinlivan 2008, 2011, among others). Notwithstanding the few exceptions discussed above, public ethics represents a blind spot in this literature, although it has been an important consideration in the Kinnock reforms. Therefore, this book, with its focus on ethics, complements existing research on administrative reform at the European Commission by advancing a relatively new angle to the study of this organization as an administrative actor. It also speaks to a more general approach in the field of European studies that translates theories and concepts from public administration scholarship to the study of European institutions (for a review, see Trondal 2007, Trondal and Peters 2013).

On the other hand, as already discussed, ethics reforms represent a democratic legitimation instrument. As such, they have contributed to a wider democratic accountability architecture that has grown within and around the Commission in the past years (see Wille 2013 for an extensive overview). They are also closely connected to other efforts meant to align the work of the Commission to the global "good governance" agenda, namely the boosting of institutional transparency and public access to information, particularly in relation to interest intermediation (see Héritier 2003, Curtin and Meijer 2006, Greenwood and Halpin 2007, Naurin 2007, Greenwood and Dreger 2013), as well as the adoption of participatory models of policymaking (see, for instance, Smismans 2006, Quittkat 2011, Kohler-Koch 2012, Kohler-Koch and Quittkat 2013). This book complements the research reviewed above, by zooming in on a less investigated component of the response mounted by the European Commission in the face of widespread criticism regarding its democratic deficit.

Finally, this book improves our understanding of the internal life of the contemporary European Commission. In exploring the thinking of officials regarding public ethics, it complements existing literature on the opinions and beliefs of Commission personnel in the first decade of the twenty-first century (in particular Kassim *et al.* 2013). It also highlights that public ethics has become a significant consideration feeding into internal processes of staff management and socialization, which the Commission had to re-invent in order to cope with the twin pressures of enlargement and administrative reform (on this, see Ban 2013).

The research presented here is also significant for the field of administrative ethics, in particular the literature dealing with the regulation of standards of conduct in government-type settings. In this area, research has lagged behind policy developments considerably. Efforts have generally gone into mapping the policies, and the array of policy instruments employed in ethics management. To this end, large surveys have been conducted – for instance, OECD's successive surveys (2000, 2011), which describe the measures adopted in its member countries, and Bossaert and Demmke (2005), Demmke *et al.* (2007) and Moilanen and Salminen (2007), which focus on ethics management in EU Member States and, partially, in European institutions. Other interesting comparative work has been conducted in the same vein but on a smaller scale, e.g., Behnke's (2002) study on ethics measures adopted in Germany, which she contrasts with the Anglo-Saxon approach, Smith's (2004) comparison of the ethics infrastructures in the US and China Palidauskaite (2005) and Palidauskaite *et al.* (2010) on the codes of conduct adopted in eastern European countries. For the most part, the literature tends to be practitioner oriented, and as such contains a mix of descriptive and prescriptive elements.

While substantial knowledge has been generated as to the type of instruments and approaches employed in ethics management, as several authors note (Lawton and Doig 2006, Six and Lawton 2013, Huberts *et al.* 2014), little is yet known about the way they function, or what impact they can have on public organizations and individuals working therein. The problem is not that such questions have not been addressed, but rather that researchers (in the US as well as in Europe) have overwhelmingly tended to focus on one, or several distinct policy instruments – for instance, municipal audit committees (West and Berman 2003), ethics training (West and Berman 2004, Van Montfort *et al.* 2013), ethics officers (Smith 2003), codes of conduct and ethical guidelines (Kaptein and Schwartz 2008, Christensen and Lægreid 2011). This kind of segmented approach is of limited value. Practitioners stress that public integrity instruments and policies should be combined into a coherent and unitary system (see OECD 1996, 2009) – the implication being that evaluation exercises need to focus on this system as a whole, rather than its individual components (on this point, see Six and Lawton 2013: 641).

The book addresses the lack of knowledge regarding the practice and impact of ethics management within organizations in several ways. Firstly, by adopting a holistic approach and offering a detailed account of how the Commission's system has been developed and implemented, it highlights the numerous difficulties and contradictions which characterize, in practice, the process of managing ethics in an organization. In particular, the analysis conducted here demonstrates that while the views of Commission officials are influenced by the arguments and concerns present in the official discourse on ethics, the vast majority remain unconvinced of the utility of ethics policies in their day-to-day work. This represents somewhat of a paradox, and calls into question the current enthusiasm surrounding such measures. The book also demonstrates that the politics behind ethics reform need to be taken seriously. It is perhaps obvious that such exercises can easily become politicized, but evaluations of ethics policy (such as they are) rarely account systematically for how politics actually matters. The analysis conducted here shows that politics matters a lot – it was key not only to bringing ethics to the Commission's reform agenda, but also during subsequent stages, as it shaped the internal implementation practice and the way staff members understood and reacted to the reforms.

The European Commission as a case study in ethics management

A few words are also in order on the significance of the European Commission as a case study. Notwithstanding its highly distinctive character as a public bureaucracy, the Commission represents a good instance to explore the above-mentioned aspects in the *practice* of ethics management, for several reasons.

Firstly, the Commission nowadays possesses an impressive arsenal of ethics policy instruments which are, by-and-large, typical and in line with international best practice.[5] Moreover, its experience with ethics reforms exemplifies a frequent pattern in national and international bureaucracies. Like many other (public and private) organizations, the Commission embarked upon ethics reforms after an external shock – in its case, the disgraceful resignation of the Santer Commission in March 1999. Introducing ethics measures in response to legitimacy crises is fairly typical – as Dobel (1993: 173) explains, "ethics codes and legislation [. . .] are usually born in scandal and passed as much to reassure the public as to accomplish any good". In fact, administrative reforms more generally are often driven by external pressures and as such constitute highly politicized exercises (Peters 2001, Pollitt and Bouckaert 2004). Furthermore, the ethics regime which emerged from the Kinnock reforms was largely compliance based. This option for a hard-line approach in the aftermath of corruption scandals is also common – for instance, Lawton and Macaulay (2009) and Roberts (2009) trace such patterns in the UK and US, respectively. And finally, Siim Kallas' attempts to redefine ethics management as the promotion of an ethical culture at the workplace (rather than crude control) is also in line with developments in OECD countries to move from compliance-based to softer, value-based approaches (OECD 2000, 2009). Because of all these commonalities, the European Commission can be considered *a typical case* (cf. Yin 2003), which can bring to light lessons for public bureaucracies facing similar conditions.

Of course, in many other ways, the European Commission is not at all a typical bureaucracy. It represents one of the most powerful international executives in the world, situated "at the heart" of a *sui generis* political system (Nugent 1997). It employs a highly multinational staff (over 33,000 officials from twenty-eight Member States), covers an impressive breadth of policy competences and exercises a mix of legislative, executive and quasi-judicial functions which would, in a national context, be split among different types of institutions. All this amounts to an internally heterogeneous organization. This differentiates the Commission from most of its national and international counterparts, but it also makes it a particularly interesting site for studying ethics management "in action". To be sure, it is unlikely that the multitude of ethics policy interventions to which the Commission has been subject over the years would not have some impact on its employees. However, due to internal heterogeneity, it is far less clear whether this would actually lead to convergence towards a common ethos. From this perspective, the Commission represents *a hard case* in ethics management, in the sense that its organizational complexities represent significant challenges (well over average) to instilling a common line among staff.

In conclusion, what makes the Commission a good choice for studying the practice of ethics management is that it showcases a typical policy intervention in an atypical organizational context. In the Commission's case, then, the so-called Sinatra inference may be applied – the impact that ethics management has in this environment can be assumed to hold with less complicated structures as well.

Research approach

The book uses *organizational socialization* (OS) as a theoretical lens. This choice reflects a view of organizations as powerful social environments, which can shape individual attitudes and beliefs. In particular, OS is defined as a process of social learning through which an individual comes to appreciate the knowledge, values and expected behaviours associated with an organizational role (see Louis 1980). Like other aspects of one's organizational role, ethics (understood here as role morality) is a subject in this learning process. Put in those terms, ethics management is analyzed as an exercise that shapes the way officials are socialized within the European Commission and which consequently can inform the development (adjustment) of their views regarding public ethics.

Following up on these points, the research project was executed in two distinct phases. The first phase was a preparatory one, dedicated to mapping the Commission's ethics system, documenting how the relevant policies were implemented, and uncovering concrete ethics issues that were considered to be particularly "tricky" in practice, and which had earned the Commission public criticism. The second phase was dedicated to mapping the views of Commission officials regarding public ethics, their perception of the specific (ethical) challenges of the job, as well as their experience with, and perception of the ethics policy instruments.

The book uses qualitative research methods, relying on a combination of interviews and document analysis. The participants interviewed in the two research phases described above differ significantly, as do the sampling strategies which were employed. For the first phase a panel of knowledgeable informants (Weiss 1994) was used, specifically twenty-eight internal ethics experts of the European Commission. This group of informants was chosen because they were the only ones with first-hand information on the development, implementation and context of ethics reforms in the Commission. Most interviewees belonged to the administrative services. Some of them were responsible for the coordination of ethics policy throughout the Commission, but most (i.e., the so-called ethics correspondents) had their attributions confined to a specific Directorate-General (DG).[6]

For the second phase of the project, a maximum variation sample was used, specifically thirty officials who did not have any specific ethics expertise but were working for the Commission in various other capacities. As the name suggests, this kind of sample is composed by deliberately selecting participants who represent instances of all important dissimilar types present in the wider population (Weiss 1994, Patton 2002, Rubin and Babbie 2009). Concretely, the sample used here exhibits variation on four key dimensions – officials' nationality, their organizational position (DG affiliation), previous professional background (public or private sector) and type of employment (temporary or permanent contract) – all of which represent factors that can generate differences in individuals' thinking about ethics and their socialization experiences. Therefore, the sample reflects, within some predefined limits, the heterogeneous nature of the European Commission, which, as argued before, poses above-average challenges in terms of ethics management.

All interviews had a semi-structured format and were conducted following preset interview guides, between March 2010 and December 2011 (a small number of follow-up interviews took place in June-July 2015). The interviews conducted during the second phase included three vignettes, i.e., detailed hypothetical scenarios on which respondents were asked to comment. Essentially, this was the methodological instrument used to elicit officials' views regarding ethics in public office. The vignettes presented ambiguous situations, which led respondents to engage in a process of reasoning, through which their views were revealed. Chapter 4 includes a detailed discussion on the characteristics of this methodological instrument and its deployment in the book. It is enough to point out, for now, that the decision to use vignettes was mainly motivated by their potential to minimize social desirability bias. Vignettes can do this because respondents are more comfortable with commenting on fictional situations than with answering direct questions about their own beliefs and experience (Finch 1987, Renold 2002). Furthermore, the vignettes used here presented ambiguous situations, where there was no predefined "right answer" to them, which afforded respondents some neutral space to genuinely consider and express their positions vis-à-vis the behaviour presented in these scenarios.

Before moving on, it is important to consider the difficulties connected to empirical ethics research. Ethics is a sensitive and loaded subject, which poses above-average problems in terms of access. Simply put, it is challenging to enlist people in a research project which could potentially be detrimental not only to themselves, but also to the organization in which they work. This is a straightforward self-protection issue on the participants' side, which requires that the researcher establishes firmly his/her credibility and trustworthiness. Research ethics is also a critical question here, because the data produced in this kind of project can, if treated incorrectly, bring harm to the participants.

Several measures were taken to address these problems. Firstly, all interviews are confidential. Names were replaced with randomly assigned numbers. The internal ethics experts in the Commission are referred to as "ethics officials", whereas the rest of the interviewees are referred to simply as "officials". In some cases, additional measures were necessary to maintain confidentiality, for instance obscuring officials' nationality and certain details regarding their job attributions. There were also cases where, sadly, the information simply could not be used. Secondly, interview protocols were strictly respected. The purpose and the conditions of the interview were explained in detail to participants. Interviews were taped only when there was explicit agreement, and in all other cases detailed reports were prepared on the same day the interviews were carried out. Thirdly, participants were recruited on a purely voluntary basis. The ethics experts were contacted using the Commission's online staff directory and, in some cases, additional internal sources. The other officials were recruited through internal channels, using recommendations from ethics experts and the snowballing technique.

Finally, it should be noted that being based on an entirely qualitative project, this book cannot claim representativeness in the same terms as a statistical work would. However, as noted above, the two groups of interviewees were selected in such a way as to allow for findings to be extrapolated if not to the entire organization, then to significant parts of it. Furthermore, what may be lost in terms of representativeness is gained through the depth and richness of data. The book presents not only a fine-grained account of how ethics management is carried out at the European Commission, but also an in-depth and nuanced report of the way officials perceive and think about ethics in everyday work-life.

Plan of the book

The book is structured around five chapters. Drawing on public administration scholarship, Chapter 1 defines the core concepts and sets out the analytical framework within which the research questions proposed here will be addressed. It also covers the organizational characteristics and complexities of the European Commission and shows how they translate in choices of research design. The remaining chapters are dedicated to the analysis of empirical data. Chapter 2 examines the structure and the evolution of the ethics management system which applies to the European Commission administrative services, by zooming in on the reform packages initiated by two Commissioners who covered successively the administrative affairs portfolio: Neil Kinnock (1999–2004) and Siim Kallas (2004–2009). It also accounts for the politics behind these reforms, especially the Commission's repeated confrontations with the European Parliament, which had proven eager to pose as an anti-corruption champion ever since the Santer resignation. Chapter 3 asks how the Commission has adapted internally to these changes. It analyzes the micro-level administrative practice connected to ethics management in the Commission, and in doing so it shows how public ethics was presented to organizational members, and the kind of messages and meanings which were associated with it. Chapter 4 is a longer piece which offers an in-depth and nuanced account of Commission officials' views towards public ethics. It uses the empirical data yielded by interviews with "regular" Commission officials (grouped, as explained before, in a maximum variation sample) to trace the patterns which pervade officials' ethics thinking and to map the lines of convergence and divergence. Chapter 5 describes the mechanisms by which the ethics management system of the European Commission influences its employees' views towards ethics. It explores whether, and how, officials' views reflect the specific concerns and framings which pervade the "official" organizational discourse on ethics (identified in Chapter 3), and discusses their direct experience with, and perception of, ethics measures. Finally, the conclusion summarizes the main research findings and relates them to broader research agendas in the fields of EU integration and administrative ethics, respectively. It also spells out lessons of general value for policy practitioners and organizations involved in ethics reforms.

Notes

1 Eurobarometer results for the past five years (2015–2011) show that on average, 43.87 per cent of European citizens distrust the European Commission (compared with 36.79 per cent who tend to trust it, and 19.33 per cent who are undecided/don't know) – see more on the European Commission Eurobarometer Interactive tool at: http://ec.europa.eu/COMMFrontOffice/PublicOpinion/index.cfm/Chart/index.
2 The term "official" is used here to refer to the administrative staff of the Commission, regardless of grade or type of employment.
3 The term "high public office holders" designates high-ranking public officials who are not members of the civil service. In a national context, this meant Members of the Government (ministers), elected Members of Parliament, Justices of the Supreme Court and Members or Directors of the Court of Audit and Central or National Banks (Demmke *et al.* 2007: 15). The institutions covered at the EU level are enumerated above.
4 But see Cini (2008) for an analysis of the European Transparency Initiative, and Cini (2014) for an up-to-date analysis of ethics management on the political levels of the Commission (i.e., the College of Commissioners).
5 The Bossaert and Demmke (2005) survey, which included all (then twenty-five) Member States, as well as the European Commission, demonstrates that the Commission's policy instruments inventory is fairly similar to that of most national public administrations in the EU.
6 The Directorate-Generals are the main organizational units of the Commission. Each DG is made up of several directorates, and these in turn consist of several administrative units.

1 Public ethics, socialization and the organizational profile of the European Commission

Drawing on public administration scholarship, this chapter defines the core concepts and sets out the analytical framework of the book. It also covers the organizational characteristics and complexities of the European Commission and shows how they translate in choices of research design.

The chapter begins by offering a basic framework for thinking about ethics in an organizational context. Specifically, it defines public ethics and its parameters, as well as the related concepts of unethical behaviour and ethical dilemmas, and shows how the latter can be used to elicit individual views relating to ethics. After establishing these conceptual reference points, I draw on the rather practitioner-oriented literature on ethics management to explore what this exercise consists of and what its boundaries are. The second section of the chapter discusses the theoretical perspective of organizational socialization and shows how it relates to ethics and ethics management and how it will be deployed in the book. It ends with a couple of observations on the treatment of socialization in EU integration research (which differs from the approach used here).

The last section of the chapter introduces the reader to the European Commission and, drawing on previous points, tackles questions of research design. It has been argued in the Introduction that the Commission represents a hard case in ethics management, because its internal heterogeneity poses above-average challenges in terms of instilling a common line among staff. In line with this argument, interviewees were selected to form a sample which reflects this internal heterogeneity – I present here the criteria on which participants were selected for in-depth interviews, the characteristics of the sample and some details regarding the recruitment method.

1.1 A conceptual framework for addressing public ethics

Generally speaking, morality is a term which refers to the nature of good or bad, right or wrong. *Ethics* (or, more precisely, public ethics), which is the focus of this book, refers to appropriate behaviour in public office. It is connected to the performance of public roles and duties. As such, it does not deal with absolute, universal principles but has a limited, *situational* character. It is best conceived of as "role morality", because it covers only a particular aspect (or role) in one's life (Rohr 1998).

It is of course a matter of debate whether it is possible – or desirable – to treat job-related normative considerations separately from the wider individual and societal moral frameworks. A good part of the literature dealing with ethics in public life highlights the possible clashes between opposing moral cues coming from different spheres of life (e.g., the fervent Catholic official who works for a government which passes legislation making abortion legal; the "dirty" policeman who tortures the kidnapper in order to save a child's life[1]). These are indeed very important questions, but they can be better answered by political philosophers. Here, the delineation of a specific sphere of public role morality – i.e., ethics – is done strictly in order to define and limit the scope of the research. It should be understood as an analytical position, not a normative one.

The parameters of "ethics" are defined in relation to the core values which ground the operation of the public service. In modern representative democracies, such values and standards often include impartiality, legality, transparency, efficiency, fairness, confidentiality and commitment to the public (see, for instance, OECD 2000). As yet, the European Commission has no official document dedicated particularly to enunciating the core values of the European civil service. However, these can be revealed in a combined analysis of the *Code of Good Administrative Behaviour* and the *Public Service Principles for the EU Civil Service* (both adopted by the European Ombudsman and applicable to all European institutions), the *Treaties*, the *Staff Regulations*, as well as the *Communication on Enhancing the Environment for Professional Ethics in the Commission*, which includes a draft statement on principles of professional ethics. Box 1.1 draws on all these official documents, but also on various flyers, brochures and training support materials used internally in the Commission.

The standards described above canvass the normative framework which applies to public office occupants – or, to put it simply, they tell us what an "ethical" official is supposed to be like. However, they do so in a rather general fashion – which means that in practice, the concrete meaning of these standards is often disputed, and what seems as clearly condemnable to some may be perceived by others as acceptable, or at least open to discussion. Significantly, a study of public ethics in EU Member States notes that "especially from a comparative point of view, there is very little common understanding about what constitutes ethical behaviour" (Bossaert and Demmke 2005: 21).

1.1.1 Ethical dilemmas and views towards public ethics

Public actors are expected to always bear in mind standards of professional ethics – that said, not all activities they perform are equally meaningful from an ethics perspective. To be clear, ethics becomes significant in situations of choice (which allow for the exercise of discretion), and only when values and standards of conduct are directly called into question, or likely to be jeopardized. Wittmer (2001) refers to these situations as ethical decisions. This book probes Commission officials' ethics thinking in the context of *ethical dilemmas*, which represent a special class of ethical decisions, where people find it difficult to judge what would constitute ethical

Box 1.1 Values and ethical standards in the European Commission services

Independence

Commission officials are expected to carry out their duties "solely with the interests of the Communities in mind", and "neither seek nor take instructions from any government, authority, organization or person outside his institution". They are also expected to avoid any situations which could cast doubts about their independence.

Objectivity and impartiality

Officials should ensure that their conduct reflects no bias. They should consistently ensure equal treatment and avoid discrimination on the grounds of nationality, sex, ethnic origin, or other factors. All parties with a direct interest should be heard. Reasons for decisions should be stated clearly and communicated to all parties.

Lawfulness

Conduct should always be in line with the laws, rules and procedures laid down in Community legislation.

Integrity

Officials should be guided by a sense of propriety and conduct themselves at all times in a manner that would bear the closest public scrutiny. This obligation is not fully discharged merely by acting within the law. Officials should take steps to avoid conflicts of interest and the appearance of such conflicts. They should take swift action to resolve any conflict that arises.

Loyalty

Staff should offer honest advice and inform management of any risks or disadvantages associated with a planned action or decision. Staff is expected to implement loyally the orders they receive from superiors, except when these are manifestly illegal. Staff should take care that their behaviour is not contrary to the interests of the Union.

Discretion and confidentiality

Staff should refrain from disclosing information received in the line of duty, unless that information is already in the public domain. They should ensure that confidential information to which they have access is adequately protected.

Transparency

Citizens have access to all Community documents within the boundaries of exceptions instituted in the specific legislation. Officials should keep proper records and welcome public scrutiny of their conduct.

Responsibility

Officials are expected to take responsibility in the performance of their duties. Public assets and resources should be used in an honest and professional manner. If they become aware of any irregularities or serious failings in the course of their duties, officials have an obligation to report them.

Circumspection

Staff has a duty to avoid delicate situations. They should inform the hierarchy of possible conflicts of interest, and obtain hierarchical permission before engaging in any outside activity. They should discourage the offering of gifts related to their professional duties.

Competence

Commission officials are expected to achieve the Commission's objectives with competence, in an effective and efficient manner. Decisions should be taken after careful consideration of advantages, disadvantages and potential consequences.

Respect and courtesy

In their dealings with the public, staff should provide quality service which is open and accessible and respects the applicable deadlines and procedures. They should treat colleagues with respect and courtesy, take their ideas and contributions into account and be ready to help them if needed. Officials should refrain from anything that could be perceived as psychological or sexual harassment.

Dignity of the service

Staff should be aware that in their private lives they may be viewed as representatives of the European institutions and should therefore refrain from any actions which might reflect adversely on their position or on the reputation of the Commission.

behaviour. Ethical dilemmas are often described as choices between competing, irreconcilable values which define the public role. As explained by Gortner, here "two or more competing values are important and in conflict. If you serve one value you cannot serve another, or you must deny or disserve one or more values in order to maintain one or more of the others" (1991: 14). Put differently, ethical dilemmas are not choices between right and wrong, but between right and right (Kidder 2009).

Ethical dilemmas should be distinguished from *unethical behaviour*, which represents deviance from appropriateness, i.e., breaking one or several of the behavioural standards which define the operation of the public service. While ethical dilemmas are inherently ambiguous, unethical behaviour is generally understood as being wrong (Maesschalck 2004b). Probably the most well-known form of unethical behaviour is *corruption*, understood here as "the abuse of entrusted power for private gain" (TI 2015b).[2] Following Lasthuizen *et al.*'s (2011) typology of "integrity violations",[3] other forms of unethical behaviour, apart from corruption, include: fraud and theft of resources; conflict of (private and public) interests though gifts or sideline activities; improper use of authority; misuse and manipulation of information; indecent treatment of colleagues, citizens and customers; waste and abuse of organizational resources; and, finally, misconduct in private time.

The book focuses on ethical dilemmas because they represent spaces where the boundaries between the ethical and unethical are negotiated. As stated in the Introduction, one of the core objectives of this investigation is to explore Commission officials' views about ethics. To be clear, the term "views" is used in a broad sense, to describe what individuals think about ethics. For the most part, it refers to judgements of acceptability regarding certain types of behaviour, but it also covers related aspects, such as the justifications evoked in assessing acceptability, or opinions on the appropriate course of action. Ethical dilemmas represent a good ground to elicit individual views about ethics because they trigger a process of evaluation (reasoning) about what is ethical and what is not, through which such views are revealed. Furthermore, if Commission officials differ in their thinking, it is reasonable to assume that those differences would most likely manifest themselves in the "grey" areas of organizational ethics represented by ethical dilemmas. To give an example, while it is very improbable that anyone would condone bribe-taking, a "grey" gift situation is much less clear-cut. As a general principle, a public servant should not receive gifts from external parties, as this may (be perceived to) damage his/her impartiality. Nevertheless, sometimes refusing a gift can be interpreted by the one who is offering it as disrespectful – maybe even to the point that the working relationship is jeopardized. In such a circumstance, it is certainly not clear whether it is still "ethical" to refuse the gift.

The approach used here is in line with the practice in empirical ethics research, where individual positions regarding ethical matters are established by presenting respondents with concrete scenarios, which lead them to engage in a process of decision-making (this is why vignettes are widely popular in this literature – see reviews by Frederickson and Walling 2001, O'Fallon and Butterfield 2005). In synthesizing several influential models in the field (i.e., Rest 1986, Treviño 1986, Bommer *et al.* 1987, Jones 1991), Wittmer (2001: 484–488) establishes that the process of ethical decision-making begins with the perception that a problem has ethical content (i.e., ethical sensitivity), continues with judgement or reasoning concerning this issue, after which a choice is made and the process ends with the

20 *Public ethics and the European Commission*

actual behaviour of the decision maker. As an aside, it should be noted that the link between ethical choice and ethical behaviour is particularly problematic, as the literature provides mixed evidence that ethical beliefs and intentions lead to corresponding behaviour (see review by Treviño *et al.* 2006).

Generally speaking, ethical decision-making, in particular ethical reasoning, is considered to be (a predominantly) rational and conscious process, but this assumption has been challenged. For instance, Haidt (2001: 818) draws attention to the importance of moral intuition, understood as "the sudden appearance in consciousness of a moral judgement, including an affective valence (good–bad), without any conscious awareness of having gone through the steps of searching, weighing evidence, or inferring a conclusion". Other parts of the literature emphasize that emotions – particularly guilt, shame and empathy (see review by Eisenberg 2000) – influence ethical decision-making in important ways. This means that individuals' ethical reasoning towards a particular situation will be supported by conscious deliberation, but also by taken-for-granted ingrained beliefs, and even emotions. This multifaceted nature of the process cautions against assuming a straightforward causal link between ethical reasoning and ethical choices, as suggested above. To use the previous example of the tricky gift situation, an individual may intuitively feel that accepting the gift is wrong (perhaps because of cultural conditioning) and will produce after-the-fact justifications (in the form of ethical reasoning) for his/her initial intuition. Because of these complexities, a choice was made here to speak of views which are *expressed* through ethical reasoning (in the context of ethical dilemmas), rather than choices which are *created* by it.

1.1.2 Ethics management in public organizations

Ethics management is understood here as a systematic, thought-out endeavour to promote organizational integrity. It is expressed, in concrete terms, in the creation of a so-called *ethics infrastructure* in an organization. This umbrella term – coined by the OECD (1996) – designates the sum of policy instruments, institutional structures and processes that, taken together, sustain ethical conduct and prevent (and punish) integrity violations. It has gained recognition in the academic literature as well (see, for example, the reviews conducted by Tenbrunsel *et al.* 2003 and Treviño *et al.* 2006, both of which identify research on organizational "ethical infrastructures" as a distinct trend in a larger body of work dealing with behavioural ethics in organizations).

An ethics infrastructure is generally assigned four important functions, namely: (a) determining and defining integrity, (b) guiding towards integrity, (c) monitoring integrity and (d) enforcing integrity (OECD 2009).[4] The first function refers to defining what standards of behaviour public servants are expected to follow, as well as to analyzing and responding to systemic risks in the organization (e.g., identifying sensitive processes such as procurement, inspections and securing against vulnerabilities). The second function denotes the need to guide and coach organizational members on the application of values and norms in daily practice. Monitoring integrity implies the establishment of channels to report wrongdoing, but also regular checks for integrity violations in the organization. Finally, the enforcement function refers to providing effective and proportional sanctions for transgressions. There is also an important distinction to be made between *core measures*, whose "main goal [. . .] is to foster integrity and prevent integrity violations" (OECD 2009: 17), and *complementary measures*, which "do not have integrity as their primary aim, but they are important to realize the goals of the integrity management framework; typically, they are instruments that fit in other supportive functions such as personnel management or financial management" (OECD 2009: 17). Considering in connection all conceptual distinctions presented above, the typology of integrity instruments in Table 1.1 emerges:

Table 1.1 Typology of integrity management instruments (based on OECD 2009)

	Functions			
	(a) Determining and defining	(b) Guiding	(c) Monitoring	(d) Enforcing
Core measures	• Risk analysis • Codes of conduct/codes of ethics • Conflict of interest policy • Gifts and hospitality policy • Post-employment arrangements • Structural arrangements (e.g., staff rotation for sensitive posts) • Analysis of ethical dilemmas • Consultation of staff and stakeholders	• Integrity/ethics training • Oaths, signing an "integrity declaration" • Specialized information and advice for staff • Integrating ethics issues in regular communication channels • Exemplary behaviour by management	• Whistleblowing policy • Complaints policy • Inspections • Integrity testing • Survey measurement of integrity violations and organizational climate • Probing for ethical dilemmas and issues among staff	• Formal sanctions • Fair and appropriate procedures for handling investigations • Communication about integrity violations • Informal sanctions
Complementary measures	• Assessing the fairness of reward and promotion systems • Appropriate procedures for procurement, contract management and payment • Measures in personnel management (e.g., integrity as a criterion for selection, promotion) • Measures in financial control (e.g., "double key", transparency of financial information) • Measures in information management (e.g., protecting automated databases)		• Internal control and audit • External control and audit	

Of course, a sound approach to managing ethics is not equal to adopting all instruments mentioned above – rather, it means that organizations will pick and choose whatever is likely to fit best with their existing systems, their culture and the wider institutional context, with due care to ensure that all four functions are reasonably fulfilled (OECD 2009). Implicitly, this means that policymakers will consider ethics management in a strategic manner.

The concept of *ethics infrastructure* is used here to delineate, within the Commission, a sphere of policy interventions that are directly relevant for public ethics. The analysis in subsequent chapters will therefore refer to the type of instruments and procedures described in Table 1.1, with an emphasis on "core" rather than "complementary" measures. It will also focus mainly on the management of ethics *inside* the Commission. Although practitioners advise that ethics policies should have in view the interlocking "layers of integrity", which start from individual values and move up to the national legal and political system (Bossaert and Demmke 2005), such an endeavour would exceed the limits of this book. To be clear, the following chapters do account for the role of external pressures in shaping the design and implementation of ethics management within the Commission – however, a full analysis of its external control environment remains outside its scope, and has been done elsewhere (see for instance TI-EU 2014)

1.2 Organizational socialization: learning ethics on the job

This book uses the theoretical lenses of organizational socialization (OS), defined as a process of social learning – more specifically, as "the process by which an individual comes to appreciate the values, abilities, expected behaviours and social knowledge essential for assuming an organizational role and for participating as an organizational member" (Louis 1980: 229–230). Simply put, OS pertains to learning what it means, and what it takes, to be part of an organization. In this view, ethics (understood as public role morality) is something that can be learnt, just like other aspects of the organizational role. To go back to the research question guiding this book, the assumption is that individuals' views of ethics are shaped in the process of learning their organizational roles.

Generally speaking, the literature which deals with the regulation of standards of conduct in public administration is concerned with individual behaviour and the impact that regulatory interventions can have on that behaviour (see Treviño *et al.* 2006: 970–971, Huberts *et al.* 2014). However, since the aim here is to uncover how individuals *think* about ethics (not necessarily how they *behave*), a theoretical framing which places emphasis on learning seems more appropriate. In this optic, ethics management – more accurately, the ethics infrastructure (which is, essentially, its "operationalization" within the organization) – represents not so much a framework which both enables and constrains behaviour, but a source from which employees learn their ethics. They receive messages from this conglomerate of managerial instruments and structures as to what it means to be "ethical". It is significant, for the point made here, that some authors have actually presented ethics management in terms of learning – for instance, Menzel (2007: 22) notes that "ethical behaviour is learned behaviour, and managers can build organizational processes and strategies that contribute to this learning effort".

1.2.1 *Formal and informal learning sources*

The book draws on a particular portion of the OS literature, which deals with the ways newcomers learn their organizational roles. In an influential contribution, Louis (1980) shows that people in a new organizational setting are likely to encounter surprises (i.e., discrepancies between anticipations and actual experiences), which trigger an effort to explain and attribute meaning to these unexpected realities (i.e., sense-making). In this effort, newcomers draw on the local interpretation schemes of the organization and on the insiders' interpretations, but also on their own past experiences and predispositions. Louis' model inspired much research on newcomers' information seeking and learning strategies (see, for instance, Miller and Jablin 1991, Ostroff and Kozlowski 1992, Morrison 1993, Chao *et al.* 1994, Ashforth *et al.* 2007). Although it focuses on novices, the theoretical insights of this literature are valuable for other organizational members as well, insomuch as one accepts that role-related learning can also occur outside the initial adaptation phase, if there are organizational changes important enough to require a readjustment.

The OS literature distinguishes among different domains in regard to which learning takes place. Despite the variety,[5] broadly speaking it is understood that learning is either role related or concerns more generally the culture of an organization. The utility of learning sources varies depending on the domain where they are employed. But – again, broadly speaking – OS research suggests that individuals employ organizationally sanctioned sources (such as manuals, guides or training programs), but also informal sources (their peers and leaders) and that the latter category is preferred over the former. For instance, Cooper-Thomas and Anderson (2006) identify, based on an extensive literature review, five learning sources – organizational literature, formal socialization programs, mentors, supervisors/ managers and colleagues. The first two are seen as formal learning sources, while the remaining ones are informal. The authors show that the level of organizational control decreases along this range of sources, with organizational literature being closest to organizationally sanctioned messages, and colleagues furthest away. In this context, "since informal sources are usually found to be more useful, when information is available from multiple sources, these informal sources are likely to be preferred" (Cooper-Thomas and Anderson 2006: 503). This opens the possibility of discrepant results, which means that the challenge for organizations is to ensure coherent messages throughout the entire range of learning sources.

How do these observations translate to the research purposes of this book? Firstly, the Commission's ethics infrastructure will be analyzed as a formal learning source. This reinterpretation is justified, given that many of the elements of an organizational ethics infrastructure are specifically designed to define and communicate the type of conduct desired from employees. Thus, an organization will typically have a code of conduct or a statement of values, which defines an "ethics" area by setting out, in a general fashion, values and behavioural standards. In addition, there will be a number of regulations on specific ethics issues, such as conflict of interests, gifts and hospitality, post-employment arrangements, etc., which will explicate how these values and standards play out in certain areas deemed of particular importance. All this ethics literature will then be communicated to staff through manuals, training, presentations and various other types of actions meant to ensure ethics guidance. Organizational practices in the area of monitoring and punishing transgressions will also signal to employees which behaviour is acceptable and which is not.

Secondly, the points in the OS literature regarding informal learning sources suggest that in an organizational context, people learn about normatively appropriate behaviour by observing those around them and, moreover, they will prefer this type of learning over using formal sources. In fact, Cooper-Thomas and Anderson's (2006) observations above correspond well with what empirical research in organizational ethics suggests regarding the role of leaders and peers. The attitudes and behaviours of peers at the workplace[6] have been proven to influence individuals' ethics (see reviews by Wittmer 2005, Treviño et al. 2006), with such influence increasing proportionally to the frequency and intensity of the interactions (Zey-Ferrell and Ferrell 1982). Among workplace peers, particularly significant are the so-called ethical role models, who inspire other employees through their personal example (see Weaver et al. 2005). Leaders are also crucial, because they represent salient authority figures in the organization and therefore are prime role models for employees to emulate (see Treviño et al. 2000, Brown et al. 2005, Brown and Treviño 2006, Huberts et al. 2007).

Clearly, then, it matters where (more precisely, with whom) in the Commission individuals learn their ethics. The Commission's tendency towards bureaucratic fragmentation, with Directorate-Generals developing distinct operating styles and subcultures (see, for example, Cram 1994, Christiansen 1997, Cini 1997 and more recently Schön-Quinlivan 2008, 2011), makes this observation all the more pertinent. In order to account for the influence of work peers and supervisors on individuals' ethical stances (and, moreover, to identify the ways in which these factors interrelate with the Commission's ethics policies), the project zooms in on administrative units, seen here as primary sites of organizational socialization in the Commission.

The administrative unit represents the smallest organizational component of the Commission – essentially, it is a team of officials who have been working closely together, for a reasonably long period of time. Arguably, these individuals have undergone organizational socialization under similar conditions – they have access to the same organizational literature and training/coaching programs, their peers and leadership are the same, they work on more or less similar issues, and they share a common group history and a common work space. In other words, we can assume that the members of an administrative unit learn their ethics under similar conditions. To be clear, interviews were carried out in four DGs, and in each of those I selected respondents who belonged to the same administrative unit, or to units which were working closely together. In this way, it was possible to capture the way officials worked together as a group and how they dealt with ethical questions in this context.

1.2.2 Socialization as acquiring role knowledge

To sum up the points made above, it can be argued, with some simplification, that individuals in an organizational context learn about public ethics from formal sources (in the ethics infrastructure) and informal sources (the people around them). The purpose here is to explore how the Commission's ethics management system feeds its employees' learning about public ethics – therefore, in order to ascertain the influence of formal sources, two elements will be highlighted.

The first is homogeneity in officials' views towards public ethics. It is reasonable to assume that people do not enter the European Commission with quite the same notions about ethics, especially given that they come from different backgrounds (in terms of nationality, work experience, etc.). Therefore, the fact that staff members think in similar terms about ethics may be considered an effect of organizational socialization. And although the process of influence is definitely more complex, official policy elements will play a role in it – after all, one of the purposes of doing ethics management is precisely to get everybody on the same page about what is acceptable and what is not. As shown in Chapter 3, the Commission clearly aimed to achieve this kind of standardization, most notably by engaging in vigorous internal awareness-raising and guidance actions after 2008. Secondly, to better isolate the effects of ethics policy interventions on the work-floor, I also look at the fit between official messages regarding ethics and the comments and positions expressed by employees on the subject. If the specific concerns and framings which pervade the "formal" discourse are reflected in the officials' ethical reasoning, this would more clearly indicate that they have learned about ethics (at least partially) from this source.

It should be clear from the above that the way socialization is approached in this book departs significantly from the standard position in EU integration research. First, the subject relative to which socialization is investigated differs. As Egeberg (2012: 939) aptly put it, the European Commission has long been treated as a "laboratory for experiments in supra-national institution-building", where researchers were interested in its capacity to instil in organizational members distinctively European features (regularly understood as supranational orientations of sorts). Different research questions have been explored around this common core, pertaining to Commission officials' attitudes or preferences regarding governance and political authority in the EU (Hooghe 2001, 2005, 2012, Ellinas and Suleiman 2011, Dehousse and Thompson 2012, Kassim *et al.* 2013, Suvarierol *et al.* 2013), their decision-making patterns (Egeberg 2006, Thomson 2008, Wonka 2008, Trondal *et al.* 2010), networking practices (Suvarierol 2008) or self-perceptions (Murdoch and Geys 2012). By contrast to all of these, the research proposed here focuses on Commission officials' views regarding public ethics. There is no overlap between the two – to put it simply, the fact that an official, for instance, favours a supranational over an intergovernmental approach says very little about his/her appreciation of what constitutes appropriate conduct in office.[7]

This distinction has consequences for the manner in which socialization is defined and conceptualized. In most Commission literature, socialization appears as somewhat of an organic process which occurs when an individual comes in contact with the organization (but see Ban 2010, 2013 for significant exceptions). This is simply because, when understood as "going native" in Brussels, socialization is not something which is planned and managed by the Commission – meaning, there are no managerial instruments expressly designed to make staff into true-blue Europeans. However, in what regards ethics, the Commission does not simply rely on its "natural" socializing capabilities, but actually has at its disposal a large array of policy instruments which can influence the thinking and behaviour of its employees. Therefore, the conceptual framework used here explicitly includes an appreciation of the organizational policies which impact on socialization (some of which are specifically designed to do so).

Furthermore, and perhaps most importantly, the EU literature generally defines socialization as value internalization, to differentiate it from instrumental calculation, or mimicking (this is true especially for authors who write from a social constructivist perspective). Value internalization means that new rules and norms cease to be foreign to the actors, so that they will comply with them even in the absence of any incentives to do so (Checkel 2005). By contrast, the theoretical framework employed here assumes that an individual is socialized when he/she has mastered how to function as an effective organizational member. In other words, the socialization outcome is role knowledge, and this does not imply a distinction between value internalization and other types of adaptive behaviour. To put it simply, one does not have to be a "true believer" to be socialized.[8] Adopting this less exigent standard is in line with the practical purposes of doing ethics management. As discussed before, an ethics infrastructure will regularly comprise instruments that create strong incentives for employees to not engage in transgressions (e.g., surveillance structures, formal and informal sanctions), as well as softer tools that aim to change the value structures in an organization (e.g., codes of conduct, ethics training). Both of these are necessary – therefore, the goal in ethics management is not to obtain sustained compliance *even in the absence of incentives* (which would imply quite an unrealistic view of human nature), but rather to achieve a good blend between "soft" and "hard" instruments. Similarly, the aim here is not to disentangle the effects of incentive-altering and value-altering mechanisms within the Commission's ethics management system, but rather to say something about their combined effect.

1.3 The officials of the European Commission and their organizational socialization

To say that the European Commission is a complex organization would probably be an understatement. The following pages offer a basic guide to the institutional functions of the Commission, its internal structure and its staff. Based on this, its characteristics as a socializing environment will be highlighted and translated to choices of research design. In particular, I will revisit the argument made earlier that the Commission represents a hard case in ethics management, owing to its internal heterogeneity, which poses above-average challenges in terms of instilling a common line among staff.

Commonly dubbed the motor of European integration, the European Commission is placed "at the heart" of the EU system of governance (Nugent 1997: 6) and, as such, it fulfils a variety of institutional roles. It affects the lives of millions of citizens, in very tangible and concrete ways – in fact, one would be hard-pressed to think of policy actors (be they public authorities, business interests or third sector organizations, in the European Union or outside of it) which would not hold a stake in what the Commission does. I distinguish here between three core institutional functions of the Commission, namely the initiation, execution, and enforcement of policy.[9]

To begin, the Commission is the place where most EU-level policy initiatives are developed. This pivotal position is due to its exclusive right to draft legislative proposals, although in doing so it often acts on the request of other European institutions (particularly the Council). The EU political system, encompassing a wide variety of actors with different interests and views, encourages the pre-cooking of decisions before entering the formal stages of decision-making. This leads the Commission, when acting as policy initiator, to engage in a lot of informal activity, from floating ideas and advocacy work, to checking the pulse in other EU institutions and inter-institutional committees, and promoting dialogue with societal interests.

Secondly, as policy executor, the Commission is mostly responsible for the coordination and supervision of front-line implementation in the Member States. This implies several different aspects. Firstly, the Commission produces implementing and delegated acts and issues a large number of guides and codes, explaining in detail the application of particular rules. Secondly, financial management is part of the Commission's executive role. The Commission oversees the collection of EU budgetary revenue, prepares the EU budget and manages expenditure. The majority of EU funds (76 per cent) are spent under shared management,[10] a system where budget implementation is delegated to the Member States, with the Commission retaining a supervisory and audit role.

Finally, the Commission also acts as "guardian of the Treaties", ensuring that EU law is implemented and respected at the national level. When checking implementation, it relies primarily on a notification system which requires Member States to report to Brussels steps taken to adapt their national legislation to EU law. Breaches are dealt with through the infringement procedure, where the Commission has the power to initiate legal action against Member States, should they fail to comply with EU law. The European Court of Justice decides on the cases. Competition policy is an exception, with the Commission being the direct enforcer (competition decisions can be contested at the European Court of Justice, although appeals rarely lead to changes in the original decision – see Nugent 2001: 285).

The functions of the European Commission – less than what a national government does, but far more substantial than those of any international secretariat – highlight the unique nature of the organization.[11] In other aspects, however, the Commission is not unusual. Its structure, for instance, is quite conventional, with a political branch similar to an executive cabinet (i.e., the College of Commissioners), an administrative branch (i.e., the Directorates-General and special services) and a system of *cabinets* situated in-between to coordinate policy-making. The DGs look like national ministries, and the Commissioners resemble ministers. Reportedly, a former Secretary-General described the Commission as "basically a structure of mini-Ministries called Directorates General" (Williamson 1991, cited in Spence 2006: 129). Of course, this analogy should not be taken too far – the College does sit at the apex of the Commission and provides its leadership, but the Commissioners are appointed, not elected, and although the Treaties provide that they be free from national pressure, in practice all Commissioners are sensitive to national interests.

The administrative services of the Commission – which this book explores – are composed of 33 Directorate-Generals and 11 special services. To borrow Gulick's (1937) famous terminology, the Commission is organized according to the principles of "purpose" and "process" – that is, each of these organizational units deals either with a specific policy area, being actively involved in making and implementing policy (e.g., DG Competition, DG Agriculture, DG Environment) or, respectively, has internal, administrative tasks or interservice coordinating functions (e.g., the Secretariat General, DG Budget, DG Human Resources, DG Translation). Another way of thinking about this is to distinguish between, on the one hand, "policy", or "operational" or "vertical" units, and, on the other, "administrative" or "horizontal" ones. There is a lot of variation in terms of size among DGs and services, with the smaller ones totalling around 300–400 staff, and the larger ones with over 1,000 employees.[12] Regularly, each DG is made up of three to five Directorates, which in turn contain between three and seven administrative units. The administrative units also vary in size, with the average being around 20 employees.

This book focuses on the "policy" or "vertical" DGs, because, as opposed to the "horizontal" ones, they exhibit the entire range of ethics challenges confronting the Commission. This is particularly true regarding the relationships with the organization's stakeholders – although the horizontal units are by no means insulated from the outside world (they deal with third parties such as contractors or lobbyists), the contact is likely to be both less varied and less intense. Generally speaking, the horizontal units are less exposed to political tugs-of-war, simply because their activity does not impact directly on Member States or societal interests (through regulation, distribution of funds, etc.).

The structure of the EU civil service is also standard from a European comparative perspective. There are three categories of officials: administrators (AD), also referred to as *fonctionnaires*, with responsibilities in policy development and execution, as well as assistants (AST) and secretaries/clerks (AST/SC), with administrative responsibilities. The career system consists of a single pay scale with sixteen grades, within which assistants and secretaries can occupy grades 1–11, while administrators can occupy grades 5–16 (European Union 2015a). The hierarchy of the European civil service resembles a traditional Weberian pyramid, with the topmost position being the Director General, followed by Director, Adviser, Head of Unit and Deputy Head of Unit, and the rest of the positions being non-managerial.

As a rule, a job in the European Commission is highly desirable. Salaries in the European administration are sizeable, complemented by advantageous social security plans and a series of additional benefits justified by relocation from one's home country. Add to that the prestige of working for an institution considered to be "the engine of Europe". Prestige also comes from the fact that entry into the Commission is preceded by a very long, demanding, and highly competitive selection procedure known as the *concours*, managed by the European Personnel Selection Office (EPSO). The strenuous conditions give the *concours* a symbolic gate-keeping function, and so those who successfully go through are considered members of a special elite (Ban 2010). It is mainly these features – complemented by a shared enthusiasm for building the institutions of Europe (Page 1997), and the common work location and lifestyle as expatriates (Stevens and Stevens 2001) – that give the European civil service its cohesive character.

1.3.1 Choosing a significant group of officials

So how exactly is the elite administrative body presented above a "hard case" in ethics management, and how do its characteristics matter for organizational socialization? After introducing the reader to the European Commission, this section analyzes the characteristics of its staff with an eye to picking out those features which matter for organizational socialization, and could determine officials to think about ethics in different ways (which, implicitly, represent hurdles for managing ethics). The analysis draws heavily on the EU literature on Commission socialization and is complemented by insights from public administration research. Notwithstanding the conceptual differences discussed previously, existing research on the Commission offers an excellent starting point for understanding the specificities of this organization as a socialization environment, the characteristics of the process, as well as the variables which matter.[13]

To begin with, *nationality* can be relevant for officials' views towards ethics. In fact, it has been the "usual suspect" for the existence of different understandings of appropriate behaviour in the Commission. In the aftermath of the Santer resignation in 1999, there was widespread talk of a "clash of cultures" in Europe, between the "clean" countries of the North and the "corrupt" ones in the South. It seemed that Commissioners, officials and Members of the European Parliament (MEPs) abided by quite different standards of public behaviour, depending on their country of origin (Pujas and Rhodes 1999). The phenomenon has also been documented in the academic literature – Maryon McDonald (1997, 2000), for instance, writes about a persistent North/South division within the Commission regarding conceptualizing the frontiers between administration and politics, public and private, ethical and not ethical. National stereotyping aside, it does not actually seem too difficult to find supporting arguments for the "clash of cultures" thesis. Even a cursory look at Transparency International's *Corruption Perception Index*[14] shows a striking divergence between the EU Member States – in 2014, the scores varied from 92 (Denmark) to 43 (Bulgaria, Romania, Greece and Italy). Also importantly, nationality (more precisely, national socialization) has been found to influence Commission officials' preferences regarding the split of political authority in the EU, as well as their economic ideologies (see Hooghe 2001, 2005, 2012), so the same might apply regarding their views about public behavioural standards.

Another important variable for socialization in the Commission is the *organizational position* that individuals occupy. Egeberg (1999, 2004, 2012) points out that unlike other international governmental organizations, the main principles of specialization in the Commission are sectoral or functional (rather than territorial/national), which means that the portfolio logic is a particularly important influence on officials' decision behaviour and, ultimately, on their identity. Empirical research on Commission officials (Suvarierol 2008), Commissioners (Egeberg 2006, Wonka 2008) and seconded national officials (Trondal *et al.* 2008) has lent considerable support to this view.

In what concerns ethics, organizational positions are relevant not necessarily as a counterweight to national orientations, but because the functions fulfilled by the European Commission entail different ethics (risk) profiles. After all, the main criticisms received by the Commission over its ethical standards do apply to some of its activities more than others. For instance, the propriety of exchanges with lobbyists is relevant mainly for the policy initiation function, while questions of financial irregularities and fraud (particularly regarding funds under shared management[15]) pertain mainly to the Commission's executive role. On the other hand, as "guardian of the Treaties" the Commission is expected to be impartial, but in reality political considerations have often been crucial in picking its legal battles. These observations make it clear that there is a possibility that officials working in different parts of the Commission do not get exposed to quite the same problems. Consequently, functional differentiation is an element to consider for case selection – if the group of interviewees is to be a significant one, it should include people who experience the entirety (or a relevant range of) ethics questions which work-life in the Commission throws up.

Another important aspect to consider is the *type of employment* contract which officials have. Most (74 per cent)[16] of those working in the Commission services are European civil servants, enjoying lifelong tenure. Apart from them, however, there are several types of non-permanent staff in the European Commission: the temporary agents (3.4 per cent) and the contractual agents (19.3 per cent), who are employed for limited periods of time, ranging between three and six years (but sometimes less). A distinctive category are the Seconded National Officials (SNEs, 3.2 per cent of total staff), who are recruited mostly from the national civil services of EU countries to spend a limited period (a minimum of six months and a maximum of four years) working full time for the Commission while continuing to be on the payroll of their original employer.

Public ethics and the European Commission   31

The type of employment contract matters because it can affect individuals' motivation to be (and stay) loyal to the Commission.[17] Tenure in the civil service has long been considered a must for achieving a professional, neutral administration able to resist pressures from the politicians of the day or from powerful private interests. Without the security afforded by a permanent position, non-permanent employees are likely to be more susceptible to such influences – even though otherwise, by comparison to tenured officials, they have fairly similar working conditions, salary/benefits[18] and disciplinary regulations.[19]

Finally, officials' *professional background* can be an important determinant for their views towards ethics. The logic is the same as for nationality, namely that individuals may bring into the Commission different understandings of appropriate behaviour – this time depending not on their country of origin, but on where they previously worked. It makes a difference whether an individual has experience in the private or public sectors, because the logics of the two sectors are fundamentally different (i.e., bottom-line profit vs. the public interest) – which means that what might be labelled as initiative in a private firm could well constitute misconduct in a public bureaucracy (OECD 1996). Therefore, individuals coming from the private sector may be less sensitive to the ethical rigours of the public service.

The literature dealing with "public service motivation" (PSM) lends further weight to this argument. PSM is generally understood as one's motivation to contribute to the common good and the well-being of society at large. It has been hypothesized that by its very nature, the public sector attracts people with such an altruistic drive (Perry and Wise 1990), which may, in turn, be connected to more ethical behaviour (Brewer and Selden 1998). Thus, an argument can be made that those who work in the private sector (or who have joined a public organization from such a position) may display lower levels of PSM, which in turn affects their ethical stances.

***

To sum up, the staff of the European Commission is a diverse body and some elements in this diversity are relevant for officials' socialization experiences with regard to ethics. Firstly, officials' nationality is significant, since EU Member States are quite diverse in their political cultures and administrative norms, which potentially translate, inside the Commission, into "clashes of culture" between North and South, East and West. Secondly, the organizational position matters, because the Commission's institutional functions may entail some variation in terms of ethics profile. Therefore, officials working in different parts of the organization get exposed to distinct questions and problems. Thirdly, the lack of tenure may weaken officials' loyalty to the Commission. Finally, the professional background is noteworthy, because those who have worked in the private sector may understand differently what passes as acceptable in order to get things done.

This being said, it is important to note that the Commission's well-defined recruitment pool, coupled with its rigorous hiring methods, make it unlikely that recruits with (very) different previous "baggage" will pass through. The very competitive and time-consuming *concours*, which candidates have to pass in order to enter the European civil service, generates a very specific profile of recruits: "a sophisticated, well-educated group, almost all with international experience, entering with considerable prior knowledge about the European institutions" (Ban 2013: 106). Among those characteristics, the previous international experience is particularly significant, as it may dislocate or weaken any specifically national views on ethics. If, prior to joining the Commission, officials are unlikely to be the "typical" French, Italian, German, Swede, or Romanian, then they are also less likely to embrace the divergent ethical standards associated with their respective national cultures.

1.3.2 Characteristics of the sample

Respondents were purposefully chosen to represent – in a balanced way and within some predefined limits – the organizational complexities of the European Commission. Specifically, a maximum variation sample[20] was used, consisting of thirty informants and displaying variation along the four variables (i.e., nationality, organizational position, type of employment and professional background) identified in the previous section as having a potential to determine differences in the way Commission officials view ethics. As Rubin and Babbie (2009: 150) show, a maximum variation sample can capture the diversity of a phenomenon with a small number of cases, which can be studied intensively. It includes cases which display significant variation along a number of criteria of interest, the purpose being to represent "all the important dissimilar forms present in the larger population" (Weiss 1994: 23). A maximum variation sample permits generalization to a larger population precisely because it contains very dissimilar cases – the logic being that any common patterns that emerge from a highly heterogeneous group would hold for the wider population as well (Weiss 1994, Patton 2002).

In terms of *nationality*, the sample includes nineteen staff members from the "old" EU-15 Member States (four British, four French, two Spanish, two Italian, two Greek, one Austrian, one German, one Danish, one Dutch and one Belgian) and eleven from the "new" Member States (three Lithuanians, two Hungarians, two Bulgarians, one Polish, one Estonian, one Slovene and one Romanian). The North–South division is also represented, with the British, German, Austrian, Danish and Dutch on the one hand, and the French, Spanish, Italians and Greeks on the other.

The recruited officials came from four DGs: the Directorate-General for the Internal Market and Services (DG MARKT), the Directorate-General for Regional Policy (DG REGIO), the Directorate-General for the Environment (DG ENV) and the Directorate General for Competition (DG COMP). These DGs were considered representative for the Commission's three core institutional functions – policy initiation, execution and enforcement (their representativeness is explained in Table 1.2 below).

Table 1.2 Selected Directorate-Generals

Commission function	Selected DG	Reason for selection	Interviews
Policy initiation	DG Internal Market (MARKT)	DG MARKT is active in one of the oldest (and most heavily lobbied) policy areas under Community competence.	6 interviews in 2 units
Policy execution	DG Regional Policy (REGIO)	DG REGIO manages spending for regional policy, which traditionally has been the second largest spending area of the EU budget, after agriculture and rural development.[21] This is also the area where the specifically EU mode of shared management is used.	7 interviews in 2 units
Policy enforcement	DG Environment (ENV)	DG ENV is active in the one area of the acquis communautaire which is generating the most significant caseload of the Commission, both in terms of open cases under investigation and in terms of infringement cases.[22]	5 interviews in 1 unit
	DG Competition (COMP)	DG COMP enjoys the highest powers in the Commission.	12 interviews in 3 units

It is important to point out that most of the Commission's operational DGs generally perform all three institutional functions (i.e., they contain administrative units, or perhaps entire directorates, dedicated to policy initiation, execution and enforcement, respectively). Thus, it would be incorrect to speak of "pure" executive or enforcement DGs, but of DGs which exercise these functions in different proportions. For instance, some are big spenders (e.g., the Directorate-General for Agriculture and Rural Development, the Directorate-General for Regional Policy, the Directorate-General for Employment, Social Affairs and Equal Opportunities), while others are more involved in policymaking (e.g., the Directorate-General for the Internal Market and Services, the Directorate-General for Taxation and Customs Union, the Directorate-General for the Information Society and Media). So, it is in this sense – i.e., the predominance of a specific function – that representativeness of the selected DGs is to be understood.

I ensured that both the units where interviewees were located as well as their DG as a whole were representative for each of the three functions. A slightly different strategy was applied for policy enforcement. Generally, Commission DGs have one or several administrative units which deal with enforcement in their respective policy areas. DG ENV is an example of this common setup. By way of exception, DG COMP was also included in the sample as it represents the only DG in the Commission dedicated almost entirely to enforcement. Furthermore, during interviews, internal ethics experts consistently indicated DG COMP as being particularly sensitive from an ethics viewpoint.

Moving on, the sample is diverse also in terms of hierarchical level and *type of employment contracts*. With one exception, all interviewees belonged to the so-called AD group. Ten people held managerial positions (Heads of Units or Deputy Heads Of Units), while the rest occupied lower ranks in the staff hierarchy. Most of them were permanent officials, with the exception of two temporary agents and two seconded national experts.

Finally, in terms of *professional background*, a bit over half of the respondents (seventeen) had previously worked in public administration, either at national or local levels, while eight had a background in the private sector, four had been employed by other EU institutions, and one held an academic position before joining the Commission. There were sixteen women and fourteen men in the group. Moreover, all respondents had at least one year worth of work experience in the Commission – which translates into a reasonable period of exposure to organizational socialization.[23]

In conclusion, the selection was sensitive to the multitude of factors which could be reasonably considered to have an influence on officials' views to ethics. This composition allows for findings to be extrapolated to other parts of the Commission. However, because of the relatively small number of interviews, the sample is not fit for isolating the individual impact of these factors (for instance, it cannot tell us whether nationality matters for the way Commission officials understand ethics). There are also further limits – because of the decision to focus on administrative units, the sample is limited to a certain hierarchical level, namely middle management (Head of Unit) and below. Largely as a consequence of this, the participants' age range is also limited – the sample includes mostly young people, with only a few officials above fifty.

1.3.3 Gaining access and recruiting participants

A few words are in order regarding the interviewee recruitment method, since research dealing with sensitive topics – such as ethics – can face significant access problems. Offering confidentiality (as it has been the practice in this project) certainly helps to garner support and trust, but it is, however, only part of the solution. Also very important is how the researcher gains entry into the organization in the first place and the routes by which he/she reaches potential interviewees. Here, access was achieved through internal channels – particularly, the entry points were the Commission's ethics officials. Interviewees were recruited either through calls for interviews circulated internally by the DGs' ethics correspondents or through the snowballing technique (i.e., acting on the recommendation of ethics officials in the Commission, I approached several Heads of Units in the desired DGs, some of whom eventually agreed to participate in the project). In parallel, hierarchical lines were used – in most cases, I contacted first the (Deputy) Heads of Units, who circulated my calls for interviews among their staff.

The recruitment method described above implied some trade-offs. The advantage was that coming through internal channels, and with the "blessing" of ethics officials and the hierarchy, the requests for interviews were met with less suspicion and more cooperation. The disadvantage was that of potential selection bias. Because ethics experts were the entry point, it is possible that they directed me towards people whom they considered to be of good standing. Moreover, as participation was voluntary, interviewees to a certain extent self-selected themselves into the project. Conceivably, the decision to participate would be motivated by a personal interest in ethics, or an acknowledgement of its importance in the organization. Finally, the investigated units enjoyed good leadership – the Heads of Units were clearly people who didn't have a problem with discussing ethics.

This being said, the risks of bias discussed above are justified given the access limitations connected to the research topic – and, furthermore, considering the aims of the project, the potential bias is not a stumbling block. Firstly, officials' views towards ethics are elicited in the context of ethical dilemmas. Given the highly ambiguous nature of these situations, the interviewees' good character would not predispose them to a particular assessment. On the other hand, the supportive leadership in the selected units does not obscure findings, since the point here is to understand how ethics management *combines* with other organizational factors to shape individual attitudes – rather than whether or not it works in separation.

1.4 Conclusion

This chapter has presented the analytical framework of the thesis. It was established that "ethics" has a situational character, referring to appropriate behaviour in public office. As such, it may be equated with the public role morality. The parameters of "ethics" are defined by reference to the core values and standards of behaviour which ground the operation of the civil service (i.e., objectivity, impartiality, loyalty, etc.). From the perspective of the individual civil servant, ethics become significant in those situations of choice where the values and standards mentioned above are likely to be jeopardized. The ethical dilemma is one such choice situation, which is particularly interesting because it features two (or more) values which are in conflict, thus making it difficult to judge what the ethical course of action is. Commission officials' views will be elicited in the context of ethical dilemmas because it is those "grey" areas that trigger individuals to seriously consider ethical aspects, and it is here where differences of views might become visible.

Taking a holistic view, the book analyzes ethics policies in the European Commission not as discrete measures, but as the expression of a coherent and deliberate effort to ensure high behavioural standards in an organization. This effort to manage ethics is manifest in a so-called organizational ethics infrastructure. The concept describes the sum of policy instruments, institutional structures and processes that, taken together, sustain ethical conduct and prevent (and punish) integrity violations and corruption. It will be used here to demarcate within the Commission an array of policy interventions that are directly relevant for public ethics.

Starting from the assumptions that individuals' views towards ethics evolve over time and that the organizational context in which they exist shapes this evolution, organizational socialization is taken up as a theoretical perspective. Namely, OS is understood as a process of social learning through which an individual comes to appreciate the knowledge, values and expected behaviours associated with an organizational role. In this perspective, ethics becomes something that – like other parts of the (public) role – can be learnt. The aim therefore is to determine whether ethics management in the European Commission shapes the process of organizational socialization, more specifically whether it informs the formation (adjustment) of officials' views regarding public ethics. This means that the Commission's ethics infrastructure is analyzed as one learning source (among others) which feeds employees as they learn about the content and limits of ethical conduct. Concretely, the analysis in the following chapters is geared to decoding the messages which the organization sent internally, to its staff, regarding the type of behaviour that is (not) acceptable and what will be (not) punished.

The last part of the chapter offered a brief portrayal of the European Commission as a public bureaucracy and tackled questions of research design. In undergoing organizational socialization, people draw on their previous experiences and understandings, but the specific conditions of employment and the local context in which they are socialized also matter. Based on these insights, and complemented by existing research on Commission socialization, a maximum variation sample was constructed along four key dimensions – officials' nationality, their organizational position (DG affiliation), previous professional background (public or private sector) and type of employment (temporary or permanent contract) – all of which represent factors that can generate differences in individuals' thinking about ethics and their socialization experiences. The sample, although small in itself, permits generalization to the larger population of the Commission precisely because it contains very dissimilar cases – the logic being that any common patterns that emerge from a highly heterogeneous group would hold for the wider population as well. Furthermore, in order to account for the influence of work peers and supervisors on individuals' ethical stances, interviews were clustered in several administrative units across four DGs considered to be representative for the institutional functions of the European Commission. Finally, informants were recruited through internal channels (more specifically, on the recommendation of ethics experts and through the snowballing technique), which meant better access but also a (tolerable) risk of having a biased sample.

Notes

1 A good discussion of these issues is offered by Applbaum (1999).
2 Generally, corruption definitions are contested. The Transparency International version was proposed here because it also covers offenses involving exclusively private actors. To be clear, corruption acts have a fairly broad spectrum (offering and receiving bribes and other undue advantages, trading in influence, nepotism, different forms of patronage), but corruption itself represents only one form of unethical behaviour.
3 Where integrity is defined as "the quality of acting in accordance with relevant moral values, norms and rules" (Lasthuizen *et al.* 2011: 387).
4 This section draws on OECD (2009) because of its explicit focus on the organizational level. However, the terminology differs somewhat. The OECD (2009) refers to an "integrity management framework", whereas I use here the term "ethics infrastructure",

which has gained more recognition in the field, among both practitioners and academics, as argued above. Although subtle differences do exist, essentially the overlap between the two concepts is large enough to use them interchangeably.
5 To give just two examples, Ostroff and Kozlowski (1992) proposed four domains of learning – task, role, group processes (social) and organization – and Chao *et al.* (1994) have six domains – people, politics, history, performance, language and goals and values. Cooper-Thomas and Anderson (2006) note that this type of scale generally requires further development and empirical validation.
6 Usually termed as "referent" or "significant others" in the literature.
7 One possible exception to this could be the independence principle (Art. 11 of the *Staff Regulations*), which requires that officials carry out their duties "solely with the interests of the Communities in mind", without seeking or receiving "instructions from any government, authority, organization or person outside his institution" (Commission 2004b: 8). Thus, an intergovernmental stance might appear ethically questionable because it departs from the "interests of the Communities".
8 It should be noted that there are also EU scholars who argue for a relaxation of the internalization standard in socialization research. Beyers (2010: 917–918), for instance, notes that focusing on internalization not only is very taxing from a methodological perspective, but also obscures the broader context in which socialization processes unfold, and their highly contingent character.
9 The EU literature generally lists five or six functions of the Commission – e.g., Nugent (2001) enumerates policy initiation, legislative functions, executive functions, legal guardianship, external representation, mediation/brokerage of interests and mobilization of policy support. There is, however, significant overlap between those functions to justify a more crisp approach (for example, policy initiation implies a legislative exercise, as well as consensus-building, brokering between opposed interests, etc.). Admittedly, the classification used here neglects the attributions of external representation, although there are reasons to consider them part of the Commission's managerial/executive role (Cini 1996: 25).
10 For more on this, see: http://ec.europa.eu/budget/explained/management/managt_who/who_en.cfm.
11 It is no coincidence that precisely this state of *in-betweenness* is what usually causes scholars to affirm the *sui generis* nature of the EU political system. This is clear in celebrated definitions such as "less than a federation, more than a regime" (Wallace 1983: 403), "neither a state, nor an international organization" (Sbargia 1992: 257) or "the middle ground between the cooperation of existing nations and the breaking of a new one" (Scharpf 1988: 242).
12 As of 2015, the smallest unit was the Bureau of European Policy Advisers, with 35 staff, while the largest one was DG Translation, with 2,275 employees – for more on this, see the European Commission staff figures, available at: http://ec.europa.eu/civil_service/about/figures/index_en.htm.
13 It bears mention that research in ethical decision making (see reviews by Ford and Richardson 1994, Loe *et al.* 2000, O'Fallon and Butterfield 2005, Tenbrunsel and Smith-Crowe 2008) suggests that a number of individual-level variables can influence individuals' ethics. Among those are psychological traits (for instance, the level of cognitive moral development, the locus of control, ego strength), demographic variables (particularly age and gender) and personal value systems, moral philosophies and religion. Although age and gender were considered when choosing interviewees, scanning systematically for all these individual-level variables (particularly psychological characteristics) was impractical and beyond the scope of this project. Furthermore, focusing on existing Commission research allowed the articulation of a set of selection criteria contextualized to the specificities of this organization.
14 The *Corruption Perception Index* (CPI) is a composite index drawing on corruption-related data from expert and business surveys carried out by a variety of independent and

reputable institutions. The CPI ranks countries based on the degree to which corruption is perceived to exist among public officials and politicians. It uses a scale of 100 ("completely clean") to 0 ("completely corrupt"). For more on this, see: www.transparency.org/research/cpi/.

15 Funds under shared management have represented probably the single most important reason why, for many years, the Commission has failed to obtain a clean bill of health in the annual audit reports of the European Court of Auditors. The Court has regularly mentioned, in the "Statement of Assurance" which accompanies its annual audit reports, that certain payments in this category were "materially affected by error" (i.e., not all formal rules had been respected), which signals that supervisory and control systems are "partially effective".

16 The percentages are calculated based on the European Commission staff figures of 2015, available at: http://ec.europa.eu/civil_service/about/figures/index_en.htm.

17 In the EU literature, this argument has been made in relation to SNEs, assumed to retain allegiance to their national civil services while working for the Commission (Cox 1969, Coombes 1970). In fact, SNEs are sometimes used as a crucial test group for Commission socialization, precisely because they are thought to be the least likely to develop supranational loyalties (see, for instance, studies by Trondal 2006 and Trondal et al. 2008).

18 This is broadly speaking. In particular, temporary agents do enjoy the same conditions as permanent officials. Contract agents have their salaries capped at €5,800, but otherwise have the same benefits as temporary agents. SNEs remain covered by the social security provisions of their home employer, but the Commission offers compensation costs for living and working abroad, which can be very significant in some cases.

19 To avoid conflicts of interests, there are special additional restrictions applying for SNEs. For instance, they assist Commission officials and temporary staff, but cannot themselves occupy middle or senior management positions.

20 Sometimes called a maximum diversity sample, or a maximum heterogeneity sample. Generally, this strategy is recommended as an alternative to random selection, if the researcher is working with a small number of cases (less than or about thirty) (List 2004).

21 Agriculture and rural development make up 43 per cent of EU budget expenditure, while regional policy represents 27.7 per cent. For more on this, see: http://ec.europa.eu/budget/figures/fin_fwk0713/fwk0713_en.cfm#cf07_13.

22 On average, 20 per cent of Commission infringement actions are handled by the DG ENV. For more on this, see: http://ec.europa.eu/environment/legal/law/statistics.htm.

23 OS research shows that the effects of socialization occur rather quickly after newcomers join the organization (approximately one month), and after six to ten months on the job, newcomer socialization can be considered complete (Saks and Ashforth 1997).

2 Change, continuity and the politics of ethics reforms

This chapter examines the structure and the evolution of the ethics management system which applies to the European Commission administrative services. It employs as a conceptual reference point the so-called compliance-integrity continuum, which currently represents the most commonly used analytical device for classifying approaches to ethics management. The focus is on the reform packages initiated by two Commissioners, who covered successively the administrative affairs portfolio: Neil Kinnock (1999–2004) and Siim Kallas (2004–2009). Kallas proposed an agenda of change, namely to move away from a focus on control (inherited from the Kinnock reforms) to a "modern" ethics management style, based on guidance and shared values. After a review of the relevant measures, the second part of the chapter evaluates whether and how the Commission has achieved this proposed change. In this connection, the chapter dwells on the increasingly aggressive external scrutiny to which the Commission has been subject since the early 2000s, and on the political dynamics that have accompanied the introduction and implementation of ethics reforms.

Methodologically, this chapter as well as the following one rely on document analysis and semi-structured interviews with Commission ethics experts. Broadly speaking, two classes of documents were analyzed: (1) official regulations, Commission legislative initiatives and their preparatory papers (retrieved through the Commission's online database of internal documents (http://ec.europa.eu/dorie/home.do), as well as Commission activity reports, and (2) internal texts (such as notes, codes of conduct, administrative guides, training materials, various brochures and flyers) which were obtained in hardcopy during fieldwork in Brussels. I used the first category of documents to trace the content of ethics reforms in the European Commission, as well as their framing within the official discourse. The second category of documents offered an insight into the administrative practice these reforms had engendered, and the message which eventually reached the work-floor.

Additionally, twenty-eight interviews were carried out at the European Commission, with officials who deal with public ethics as part of their regular job attributions – they are, so to speak, the "ethics brigade" of the Commission. Most of the interviews were carried out in 2010, and a small number of follow-up interviews were done in 2015. The majority of interviewees belonged to the administrative services; however, the sample also included a representative from the Commission's political tier. Some of the interviewees were responsible for the coordination of ethics policy throughout the Commission – this group was located in the Directorate-General for Human Resources and Security (DG HR), the Investigation and Disciplinary Office (IDOC), the Secretariat General (SG) and the Kallas cabinet. The majority, however, had their attributions confined to a specific Directorate-General – this is the group of the so-called ethics correspondents, an institutional role established by the *Ethics Communication*. For this category, a total of seventeen DGs were surveyed.[1]

Internal experts were chosen for interviews, as they are the only informants with first-hand information on the development, implementation and context of ethics reforms in the Commission. Some of the veterans in coordinating positions had been involved with both the Kinnock and the Kallas packages, and thus could offer a comparative perspective. The ethics correspondents, on the other hand, explained the DG-level approaches, allowing the researcher an unprecedented opportunity to delve deep into the internal dynamics of the Commission, and grasp a fine-grained understanding of "ethics in practice". Internal experts, however, may well be ethics enthusiasts, prone to overestimate the importance and impact of their work. Responding to this possible bias, the analysis relies predominantly on the factual information obtained during interviews, rather than the respondents' perceptions and opinions regarding changes in ethics management at the Commission.

In addition to document analysis and expert interviews, this chapter also draws on a small number of media sources. These were employed for tracing the Commission's history of ethics-related scandals, which is presented in brief in section 2.3.2.

2.1 The compliance-integrity continuum

In order to make sense of the ethics system in place at the European Commission services, I will use as a conceptual device the so-called compliance-integrity continuum (also known as the distinction between rules-based and values-based systems, or between "the low road" and "the high road").[2] It has been consistently used to survey ethics measures in OECD member states (OECD 1996, 2000) and has been deployed for analyzing ethics at the Commission (see particularly Cini 2007a, 2007b, 2010). The essential distinctions are the following:

> The rules-based approach to integrity management emphasizes the importance of external controls on the behaviour of public servants. It prefers formal and detailed rules and procedures as means to reduce integrity violations and prevent corruption. The values-based approach focuses on guidance and 'internal' control, i.e., control exercised by public servants on themselves. This approach aims to stimulate understanding and daily application of values and to improve ethical decision-making skills though interactive training sessions, workshops, ambitious codes of values, individual coaching, etc.
>
> (OECD 2009: 12)

Figure 2.1 The compliance-integrity continuum

Typical compliance instruments are detailed legislation and procedural codes, as well as extensive control mechanisms (both internal and external to the organization), while the integrity-based style recommends the use of interactive ethics training sessions, ethics counselling and ambitious codes of values (Maesschalck 2005). The two opposing ends of the continuum reflect diverging strategic approaches – focusing on *what not to do* or on *what to do* (Pope 2008) – which have concrete implications for policy design. Unsurprisingly, the OECD (1996: 59) suggests that the traditional, Weberian model of public administration (where the principles of legality and hierarchy form the core of bureaucratic control) fits with a compliance-based approach, while the integrity style is better suited to the NPM model (which cultivates use of discretion by public administrators and a results-based control system).

It is evident that the discussion around compliance and integrity-based ethics management reflects broader theoretical debates on the determinants of human behaviour – more specifically, the time-honoured dispute between economics-inspired perspectives, which portray individuals as utility maximizers, and sociological explanations, which emphasize the centrality of values and group ties. To be clear, in the compliance approach the manipulation of incentive structures is seen as the principal means of obtaining the desired conduct from employees, while the integrity side emphasizes instead the internalization of values and norms by public employees (Cini 2007a: 19). To borrow March and Olsen's (1989, 2006) famous terminology, "low road" ethics is consistent with the logic of consequentiality, while "high road" ethics reflects the logic of appropriateness. Because most people, most of the time, are motivated by some combination of incentives and norms, the practitioners' recommendation is that, in practice, the compliance and integrity approaches should be combined in a mutually reinforcing manner.[3] Cooper (1998: 163) explains it eloquently in the following terms: "there must be enough control from outside the individual to discourage those inclinations towards indulgence of self-interest, but enough internal control to encourage the most socially constructive, idealistic, altruistic and creative impulses."

2.2 The development of ethics management in the European Commission services

This section traces the gradual interventions which, over time, have engendered a rather comprehensive ethics infrastructure in the Commission. It does not offer a complete analysis of the system (such an endeavour would well exceed the limits of the research), but rather zooms in on the core instruments of the Commission's ethics infrastructure (although changes in complementary systems, specifically human resource management, audit and financial control, are also minimally covered). I take as a starting point the resignation of the Santer Commission in 1999, generally considered as the watershed that put public ethics on the reform agenda. The focus is on the mandates of Neil Kinnock (1999–2004) and Siim Kallas (2004–2009), both of whom covered administrative affairs portfolios and contributed substantially to the development of ethics management in the Commission – although, as already hinted above, with different visions and priorities. Because the implementation of the program initiated by Kallas was carried on by his successor, there is also some coverage of the period 2010–2014. Given that accounts of the Kinnock era can be found in the existing literature (see particularly Dercks 2001, Hine and McMahon 2004 and Cini 2007a), in what follows I will dedicate substantially more space to the recent years.

2.2.1 The Kinnock reforms: a rule-based ethics system

The fall of the Santer Commission was probably the most damaging public scandal the Commission has ever known. Following the events of March 1999, it found itself hard-pressed to demonstrate credible commitment to securing high behavioural standards. As a result, the concern with enhancing ethics is clearly visible in the *White Paper on Reforming the Commission* – the key principles of "good governance" laid out in the beginning of the document (independence, responsibility, accountability, efficiency and transparency) evidently point this out. Overall, however, the ethics dimension of the so-called Kinnock reforms was subsumed to a larger administrative modernization of the Commission, guided primarily towards efficiency and effectiveness (Cini 2007a). This meant that only a small number of measures addressed ethical behaviour explicitly, but many of the reforms in the human resources and financial control systems had an implicit ethics perspective (Hine and McMahon 2004).

The measures which were most visibly linked to public ethics prove that reformers were largely favouring the compliance-based policy repertoire. For example, the revisions to Title 2 of the *Staff Regulations*, dealing with officials' rights and obligations, reflect a focus on defining the standards of expected behaviour, and particularly on tightening controls. Officials were forbidden to "deal with a matter in which, directly or indirectly, they have any personal interest such as to impair their independence and, in particular, family and financial interests" (Commission 2004b: 9). Declaring interests became mandatory for officials and their spouses in gainful employment. Closely related were the post-employment restrictions, by which officials were required to inform the Appointing Authority (AA)[4] of any occupational activity undertaken within two years of leaving the service of the Communities. The AA could forbid such activity if it "could lead to a conflict with the legitimate interests of the institution" (Art. 16). The AA's approval was also required in case of engaging in work assignments outside the Communities, whether paid or not (Art. 12b), accepting payments, gifts or honours of any kind (Art. 11), running for public office (Art. 15) or publishing any materials which refer to the work of the Communities (Art. 17a).

In the same spirit, the Kinnock package produced a boost of organizational capacities for monitoring and punishing transgressions. In 2002 the Commission's disciplinary office, IDOC, was established. Provisions on disciplinary action were significantly revised, and a policy framework for whistleblowers was introduced (SR, Art. 22a and 22b). Particularly significant was a modification of Art. 22 of SR, which made staff financially liable for any damage suffered by the Communities as a result of their "serious misconduct". Later on, measures were taken to "review and consolidate information circuits between services and the political level on the one hand, and between central and operational services on the other hand" (Commission 2004a: 14). Among others, the *Code of Conduct for Commissioners* was revised to clarify communication between the political and administrative sides. Also, a 'Public Service Ethics' unit was created in the SG in 2005, to serve as a liaison point between the Commission, the European Anti-Fraud Office (OLAF) and IDOC (Ethics official #21).

On the softer side of the ethics policy spectrum, the *White Paper* focused on standard-setting, as part of a larger objective of creating a "culture based on service" (Chapter II of the Action Plan annexed to the *White Paper*). In what regards the services, this was done via the *Code of Good Administrative Behaviour*, adopted in September 2000, following an earlier recommendation of the European Ombudsman (Commission 2000). The document, however, does not cover ethical standards in a broad sense but focuses specifically on dealings with the public, and emphasizes the following principles of "good administration": lawfulness, non-discrimination and equal treatment, proportionality and consistency. Furthermore, it deals in large part with procedural aspects, such that "even with a rather broad understanding of ethical issues [. . .] the Code does not directly concern ethics" (Cini 2007a: 130).

On the other hand, as noted before, the most important contribution of the Kinnock package (in terms of ethics management) was in areas which were not flagged as dealing with ethics – particularly in human resources and financial control systems. It is difficult to do justice to the complexity of these reforms in the confines of this chapter – therefore, in what follows I will discuss only the most important (i.e., ethics-relevant) characteristics.

In regard to human resources management, the *White Paper* reworked the entire spectrum of staff policy, from recruitment to retirement. Some of the most significant revisions were: making recruitment more efficient, transparent, and geographically balanced, by creating a recruitment office common to all institutions (i.e., the EPSO); the introduction of a new staff appraisal system, the Career Development Review, which tied career advancement to performance, rather than length of service alone; and the encouragement of mobility, especially for senior managers and "sensitive" jobs (e.g., in the areas of contract and subsidies awards).[5] As for the financial management, the *White Paper* increased internal managerial responsibility by moving to a decentralized system, where expenditure authorization and control is done at DG level. Additionally, it separated the functions of internal control and internal audit, which meant an additional pair of eyes checking on money management.[6] It is interesting to note that the coverage of the audit system was later expanded beyond financial aspects, to broader governance issues, ethics included. Thus, following revisions in 2007, a new internal control standard (i.e., Internal Control Standard 2) was introduced, dealing specifically with "ethical and organizational values". The changes brought about by the Kinnock reforms are considered to have created a strict and sophisticated control environment – perhaps excessively so, given the amount of time and people now committed to it (Ethics official #23). Also significant is that the *White Paper* was peppered with references to transparency and open government, seen as a means of improving connections between the Commission and the European citizenry, and strengthening accountability. It proposed the creation of an "e-Commission" through boosting the usage of information and communication technologies, and prompted the introduction of legislation on public access to documents in the European institutions.

In conclusion, the *White Paper* installed the building blocks of the Commission's ethics management system, and in doing so it has engendered a compliance-based ethics regime, at least in regard to the administrative levels. Earlier assessments in the literature converge on this point. Thus, Hine and McMahon (2004: 2) concluded that the style of ethics management was "congruent with the rule-based organizational culture of the Commission", while Cini (2007b: 129) notes that despite the introduction of some integrity instruments, "control is much more the norm when it comes to managing Commission ethics in this area". Sources in the Commission also acknowledge that until 2004/5, the ethics framework was heavily rules based (Ethics officials #23, #24).

This preference toward a hard-line approach is not surprising. The *White Paper* did come in response to a major legitimacy crisis, which it sought to address in a concrete and visible way, by limiting officials' discretionary power (Ellinas and Suleiman 2008: 722). With important loopholes in the accountability and control architecture (as documented abundantly in the CIE reports), the Commission needed immediate and ample structural fixes. Hence reformers could not afford the "luxury" of treating ethics lightly, as a question of values.

2.2.2 The Kallas package: moving to a trust-based ethics system

The *European Transparency Initiative* (ETI), introduced in 2006 by Kinnock's successor, Commissioner Siim Kallas, had three pillars: (a) anti-fraud and financial management (i.e., publishing information on the end beneficiaries of EU funds), (b) interest group activity (i.e., the creation of a lobby registration system inside the Commission and adoption of a code of conduct for interest representatives) and, finally, (c) rules and ethical standards for EU officials. Overall, the ETI was presented as a review of the Commission's overall approach to transparency, building on what had already been achieved in the previous years, with transparency itself seen as a key tool to securing citizens' trust:

> The Commission believes that high standards of transparency are part of the legitimacy of any modern administration. The European public is entitled to expect efficient, accountable and service-minded public institutions and that the power and resources entrusted to political and public bodies are handled with care and never abused for personal gain.
>
> (Commission 2006a: 2)

By using transparency as a generic placeholder, the ETI in fact banded together rather different initiatives, with only its last pillar being directly relevant to ethics management in the Commission services. As a part of it, the *Communication on Enhancing the Environment for Professional Ethics in the Commission* was adopted in 2008. Since its launch, it has been the anchor point for all ethics policy in the European Commission.

The *Ethics Communication* was presented as a reform package which broke away from the tradition of control characteristic of the Kinnock ethics regime. This is clear from its introductory remarks: "the main goal of the initiative [. . .] is to consolidate and promote an ethical culture within the Commission, [. . .] to support responsibility, and not to create tools which may be understood as new ways to control staff members" (Commission 2008a: 3). The *Communication* was born in the aftermath of the "Ethics Day" in 2006, a Commission large-scale internal event aimed at debating practical ethical cases. As the preparatory *Note to the College* reveals, the Ethics Day had thrown into sharp relief the staff's need for simpler rules and better ethics guidance, which served to validate Kallas' push for a change of optic in ethics management. A further argument was the necessity to conform to modern practice: 'in public and private organizations alike there is a trend to discuss values and corporate identity and to create ethics offices. The Commission always strives to be a model administration and cannot afford to lag behind best practice' (Commission 2007: 1).

The *Ethics Communication* suggests that ethics policy is more than just preventing and punishing transgressions – it extends to the realization of values and behavioural standards in everyday practice. As some of the interviewees explained, the objective was to have people behave ethically not because they were afraid, but because they genuinely wanted to (Ethics officials #14, #16). The *Communication* sought to achieve a common understanding of ethical values and more trust within the Commission while avoiding the production of new rules. As Kallas explained in a speech delivered at the Staff Forum in 2007:

> I believe that a lively discussion on professional ethics is crucial. [. . .] Common sense and values are often a more efficient guide than long rulebooks. So I hope that in our discussions on ethics we can reach agreement on key

common ethical principles, which should help avoid scandals sending us into 'regulatory overdrive'.

(Kallas 2007: 10)

However, this "more values, no more rules" objective had to be achieved within the confines of an elaborate compliance regime. Consequently, the *Ethics Communication* binds together several truly innovative measures with some others which are clearly a follow-up of the Kinnock mandate. Conceptually, the *Communication* is an even-handed mix of continuity and innovation in ethics policy.

The genuinely novel part is represented by initiatives meant to boost organizational communication and guidance to staff in the area of ethics. Thus, the adoption of a *Statement of Principles of Professional Ethics* was proposed, which 'without prejudice to the *Staff Regulations* should reflect the standards and expectations that underpin the obligations incumbent on all officials' (Commission 2008a: 3). Other measures were the creation of a single "Ethics Website" where all ethics-relevant information would be centralized, and the extension of ethics training programs beyond the induction stage (i.e., compulsory training for sensitive posts and systemic training for managers). Finally, the *Communication* instructed that each DG would appoint a so-called ethics correspondent, i.e., a person who would serve as a point of contact for all ethics-related issues, with strictly advisory attributions.

On the other hand, the measures which related to the Kinnock package were meant to correct some of the negative consequences which appeared during its implementation. Thus, a one-stop shop electronic approval system was recommended, for all staff requests needing authorization from the Appointing Authority. This was considered to not only make the entire procedure more efficient and transparent, but also bring harmonization of authorizing practices across DGs, rectifying the discrepancies which had been noticed (Ethics official #24). Along similar lines, the *Communication* mentioned the creation of a checklist that would help officials better identify conflicts of interest, and the revision (simplification) of existing regulations on favours, gifts and hospitality on the one hand and outside activities and assignments on the other.

It is evident that despite a discourse of radical change, content-wise the *Ethics Communication* represents a more toned-down effort to smooth the edges of the Kinnock legacy, and enrich it with elements of guidance and awareness-raising. Indeed, in terms of concrete changes to the Commission's ethics infrastructure, building up ethics guidance for staff was the most important achievement. Whereas the Kinnock reforms left this front largely uncovered (Cini 2007a), nowadays the Commission has much more to offer. Following the points outlined in the Kallas package, DG HR has made available a reader-friendly internal Ethics Website, which consolidates, explains and illustrates by hypothetical cases the relevant legislation. Moreover, specialized ethics training is offered regularly (i.e., the two-day course "Ethics and Integrity", mandatory for newcomers, plus a program on "ethical leadership" which targets staff in management positions).

Finally, and most importantly, a structure for managing ethics inside the DGs was created with the appointment of local ethics correspondents. Organized in a network coordinated by DG HR, the correspondents represent the "transmission belt" between the central ethics structures of the Commission and the staff on the work-floor. Thus, for the vast majority of officials, they were the "face" of Kallas' new policy – in this respect it is significant that although sparse in outlining their job description, the *Ethics Communication* did emphasize the element of trust:

> Every DG should therefore appoint an "ethics correspondent" to serve as the focal and first contact point for all ethics-related issues, both for the services and their staff. When dealing with queries from staff the ethics correspondents *act in confidence*.
>
> (Commission 2008a: 4, emphasis added)

Reflecting this concept, there was much local discretion in the appointment process, as DG HR did not transmit any specific criteria but merely recommended that the person should already be knowledgeable of, or have some experience with, ethics issues (Ethics officials #1, #20, #24), and have a positive reputation among staff in the DG (Ethics official #6). The ethics correspondents are located in either human resources or internal control units, and many of them are in managerial positions. The new attributions came as an addition to the regular (full) work schedule.

With the new post, concrete responsibility for ethics management was assigned, which has led to an explosion of ethics initiatives within the DGs – basically filling up a vacuum, as there is little to suggest the presence of anything similar before. The repertoire of instruments is characteristic of the integrity management toolkit, with some commonly encountered examples being: an ethics-dedicated section on DG intranet; DG-specific ethics codes and guidelines; and short ethics training and one-off awareness-raising events (e.g., "Ethics Days", ethics workshops, lunchtime debates, visits by the ethics correspondent to weekly unit meetings). Moreover, activities are quite similar across DGs, which is not surprising, since the network of ethics correspondents is an environment which stimulates sharing of best practices (Ethics officials #1, #9, #15).

2.2.3 The Kallas package after 2010

After 2010, Maroš Šefčovič, the new Vice-President for Inter-Institutional Relations and Administration, followed through on the *European Transparency Initiative*, where many points had been left open at the time the College changed. Thus, during the Barroso II Commission (2010–2014), the *Ethics Communication* continued to serve as the political basis for ethics policy in the Commission services. Overall, however, it did not constitute a priority action line for this period. On the one hand, other elements of the ETI received more attention, in particular the second pillar relating to lobby regulation, as the Commission and the European Parliament merged their respective registration systems in 2011 creating the so-called *Transparency Register*. On the other hand, the Šefčovič cabinet oversaw an extensive revision of the *Staff Regulations*, started in early 2011 and eventually completed in 2013. The revision constituted a response to the sovereign debt crisis which hit the European Union in the aftermath of the global financial meltdown of 2008 and created pressure for the European institutions to show solidarity with national public administrations by introducing cost-cutting measures. This was the core purpose of the reform, eventually achieved by increasing working hours to forty per week without additional compensation, raising the pensionable age, changing the method for adjusting salaries and pensions in reference to those in the civil services of the Member States, along with other, more minor measures. Another important plank was represented by upgrading human resources processes, in order to preserve a high standard of service and the attractiveness of jobs in the European administration despite the less appealing financial aspects. This entailed some readjustment to the career structure and the way performance management was carried out, plus more flexible arrangements around non-permanent contracts (for an overview of relevant measures, see Commission 2013a).

As regards ethics measures, the years of the Barroso II Commission were characterized by a continuation of the awareness-raising and guidance efforts commenced during Kallas' term. The focus has been on specialized guidance for topical issues. Thus, in 2012, two communications from Vice-President Šefčovič were issued, one regarding the handling of gifts and hospitality from third parties, and the other on whistleblowing, with awareness-raising campaigns following each of them. In 2013 a revised *Decision on Outside Activities and Assignments* was issued, with the purpose of streamlining the internal practice by defining categories of ancillary activities that could, in principle, be approved, and others which would not receive AA approval (Ethics official #24). Additionally, targeted guidance on a number of other topics (e.g., staff conduct during the campaign for the EP elections in 2014, the use of social media, engaging in volunteer activities) was issued on a more ad-hoc and low-key basis. Awareness-raising continued with a new series of master classes delivered by external experts (Commission 2012c), a program of DG visits carried out by representatives of IDOC and DG HR since 2013 (Ethics official #24), various articles published in the internal Commission magazine and the regular updating of the special Ethics Website. Notably, in 11–15 November 2013 a Commission-wide Ethics Week was organized, following the precedent of the Ethics Day in 2006 but using a different template. By comparison, the Ethics Week had much more of a grassroots feel, with ethics correspondents organizing local events in their respective DGs and Directors-General issuing statements to their services on the importance of ethics (Ethics official #24). The event was topped off with a conference and a video discussion with Vice-President Šefčovič and Commissioner Barnier (Commission 2014a).

Alongside all this, the one-stop shop electronic system for declarations and requests of authorization to the Appointing Authorities, which had been proposed in the *Ethics Communication*, was developed almost entirely during these years. An internal IT platform was used for the purpose, where different modules were added gradually, relating to outside activities, gifts and hospitality offers, spouses' employment and ad-hoc conflicts of interests (Commission 2015a). The network of ethics correspondents was boosted by setting up an electronic share-point in 2012, where all relevant legislation and guidelines were stored and which was used to exchange practices and address questions on specific cases to the coordinating unit in DG HR (Ethics official #26). Additionally, since 2012 ethics correspondents were given the additional responsibility to offer guidance on whistleblowing issues (previously this was mostly covered by OLAF, and the specialized services in DG HR and the Secretariat General).

Apart from these activities, which represent the realization of specific points in the *Ethics Communication* or otherwise follow the line and tone set by it, the revision of *Staff Regulations* occasioned other changes in the ethics system applying to the services, which, importantly, were neither initiated nor planned by the Commission. Specifically, new formalities were introduced related to conflict of interest prevention. An obligation was created for all AAs to examine, before making new recruitments, whether the candidates faced any potential or actual conflicts of interests – to that end, candidates are now asked to complete a specific interest declaration form (Art. 11). Furthermore, former senior officials were prohibited, in principle for a period of twelve months after leaving office, from engaging in lobbying and advocacy activities vis-à-vis their former colleagues, with European institutions obliged to publish annually information on the implementation of this provision, including a list of the cases assessed (Art. 16). A similar restriction was introduced for staff members on leave on personal grounds,[7] who were also required to undergo a conflict of interests check upon return to active service (Art. 40). Finally, the European institutions were obliged to establish internal procedures for handling whistleblower disclosures and for protecting the legitimate interests of staff members who engage in such activities (Art. 22(c)).

***

In conclusion, looking retrospectively at the measures implemented after the traumatic Santer resignation, it is evident that the European Commission has acquired a comprehensive system of ethics management. This system was built up incrementally: it started out as a less emphasized component of a large effort of administrative modernization and only later, with the *Ethics Communication*, entered the policy agenda as an item with more visibility. The Kinnock reforms laid the foundations of ethics management in the Commission, and on this basis the *Communication* developed ethics guidance for staff, a trend which continued during the Barroso II Commission as well.

2.3 The *Ethics Communication* and the delivery of change

At the level of official rhetoric, the *Ethics Communication* proposed to bring the Commission closer to a "modern" management style based on guidance and shared values. This was clearly explained in the preparatory notes: "only if we agree on a common set of principles can we move from a rules based system to a trust based system in conformity with a modern management structure" (Commission 2007: 1). However, judging by the actual content of this package, as well as the administrative practice which it has engendered within the Commission, it is clear that the agenda of change was not fully realized. As illustrated amply in the previous sections, the *Ethics Communication* has brought about major improvements in the Commission's ethics system, particularly in what regards ethics guidance. There is undoubtedly more "ethics talk" now compared with the "old days", when newcomers received a copy of the *Staff Regulations* and started working the next day (Ethics official #21). However, more communication is not necessarily equal to more values and trust in ethics management. Commission officials remain bound by a wide variety of restrictions (in regard to outside activities, speeches and publications, declaring their financial and family interests, etc.), which have only grown with the most recent revision of the *Staff Regulations*.

To come back to the distinction between compliance and integrity-based ethics management, discussed at the beginning of this chapter, an integrity-based management style "means giving up some control" (OECD 1996: 59) and instead focusing on building a supporting culture in the organization where employees can be *trusted* to behave ethically. From this perspective, ethics is not restrictive but becomes a resource which helps public servants deal with discretion. While it is common to draw parallels between these two approaches to ethics management and concrete policy instruments (as shown in section 2.1), one should also consider that it is entirely possible that the same policy instrument can be used in different ways according to where the emphasis lies in a particular ethics system. To give just one illustration of this, consider the distinction that Longstaff (1994) makes between ethics training and ethics education: while the former is designed to impart to people the knowledge and skills necessary to behave according to the organizational ethos, the latter aims to develop individual moral autonomy, so that people would more authentically and *on their own* approach ethics questions in their organization. Therefore, the difference between the two styles is to be found (also) in the deeper assumptions on which they are based – namely, while in a compliance optic, ethics is achieved through rule-compliant behaviour, the integrity-based style is more about stimulating individual ethical competence and agency (on this point, see also Weaver and Treviño 1999, Huberts *et al.* 2014: 240).

It is when considering these more fundamental aspects that I find that the Commission did not manage to turn the corner, as suggested by the official discourse. It is significant that rolling back controls was neither proposed nor achieved, even though it was at least implied, at the launch of the *Ethics Communication*, that these aspects created an uneasy situation within the Commission. What the *Communication* settled for, instead, was to stop the regulatory inflation and adapt internal systems to handle the existing administrative burden, which was already substantial. The fact that an electronic database (i.e., the one-stop shop approval system) had to be built specifically for this purpose is very telling. It is also significant that the purpose of the massive internal communication effort engendered by the *Ethics Communication* was simply to make sure that staff members were well acquainted with their statutory obligations. These aspects will be discussed at length in the following chapter, but for now, in order to illustrate this point, it is instructive to look at the characteristics of the interaction between ethics correspondents and staff members. As provided in the *Ethics Communication*, and amply confirmed though interviews, ethics correspondents are responsible for advising, in confidentiality, on any ethics-related inquiries coming from staff. The correspondents demonstrate ownership over this role, describing themselves as an internal point of contact on ethics issues (Ethics officials #3, #4, #9, #14, #19), somebody colleagues can turn to if they have a more delicate problem (Ethics official #3), or somebody who lends a friendly ear in confidence (Ethics official #6). When asked about the issues on which staff requests guidance most frequently, ethics correspondents rather unanimously pointed to: external activities (anything from teaching assignments to honorary membership in voluntary associations), publishing and public speeches, dealing with gifts and hospitality, and potential conflicts of interest. Essentially, all of these are subjects on which AA authorization and/or the completion of specific forms is required. Indeed, since the objective was to ensure that 'everybody knows the rules', it is only natural that staff inquiries flock in areas where compliance is formalized in some way.

In conclusion, what the *Ethics Communication* achieved was simply a diversification of ethics management instruments in the Commission, while keeping intact the compliance philosophy behind the system. In this regard, not much has changed since the Kinnock years. But why exactly was it that the more fundamental transformation suggested in the official discourse remained out of reach? This is a puzzling question, because the internal conditions were all favourable, in terms of political leadership, know-how and organizational resources. Siim Kallas was a committed policy entrepreneur – as Cini (2008: 755) notes, in the absence of clear priorities on the administrative agenda of the Barroso I Commission, Kallas took the initiative and made the ETI into "his pet project". Maroš Šefčovič, his successor, pushed on faithfully with the implementation of the ETI. On the other hand, the Commission was fully able to mobilize the resources needed to implement the *Ethics Communication*. Without a doubt, the remarkable amount of ethics initiatives within the DGs in the past years proves this, all the more so because they represent a major innovation.[8] Finally, the ethics officials clearly understood what integrity-based ethics management entails. Thus, some of the interviewees remarked that ethics should not be a burden, but a normal reaction for everyone, a reflex for identifying dangerous situations and reacting appropriately (Ethics officials #3, #6). Others argued that being "ethical" boils down to using one's own good judgment, and consulting when in doubt (Ethics officials #6, #7, #16, #19). There was a clear awareness that regulation becomes counterproductive after a certain point (Ethics officials #14, #19). Several interviewees even admitted that the internal capacities for monitoring employee conduct are limited, so it becomes necessary to rely on people's understanding of ethical principles, their "good will" to behave correctly (Ethics officials #1, #6, #16).

The core argument advanced in the remainder of this chapter is that in order to understand the character of the ethics system in the Commission services, one must look to the external conditions under which the Commission operated. On the one hand, it found itself under increasingly aggressive public scrutiny, made possible by the development of investigative journalism and the emergence of anti-corruption watchdog groups in the Brussels sphere. On the other hand, the assertiveness of the European Parliament, eager to establish itself as an up-and-coming accountability forum in the EU, meant that episodes of bad publicity were transformed into political costs. These pressures, explored in more detail in the following two sections, have restricted the Commission's autonomy to define its own line in ethics management, and in particular rendered any sort of relaxation of controls unfeasible.

2.3.1 Public scrutiny and ethics scandals

An important factor which contributed to the increased public scrutiny facing the Commission was the development of investigative journalism in the Brussels sphere. As Shore (2007: 200) argues, one of the reasons why "the internal life of this most public of administrations remain[ed] so private" before the Santer resignation was that journalists were "all part of the system". Around that time, however, the situation began to change – the national media proved a growing interest in EU affairs and unearthed the EU fraud stories of the late 1990s, which were then avidly relayed by the Brussels press corps (Cini 2007a). This section provides an overview of the ethics scandals which have periodically punctuated the evolution of the Commission's ethics system and thus illustrates the increasingly important role that the media has had in this regard.

Quite naturally, with the events of 1999, the Commission received a great deal of bad press – as Cini (2004: 43) notes, "both Commissioners and Commission officials were tarred with the same brush, the assumption being that unethical conduct of various kinds was rife within the EU institutions". It did not help that the reports of the Committee of Independent Experts, which had precipitated the Santer resignation, contained a strongly moralistic tone. At the time, the media focused particularly on the case of the French Commissioner, Edith Cresson, who had appointed Mr. Berthelot, her personal dentist and family friend, to a position of "visiting scientist" in the Commission, for which he was obviously not qualified. Cresson refused to assume responsibility for any wrongdoing and stated, in her defence, that she had only tried "to do something for Europe" (for extensive press coverage, see Shore 2005: 144). It was perhaps this public attitude of defiance that did the Commission the most damage, since, as one official noted, Cresson "made us all look like crooks" (Ethics official #8).

Later on, for much of 2003, the so-called Eurostat affair held the headlines. It remains, to this date, the most severe crisis the Commission has faced since the Santer resignation, although the scale is clearly not the same – as one interviewee put it, "the Commission stumbled, but did not fall" (Ethics official #24). With this episode, the trend of bad publicity continued, as it was demonstrated that many of the issues singled out in the CIE reports had still not been solved. Concretely, the allegations related to the relationship between Eurostat (the Commission's statistical office) and several of its contractors. There were accusations of manipulating tender procedures to favour certain companies, and blatant conflicts of interests, as Yves Franchet, Eurostat's Director General at the time, was the founder of two firms which benefited repeatedly from Eurostat contracts. One case in particular stood out, concerning the establishment, by senior Eurostat officials, of a savings bank account into which around €900,000 of EU funds were put. The money apparently came from the sale of EU data products by Planistat, a French company under contract with Eurostat.[9]

After 2004 the turmoil eased up, but the press continued to display a growing appetite for sleaze stories. An illustrative albeit extreme example of this is the *Sunday Times*, whose journalists have been actively "hunting" for subjects by going undercover. They managed to create quite a damaging story with the case of Fritz-Harald Wenig, a former Director in DG TRADE, which made the headlines in 2008. Wenig leaked highly sensitive, confidential information to two undercover journalists posing as lobbyists for a Chinese company and did so over lavish dinners at Brussels' elite restaurants, and apparently with the promise of a financial reward of €100,000 waiting in a frozen bank account (*Sunday Times*, 07.09.2008). In 2012, the Commission was again embarrassed over its dealings with private interests, this time in a more high-profile case involving John Dalli, the Maltese Commissioner for Health and Consumer Policy. Tobacco producer Swedish Match reported to the Commission that an associate of Dalli had asked them for a €60 million bribe in exchange for a favourable intervention in the revision of the controversial Tobacco Products Directive (*Reuters*, 24.10.2013). Although the reaction was very quick and decisive – Dalli resigned shortly afterwards on Barroso's request – the reputational damage had already been incurred. What is more, the affair dragged on, as the European Parliament took issue with the quality of the OLAF investigation into the matter (*EurActiv*, 29.04.2013), and Dalli opened a lawsuit claiming that he had been "ambushed" by the Commission President into resigning (*EurActiv*, 08.07.2014).

Closely connected to these instances of unsavory behavior towards lobbyists, the media also devoted attention to the "revolving door" phenomenon, which refers to individuals taking up private-sector jobs after leaving public employment, or vice-versa. These moves raise ethics concerns insomuch as the overlap between the public and private positions occupied by the same person is large enough to create conflicts of interests. Although to some extent this subject had always stirred some controversy, it captured the public attention more fully after the first Barroso Commission finished its term in office in 2010. On that occasion, some ex-Commissioners were hired by companies in the industry fields over which they previously had regulatory authority. One prominent example was Gunther Verheugen, former Commissioner for industry, who had secured executive positions with a number of banks and consultancy firms, and also established his own lobbying consultancy – the "European Experience Company" – shortly after leaving the Commission (*EUObserver*, 31.08.10). Another was Charlie McCreevy, ex-Commissioner for Internal Market, who joined the executive board of the British investment bank NBNK, as well as taking a position with low-cost airline Ryanair – although he was eventually forced to resign from NBNK (*EUObserver*, 08.10.10). Later on, same media coverage was also given to the "revolving door" in the higher echelons of the Commission services, including the case of a former

DG TRADE official who had moved on to Huawei, China's biggest telecommunications company, with the Commission soon thereafter opening investigations against the same company on suspicions of price dumping (*Der Spiegel*, 09.10.2013). All these cases were problematic because the network of contacts and the related political leverage of those who had worked in the Commission provided their new employers an unfair advantage over competitors.

In parallel to the rise of investigative journalism, the Brussels NGO scene changed considerably, with watchdog groups becoming very vocal. This, too, contributed to the trend of increasing scrutiny over Commission business. Civil society activism on anti-corruption issues was rather minimal during the Prodi Commission, but the launch of the European Transparency Initiative provided the spark for the coagulation of Brussels' strongest watchdog coalition in the field, the Alliance for Lobbying Transparency and Ethics Regulation (ALTER-EU). ALTER-EU now consists of approximately 200 civil society groups, trade unions, academics and public affairs firms, which share a concern for "the increasing influence exerted by corporate lobbyists on the political agenda in Europe"[10] (ALTER-EU 2015). Another noteworthy presence is the EU branch of Transparency International, which opened in 2010 – although a later arrival in Brussels, the TI EU Office represents a heavyweight with a global network at its back and a reputation to match. It too holds an interest in (undue) lobby influence in EU institutions, but overall the agenda is broader, including public access to documents and management of the EU budget and public integrity beyond the EU institutions.[11]

Civil society actors were often successful at profiling certain issues as integrity risks for the European Commission, shaping the public discourse around them, and eventually mobilizing other actors for political action on these agendas. One telling and rather recent example of this relates to the revolving-door phenomenon, portrayed by activists as a particularly insidious and widely used channel by which powerful and moneyed private interests obtained privileged access to the Commission. Riding (and sometimes feeding) the wave of publicity regarding this issue, ALTER-EU carried out continuous monitoring,[12] periodically issued reports (see ALTER-EU 2010, 2011) and, through several of its core groups, placed multiple strategic complaints to the European Ombudsman. One such case was opened in 2013 and concerned the Commission's generic treatment of post-employment issues in the services. Based on the inspection of fifty-four individual files, the Ombudsman found that a solid procedure to review potential conflicts of interest in those situations was lacking (European Ombudsman 2014a). Another case that same year, also originating from a complaint filed by NGOs affiliated with ALTER-EU, found that the Chairman of the Ad-Hoc Ethical Committee, the body that decides on Commissioners' post term-of-office activities,[13] was unfit to occupy this position, as he himself was exposed to conflicts of interest (the person in question worked for a law firm where he was representing the interests of private actors before the Commission) (European Ombudsman 2013a). A little earlier, the Ombudsman had handled a very similar complaint, concerning the European Food Safety Agency (the head of the division dealing with genetically modified organisms had moved on to a biotechnology company), and invited the agency to strengthen its internal procedures (European Ombudsman 2013b). These inquiries, coupled with media attention and more direct lobbying by NGOs, shaped the background against which the European Parliament seized the opportunity offered by the revision of the *Staff Regulations* to introduce stricter provisions regarding post-employment situations, and the management of conflicts of interest more generally (see section 2.2.3 above).

In conclusion, the brief (far from exhaustive) overview provided above illustrates that ever since the Santer resignation, the European Commission has had to deal with an incisive press and NGO scene, as well as periodic public scandals, which raised doubts about the standards of conduct practiced by its staff members (and Commissioners). This has clearly created pressure for the Commission, which began to attach a lot of importance to the way it was publically perceived. With a public image issue that had to be addressed, it is no wonder that the theme of public trust was often emphasized in connection to ethics regulation. As expressed by Maroš Šefčovič in a discourse delivered to the ethics correspondents in the Commission:

> If you follow the media, you see the debate of the alleged influence of lobbies in the decision-making in the EU, but also on national governments and parliaments; we have regular criticism from some NGOs, MEPs and media about alleged conflicts of interests and we must take this very [seriously], even if we think it is not true. It is not only important that the professional behaviour is without reproach, but also that the greater public perceives it like this. This is essential to have the trust of the people.
>
> (Šefčovič 2013: 2)

Indeed, ethics officials are all too aware that the Commission is permanently watched, that the perception of wrongdoing is as damaging as wrongdoing itself (Ethics official #9) and that "in communication, coping with fantasy is the most difficult thing to do" (Ethics official #8).

2.3.2 Ethics as a political liability

As the Commission became monitored more and more for its standards of conduct, the European Parliament grew eager to pick up and capitalize on its (apparent) ethical shortcomings. Its growing interest meant that ethics was not only, as portrayed above, a problem of public reputation (with negative repercussions on the Commission's legitimacy vis-à-vis European citizens), but also a liability in its political confrontation with the Parliament.

As Judge and Earnshaw (2002) point out, the Santer resignation represented a resounding victory for the European Parliament in relation to the Commission and was interpreted by commentators at the time as a huge leap taken by the Parliament towards establishing itself as a democratic force in the EU. The events of 1999 put the Commission on the defensive vis-à-vis the Parliament – a trend sustained by the Eurostat affair, which represented another important occasion for the Parliament to attack the Commission on the issue of standards of conduct. Numerous hearings were held by the Budgetary Control Committee in the course of 2003 and 2004, and rumours swirled regarding the resignation of the Commissioners involved, although eventually this did not happen (Cini 2007a).

Later on, the Parliament repeatedly used its leverage on budgetary matters to push the Commission on ethics. For instance, in 2011 and later on in 2014 it voted to freeze part of the budget for the European Commission's expert groups[14] until measures were put in place and consistently applied to enhance transparency and avoid capture by special interests (*EUObserver*, 22.10.2014). In 2010, after the slew of revolving-door scandals which followed the departure of the Barroso I Commission, the Parliament threatened to withhold the transitional allowances paid out to Commissioners after their mandate ended, unless changes were introduced into the *Code of Conduct for Commissioners* (*European Voice*, 30.09.2010).

The budgetary discharge procedure has in fact regularly been used to request action on ethics matters from the Commission. Most recommendations contained in the annual discharge reports are, unsurprisingly, linked to financial management and control systems and the effective use of public funds – but, over time, the Committee on Budgetary Control has also included points that pertain more directly to ethics management (both in the services and in the College). For instance, the reports for the financial years 2009 and 2013 both call on the Commission to ensure that its staff is well aware of the relevant SR articles relating to whistleblower protection, and that the rights of whistleblowers are fully upheld (European Parliament 2011, 2015). The reports for 2005, 2006, 2007 and 2008 all include specific points on revising the *Code of Conduct for Commissioners*, with the last one explicitly stating that the Parliament expects to be consulted on these revisions (European Parliament 2010). The discharge report for the financial year 2012 covered in-depth the unsatisfactory management of conflicts of interests in EU agencies, deploring the lack of a comprehensive regulatory framework that would impose basic requirements applicable to all agencies, and calling on the Commission to initiate action in this regard, again in consultation with the Parliament. Measures on post-employment restrictions were also requested, this being deemed a continuing problem not only for the agencies, but for the Commission as well (European Parliament 2014).

Apart from the power of the purse, the Parliament has also employed more mundane (but no less effective) channels, such as the organization of hearings and workshops, to increase visibility around certain ethics issues. The reporting of misconduct witnessed at the workplace – "blowing the whistle", or whistleblowing, as it is commonly referred to – represents an interesting (although not necessarily typical) example of this. The Parliament had held a long-standing interest in this topic, with the Budgetary Control Committee being instrumental in sparking a debate around the effectiveness of the whistleblower framework provided for in the *Staff Regulations* (Art. 22a and 22b). Two separate studies on the matter were commissioned, the first to come out in 2006 (RCC 2006) and the second five years later (PricewaterhouseCoopers Belgium & iForce 2011). Both were critical of the existing provisions, highlighting, among others, their insufficient coverage, the modest protection offered to whistleblowers and, consequently, the failure to encourage or even facilitate disclosures. The latter study also made a point of the complete lack of internal programs within European institutions to implement the existing articles in the SR, deficient as they were (PricewaterhouseCoopers Belgium & iForce 2011: 64–69). As a follow-up, the Committee organized public hearings and workshops in the course of 2011, and, finally, it used the window of opportunity created by the SR revision in 2013 to introduce a new provision (Art. 22c) by which EU institutions were required to put in place procedures for handling complaints made by whistleblowers regarding the treatment received after making a disclosure. Significantly, the *Guidelines on Whistleblowing* adopted by the Commission in 2012 were a partial reaction to this continued criticism but also the result of internal reviews which had revealed that many disclosures regarded trivial matters, and too few cases of "proper" whistleblowing had occurred over the years (Ethics official #24).

Along with the Parliament, and often in cooperation with it, the European Ombudsman has also taken a long-standing interest in the Commission's treatment of public ethics. This was done via two channels. Firstly, the Ombudsman has used its investigative powers to make a stand on specific ethics questions – this was achieved either by following up on strategically placed complaints (as exemplified above with the revolving-door cases) or, as has been the case especially since 2013, through own-initiative inquiries (e.g., on the composition and transparency of expert groups, on rules to protect whistleblowers). Secondly, the European Ombudsman was active in setting horizontal standards of conduct for the European administration (and, implicitly, for the Commission services). In the context of the Kinnock reforms, it produced the *Code of Good Administrative Behaviour*. Later on, in 2011, the *Public Service Principles for the EU Civil Service* were issued, a document described as a "high-level distillation of the ethical standards for EU civil servants" (European Ombudsman 2012: 3).

***

In conclusion, the political environment of the Commission was a constraining one, as institutions which held it accountable took a keen interest in its treatment of ethics issues. The outcomes of the *Ethics Communication* should be understood as a result of this enhanced external scrutiny, and the politics that came with it. This is somewhat ironic, because the *Ethics Communication* actually represented an attempt, from the Commission, to take back policy agency, and shift from a passive, predominantly responsive position to a more proactive approach in ethics management. To be clear, the ethics component of the Kinnock reforms had followed closely the agenda set by the CIE reports (implicitly by the European Parliament), as "the Commission contented itself with working through the Reports line-by-line, to ensure that what the Reform was about was operationalising in a practical manner the earlier document" (Cini 2007a: 212). By contrast, with Kallas, policy change was the result of a more reflective outlook towards internal organizational needs. As mentioned before, the *Communication* drew on the conclusions of the Ethics Day in 2006, as well as on the preparatory work of an internal working group, which had been tasked with articulating solutions that would render the Commission's ethics system "modern, coherent, easily accessible and easily understandable" (Commission 2008a: 3). The timing was also very significant – as one interviewee remarked, the fact that the *Communication* did not follow any scandal threatening the Commission's reputation signalled that it was now possible to "talk" about ethics in a proactive way (Ethics official #23). This meant that the Commission was now a mature organization, which had left behind the days when ethics policy was basically a response to *publicized* integrity failures, and instead assumed much more ownership and initiative over these matters.

The Commission did implement the points of the *Ethics Communication* consistently, and, as should be evident from the overview presented earlier in this chapter, it invested significant organizational resources in doing so. In keeping with the agenda of "more values, no more rules", it did not itself initiate any changes to the basic regulatory framework, and focused instead on implementing effectively the existing provisions. However, the external conditions in which it operated imposed clear limits on what was possible to achieve. Although, unlike the early 2000s, the Commission was no longer admonished over financial management and the treatment of contractors, the relationship with private interests had become a major sticking point. As shown in section 2.3.2 above, revolving-door cases regularly made the headlines, as did instances of shady dealings with lobbyists. It was not difficult to interpret these slippages as the consequence of the Commission lacking proper controls with regard to conflicts of interest and engagement with outside parties. The European Parliament – often in tandem with the Ombudsman and supported by the work of anti-corruption activists in Brussels – has certainly taken that route. In these circumstances, the Commission was ill-positioned to try rolling back the controls created in the "audit fury" of the Kinnock years. As one interviewee confirmed, the European Parliament was very keen not to see this happen, and with the power to refuse granting the annual budget discharge, it had the institutional muscle to enforce its viewpoint (Ethics official #23). In fact, the amendments introduced by the Parliament on the occasion of the *Staff Regulations* revision in 2013 prove quite clearly its preference for a tighter regulatory framework for ethics at the European Commission.

The importance attached internally to public perceptions also played a key role. Because the Commission had engaged in ethics reforms as a response to corruption (and the public image problems that came with it), the hard-line approach specific of the Kinnock years was understood to be a guarantee that irregularities of the type leading to the Santer resignation would not happen again. This framing survived in later years, as the evolution of the Commission's ethics system was periodically and significantly punctuated by episodes of scandal. For all the Commission's ambitions of being a modern administration and getting in line with international best practice (which pointed to the use of integrity-based ethics management), these contextual specificities proved important, suggesting that the right kind of framework, for an organization that kept getting into trouble, was one with strong controls. Concretely, for Kallas this meant that rolling back controls was not only politically not viable (as explained above), but also ill-advised, since it risked sending the wrong message, i.e., that the Commission was relaxing on the ethics front. All that was possible to achieve was the blending of a "high road" style of policy instruments, with an organizational message and practice that remained compliance based – in other words, the Commission did the best with what it had at its disposal.

2.4 Conclusion

This chapter has charted the system for managing ethics in the European Commission services. The first section offered an overview of the relevant administrative reforms implemented over the last decade. It has been established that ethics entered the Commission's agenda in the context of the *White Paper on Reforming the Commission*, which outlined the overhauling reform program initiated by the Prodi Commission – specifically Neil Kinnock, the Commissioner responsible, at the time, for administrative affairs. Even though the topic was not particularly highlighted, the *White Paper* did lay the foundations of the Commission's ethics management system, by amending significantly the *Staff Regulations*, establishing IDOC, introducing the *Code of Good Administrative Behaviour*, and bringing significant changes to the human resources, as well as financial control and audit systems. Kinnock's successor, Siim Kallas, continued the administrative reform agenda with the *European Transparency Initiative*. In this framework, he introduced the *Communication for Enhancing the Environment for Professional Ethics in the Commission*, which became the main anchor point for ethics policy after its launch, in 2008. Compared with the *White Paper*, the *Communication* had a more focused approach, its main achievement being a dramatic increase in awareness-raising and guidance activities throughout the Commission. In conclusion, the Commission nowadays possess a well-developed policy arsenal for managing ethics.

This being said, the agenda set by the *Ethics Communication,* to effect a transition to a system based on a common understanding of ethical values, and more trust within the organization, was not fully carried through. Findings suggest that the administrative practice fell short of the official discourse – this is demonstrated, first and foremost, by the fact that the internal awareness-raising activity focused on getting officials acquainted with the relevant rules (and their correct interpretation). Such an approach is closer to a "low road" view, where ethics is largely equated with "staying safe". On the other hand, Kallas had also intended to not create "new ways to control staff members" (Commission 2008a: 3) – but eventually this did happen as the European Parliament, egged on by anti-corruption activists and a more general public concern over the Commission's dealings with the Brussels lobby, used the revision of the *Staff Regulations* in 2013 to introduce several amendments which tightened the regime regarding conflicts of interest and whistleblower protection.

The fate of ethics reforms in the European Commission is a testimony to the importance of historical and political context. The Commission lacked neither the know-how, nor the organizational resources, nor the political leadership necessary to make the shift towards integrity-based management. The outcomes of the *Ethics Communication* are the result of path dependence. Because during Kinnock's mandate ethics reforms came on the heels of public scandal and criticism, a relaxation of controls – even after the storm had passed – proved to be out of the question. The high level of public scrutiny to which the Commission was subject, and the importance attached internally to public perceptions, also reinforced the status quo.

The type of ethics management practiced by the Commission, explored in this chapter using the compliance-integrity continuum as a reference point, matters for officials' socialization because, as argued previously, the "high road" and "low road" ethics represent – and may signal to organizational members – very different notions about what ethics is. Furthermore, as mentioned in Chapter 1, values and ethical standards tend to be quite abstract and undisputed, gaining substance only in context. Therefore, accounting for contextual factors and their influence on the Commission's ethics system, as done in these pages, is also important for an adequate understanding of what ethics means nowadays for this organization and its employees. The following chapter will build on the findings presented here to explore the messages communicated internally about ethics and the subjects deemed as particularly important in this context.

Notes

1 The seventeen DGs were: the Directorate-General for the Internal Market and Services, the Directorate-General for Justice, Freedom and Security, the Directorate-General for Regional Policy, the Directorate-General for Enterprise and Industry, the Directorate-General for the Environment, the Directorate-General for Competition, the Directorate-General for the Information Society and Media, the Directorate-General for Health and Consumers, the Directorate-General for Taxation and Customs Union, the Directorate-General for Economic and Financial Affairs, the Directorate-General for Humanitarian Aid, the Directorate-General for Trade, the Directorate-General for External Relations, the Directorate-General for Enlargement, the Secretariat General, the Directorate-General for the Budget and the Directorate-General for Interpretation. Of these, fourteen were "operational" (i.e., active in policymaking and implementation, in the areas of both internal market and external relations) and three "administrative" (i.e., with predominantly managerial tasks). Thus, the collected information can be considered representative for a wide range of activities and functions performed in the Commission. As an aside, the reader will notice that this book uses the names which various Commission DGs had at the time when fieldwork was conducted. This is done for reasons of historical accuracy; however, it should be noted that DG names, and indeed some of their competences, are subject to change over time – for instance, the Directorate-General for the Internal Market and Services has become since 2014 the Directorate-General for Internal Market, Industry, Entrepreneurship and SMEs (DG GROW), while the Directorate-General for Health and Consumers is nowadays called the Directorate-General for Health and Food Safety (DG SANTE).
2 The Organisation for Economic Co-operation and Development (OECD) has probably been the most prominent voice publicizing the compliance-integrity continuum. However, the distinction does not originate with the OECD but is a fundamental one in the literature on ethics management (see, for example, Rohr 1978, Lewis 1991, Paine 1994).

3 For example, point 9 in OECD's *Recommendation on Principles for Managing Ethics in the Public Service* (1998: 4) states: "government policy should not only delineate the minimal standards below which a government official's actions will not be tolerated, but also clearly articulate a set of public service values that employees should aspire to".
4 Basically, the Appointing Authority (AA) designates the employer. The AA exercises a wide range of attributions related to the officials' careers, rights and obligations, disciplinary action, etc. It is up to each institution of the European Communities to decide which unit(s) within it will serve as AA. In the European Commission, DG HR serves as AA in some cases, but for most officials the AA is their Director General.
5 Officials in the top senior positions should move to another post after five or, in exceptional cases, seven years. For staff in sensitive positions, mobility is compulsory. For more, see: http://ec.europa.eu/reform/2002/index_en.htm.
6 All of these changes necessitated, among others, the amendment of the *Financial Regulation of the European Communities*, in 2002, the establishment of the Internal Audit Service (IAS) of the Commission and of the Audit Progress Committee (its role is to ensure effective follow-up of internal and external audit recommendations), the setting up of an independent financial irregularities panel and of a Central Financial Service in DG Budget.
7 The leave on personal grounds (or *congé de convenance personnelle*, CCP) is a facility enjoyed by European civil servants, to take an unpaid leave of absence for various personal reasons. The CCP is granted for a maximum of one year, after which the official in question is required to apply for an extension; the total amount of time spent on CCP cannot exceed twelve years (it used to be fifteen years before the latest changes to the Staff Regulations).
8 With the exception of DG COMP, which adopted its own code of conduct in 2005, well before the trend was picked up by others.
9 Allegedly these funds were never used for private purposes (but for covering Eurostat expenditures for salaries, public relations, etc.); however, since the bank account could not be scrutinized by the EU's financial controllers, its existence was illegal. A detailed factual account of the Eurostat affair can be found in Cini (2007a: chapter 4).
10 As part of this agenda, the coalition advocates for improving the lobby registration system (specifically, the now joint Commission/Parliament *Transparency Register*), a more balanced membership of the Commission's expert groups, as well as tightening conflict of interest rules in response to the "revolving door" phenomenon.
11 The TI EU Office advocates, for instance, for police and judicial cooperation within the EU regarding cross-border corruption crimes and fraud, on corruption risks (and management) in specific EU policy areas, such as international development, climate change and the European Neighbourhood Policy and engages with anti-corruption and unethical practices in the private sector in the EU – see: www.transparencyinternational.eu/focus-areas/.
12 For instance, the Corporate Europe Observatory, one of the core ALTER-EU groups, runs an online database on Commissioners, MEPs and officials who have gone into lobbying or industry jobs after leaving the European institutions – see: http://corporateeurope.org/revolvingdoorwatch#.
13 The Commission's Ad Hoc Ethical Committee is made up of three members and delivers consultative opinions on general questions concerning the interpretation of the *Code of Conduct for Commissioners*, including the Commissioners' post term-of-office activities.
14 Expert groups are bodies set up to provide the Commission, or specific departments in it, with policy advice and expertise, which meet more than once. The Commission's register of expert groups is available online at: http://ec.europa.eu/transparency/regexpert/faq.cfm?aide=2.

3 "You are the human face of the Commission"

Ethics translated in internal administrative practice

This chapter shows how the European Commission has adapted internally to the successive ethics reforms operated since the early 2000s. It analyzes the micro-level administrative practice connected to ethics management, and in particular the messages which pervaded the Commission's internal communication regarding ethics. This focus is necessary, in light of the arguments made in Chapter 1 on employing organizational socialization as a theoretical perspective: as established, this framing requires that the Commission's ethics infrastructure be regarded as a source which feeds individuals' learning about their organizational roles (ethics included). Therefore, drawing out the messages which were sent internally sheds light on what employees were "taught" about ethics.

As demonstrated previously, the *Ethics Communication* has led the Commission to build up ethics guidance almost from scratch. The multitude of training sessions, presentations, codes of ethics and so on, which sprang up at both central and local (DG) levels after 2008, were designed to signal the importance of ethics in organizational life and to transmit to staff the standards of conduct which are expected of them. They represent a channel (not present in previous years) by which the Commission explicitly defined its message and standing regarding ethics. Therefore, the emphasis in this chapter will be on these activities. To be clear, the analysis covers the official documents of the Commission (e.g., the *Staff Regulations*), the internal materials intended for staff use (such as codes of conduct and administrative guides, training manuals, presentation leaflets), as well as the characteristics of the communication between the internal ethics experts and "regular" officials. This coverage is in line with the norm in organizational socialization research, which generally takes into account those instruments and strategies that are designed by organizations specifically to socialize new members (e.g., induction training).

In terms of structure, this chapter starts with a discussion of the general characteristics of the Commission's internal communication regarding public ethics, and the core messages transmitted to the work-floor. Following up on these points, the next section zooms in on the internal guidance relating to specific ethics issues which, in the context of the European Commission, are more likely to generate grey (dilemmatic) situations in practice. The presentation of these issues follows a typology of ethical dilemmas based on the relationships an ethical problem applies to, starting from the individual official, as a central reference point, and considering the links with the official's organization, his/her colleagues and external stakeholders. This selection of topics will serve as a basis to construct the vignettes which, in the following chapter, will be used to elicit the views of "regular" officials regarding public ethics.

3.1 Ethics in internal communication: rules and the public image of the European Commission

As revealed in interviews with Commission ethics officials, the general objective in the flurry of ethics activity which followed the *Ethics Communication* was prevention – ensuring that staff members knew the relevant ethics rules (or knew where to find them), so that lack of knowledge could not be a plausible defence against wrongdoing. The focus, in this effort, has been on compliance: what was essentially transmitted to staff was that the Commission had a number of regulations in the ethics area, which they should be aware of and respect.

This point is well illustrated by a brief analysis of the codes of conduct, or ethics guidelines which have been adopted at the DG level. When fieldwork was conducted in 2010, seven of the surveyed DGs had such a document. As a general trend, these are quite prescriptive documents, although their length varies. I take as an example here the *Code on Ethics and Integrity of DG COMP Staff*, introduced in 2005 and revised twice since (in 2008 and 2010, respectively), which served as a model for the codes in the Directorate-General for Trade (DG TRADE) and the Directorate-General for Justice, Freedom and Security. The declared aim is "providing guidance to DG COMP staff via a single document on the application of the different Commission's ethical rules" (Commission 2010b: 3). Out of thirty-six pages (excluding annexes), about two are dedicated to outlining general principles of staff conduct, while the rest contain detailed explanations of internal ethics regulations, practical advice, and hypothetical examples. The tone is heavily prescriptive, e.g., "you are advised to be particularly careful when gifts/favours/donations are offered in relation to your work at the Commission. […] [It] is recommended that you decline all such offers that have more than merely symbolic value" (Commission 2010b: 17). DG COMP is not a singular case. Actually, it is not difficult to find evidence that strictness and emphasis on procedures is a rather general characteristic of ethics guidance in the Commission – rather than adaptation to a peculiarly high-risk job. For example, the *Practical Guide on Staff Ethics and Conduct*, which has Commission-wide applicability, reads much along the same lines.

On the other hand, it is also significant that documents with a more lofty and abstract content were not prioritized. The fate of the *Statement of Principles of Professional Ethics* is telling in this regard. The *Statement* was a one-page document included in the Kallas package, which enumerated succinctly the core values and principles of the EU administration, and thus resembled closely the brief, high-minded codes of ethics specific to integrity management regimes.[1] Despite the internal interservice consultation being completed by the summer of 2009 (Ethics official #20), it was never adopted at the political level. Justifying the delay, some ethics officials observed that the *Statement* actually served as a stimulus for an internal ethics discussion in the Commission (Ethics officials #17, #18, #20) – the implication being that it matters less whether it is actually adopted, as long as the objective of awareness-raising has been achieved. One official even expressed doubts on the utility of such a document, remarking that targeted guidance on concrete cases is much more useful (Ethics official #17). In time, the gap was filled by the *Public Service Principles for the EU Civil Service*, issued by the European Ombudsman in 2011, which is now integrated into internal guidance materials – however, the fact that this document was formulated outside the Commission is significant.

Importantly, the emphasis on procedures and rules does not mean that in the Commission being "ethical" was narrowly equated with rule obedience. More precisely, it was about rule *awareness* – what was required of staff was not that they be fully conversant with the organization's ethics regulations but that they have an attitude of prudence and "ask when in doubt". This is clearly expressed in the principle of circumspection set out in the *Practical Guide on Staff Ethics and Conduct* and other, similar materials: "stopping and reflecting on the possible consequences and implications of potential actions, showing a proper sense of moderation and conducting oneself at all times with a due sense of proportion" (Commission n.d.: 6). One interviewee even implied that rule knowledge is not as important as acting with circumspection, because in this way one "will not fall in too many traps" (Ethics official #19).

It is important to note that communicating effectively about ethics was a commonplace concern among the Commission's ethics bureaucracy. There seemed to be a general understanding that as one official plainly put it, "rehashing the rules is really boring, people fall asleep" (Ethics official #24). For example, ethics correspondents who delivered ethics trainings said they regularly included discussions on concrete cases (hypothetical or based on real experience), to familiarize people with the kind of situations they could realistically face (Ethics officials #8, #9). Those who introduced codes of conduct into their DGs (or intended to do so) regularly invoked the need to have all essential information in one document, and contextualize it to the specific activity of the DG (Ethics officials #1, #17). Other interviewees declared that raising awareness on ethics is not a one-off endeavour, but rather a continuous effort (Ethics officials #14, #21). The importance of seeking advice and a second opinion when faced with an ethical problem was stressed across the board.

Interestingly, ethics (and ethics regulation) was interpreted and justified internally to staff members as a means towards achieving and keeping a good institutional reputation for the European Commission. The concern with its public image represents a constant in all organizational communication on ethics. Significantly, the *Ethics Communication* stated, in its opening lines, that "meeting the highest standards of professional ethics is of paramount importance with respect to the accomplishment of the Institution's tasks and its credibility and reputation" (Commission 2008a: 1). In one form or another, this same point was conveyed in the various codes of conduct and internal ethics guidelines adopted at DG level.

For instance, a brochure in the Secretariat General advises staff to "always bear in mind that you are the human face of the Commission, and make sure that your conduct is beyond reproach" (Commission 2010d: 5), while a note from the Director General to the staff of the Directorate-General for Health and Consumers states that "we must behave, internally and externally, in a way that our reputation and credibility are preserved" (Commission 2009: 1). Along very similar lines, the manual for newcomers' ethics training highlights that "high ethical standards and behaviour help to improve the reputation of the Commission and its staff" and that "the diffusion of a good image stimulates higher ethical performance" (Commission 2006b: 5), and goes on to explain the internal and external controls to which the Commission is subject. The internal codes of conduct in DG COMP and DG MARKT add that the ethics rules are meant to protect Commission staff members from "malicious allegations or misrepresentations" (Commission 2010c: 1).

However, for all the emphasis placed on the Commission's public image and its reputation, there is not much in internal communication concerning the internal monitoring and enforcement processes, which essentially represent the Commission's line of defense against such ethics violations. Apart from whistleblowing channels (discussed below), other reporting and complaints mechanisms are not featured in communication activities. IDOC and OLAF, the two bodies tasked with enforcement in the Commission, are also minimally covered.

The only significant exception here is represented by the circulation of IDOC's annual activity reports as an awareness-raising exercise. Since 2007, the reports have included qualitative data (i.e., a section where anonymized cases are shortly presented), and more recently, IDOC used their case material in a series of interactive training sessions delivered locally to various DGs (Commission 2013b). The qualitative section was simply meant to showcase the kind of conduct that can lead to disciplinary consequences, and therefore it contains an extremely varied selection, in terms of both offences and the sanctions imposed. On the other hand, the statistical information in these reports makes it clear that the number of people in the Commission services who undergo disciplinary investigations is very small, and the number of those who are found guilty of (serious) offences is even smaller. IDOC's annual caseload represents only a fraction of the total population working in the Commission, although it has grown constantly over the years, from 45 new cases in 2005 to around 100 in 2014.[2] Furthermore, only about 30 per cent of cases end with the imposition of some form of sanction, be it light (such as a written warning or a reprimand) or more severe (downgrading, dismissal, the reduction / withholding of pension). Very grave sanctions are rare – for example, between 2011 and 2014, only 12 employees were dismissed or removed from their posts.[3]

These data should be interpreted with caution. It does not necessarily suggest that the Commission is "doing well" in what regards ethics, in the same way as it does not mean that the enforcement function is weak. From a communication perspective, irrespective of how many disciplinary cases are opened and what sanctions are imposed, IDOC's outreach activities do send a message internally that wrongdoing is being observed, reported and punished. Thus it is important because organizational members should be assured that ethics policies are not mere window-dressing – as Treviño and Weaver (2003) observe, if there is a perception that in spite of lofty declarations, integrity violations are not punished, this can affect negatively employees' ethical behaviour. However, given the overall trends discussed above, it is safe to assume that monitoring and enforcement play a secondary role in the overall economy of the messages sent by the Commission internally, on the subject of ethics.

To be clear, the point here is not about the performance of the monitoring and enforcement functions as such, but rather what information Commission employees are likely to receive regarding these aspects. This is what matters, considering the social learning perspective adopted in the project. And apart from the aspects discussed above, it is unlikely that officials would have more information. As some ethics correspondents observed, Commission employees would only find out about someone incurring (disciplinary) sanctions informally, by word of mouth, and most likely if the case relates to their immediate work circle (Ethics officials #12, #18). One reason for this is the confidentiality that surrounds the relevant procedures. For instance, the identity of whistleblowers, as well as the content of their disclosures, will be known only to the few bodies/persons that can legitimately act as recipients. Both OLAF and IDOC investigations are conducted in confidentiality. IDOC will communicate personal data regarding the official concerned by an administrative inquiry or a (pre-)disciplinary case only on a "need-to-know" basis; everyone who is involved in the proceedings is bound by a duty of discretion, which continues to apply after the case is closed (Commission 2014c). What is also important is that in the absence of EU-level criminal law, offences with a criminal character involving members of European institutions are dealt with in the national judicial systems (involving proceedings of different lengths and outcomes), which constitutes another hurdle for information to reach Brussels.

***

To recapitulate, findings show two central, interrelated features in what the Commission communicated internally about ethics. Firstly, officials were expected to be aware of regulations in the area of ethics and to have an attitude of prudence and circumspection towards such questions. Secondly, the Commission's reputation was emphasized – from this perspective, officials represented the "human face of the Commission", and their conduct had to be beyond reproach. These features constitute another indication that the switch suggested by the *Ethics Communication* was not fully carried though. A "high road" integrity-based management style presumes that ethics becomes a resource which helps public servants deal with discretion. It is about promoting, not stifling, individuals' ethical agency. The Commission's focus on regulation, however, suggests anything but encouraging ethical agency – in fact, ethics remains a constraint for its administrative services, except that nowadays these constraints are probably better known. Qualitatively, there is a clear difference between the actual practice in the Commission and what was proposed with the *Ethics Communication*, i.e., stimulating discussions on the common ethical principles and values *underpinning the rules*.

The organizational communication was in keeping not only with the compliance-based character of the ethics regime, and also with the contextual constraints facing the Commission. As demonstrated at length in the previous chapter, the organization found itself operating in an environment of sharp scrutiny, with the European Parliament eager to transform episodes of bad publicity into political costs. In these conditions, the preoccupation with public image represents a deliberate choice to send a strong message, internally, as to what was at stake, when it came to ethics. It also explains, in part, why the implementation of the *Ethics Communication* has focused on "knowing the rules". Simply put, rule awareness serves to standardize staff's reactions and behaviour, so that, as one ethics official explained, although one cannot guarantee that nothing will ever go wrong, risks are minimized (Official #20).

3.2 Ethics "hot spots" in the European Commission

Following up on the points made above, this section presents the ethics issues in connection to which ethical dilemmas are more likely to form. Having an appreciation of what really matters, from this perspective, is essential for defining the topics relative to which the views of those on the work-floor will be explored, in the following chapter. The guidance officials receive on these ethics "hot spots" is detailed in the following pages – in doing so, this section illustrates how the twin messages of rule awareness and care for public reputation (discussed above) are translated to topical issues.

To determine the issues which are more likely to give rise to ethical dilemmas, I rely mostly on interviews with internal ethics experts. In the absence of a more systematic diagnosis, the views and experiences of the Commission's ethics bureaucracy remain the only source of first-hand information regarding this aspect.[4] The ethics correspondents in particular were a valuable asset, because, as indicated before, an important part of their job is to advise on ethics-related inquiries coming from staff. As such, they were ideally placed to develop a well-informed view on the subjects which can engender dilemmas, or prove to be more "tricky" to handle in practice. Additionally, the selection of topics was sensitive to the public criticism received by the Commission over the years regarding standards of conduct – as the previous section made clear, the Commission was sensitive to these matters as it developed its ethics management system and internal communication on ethics.

3.2.1 Types of ethical dilemmas

In order to navigate the complex ethics universe of the Commission, I employ a typology of ethical dilemmas which focuses on the relations to which they apply.[5] Drawing on Kaptein and Van Reenen (2001) and Kaptein and Wempe (2002), I distinguish among three types of ethical dilemmas.

Firstly, type 1 dilemmas refer to the relationship between the public official and the organization, which highlights the official's responsibilities *towards* the organization where he works, as a whole. Here, ethical problems arise where there is a conflict between the personal (private) interests of the employee and the interests of the organization. Issues in this category include: conflicts of interests and external activities (i.e., engagements outside the working program, remunerated or not – e.g., part-time teaching), private-time behaviour which can reflect negatively on the image of the organization, officials' individual freedom of expression and use of office resources (e.g., using the office telephone for private calls).

Moving on, type 2 dilemmas refer to the relationship between the official, the organization, and his/ her colleagues, highlighting the official's responsibilities *within* the organization. Here, ethical problems arise when the interests of the organization slip between the employees' individual duties. Issues in this category include: whistleblowing (i.e., reporting misconduct witnessed at the workplace), tendering fair and impartial advice to superiors, discrimination or favouritism in the area of human resources (hiring, firing, promotions, etc.), inappropriate or illegal orders and psychological and sexual harassment.

Finally, type 3 dilemmas refer to the relationships among the official, the organization, and external actors (i.e., the organization's stakeholders, the public, the press), highlighting the officials' responsibilities *on behalf* of the organization, towards external actors. Issues in this category include: dealing with gifts and hospitality, handling sensitive information in relation to stakeholders and the press, improper treatment of citizens, contractors, etc.

The typology is succinctly presented in Figure 3.1.

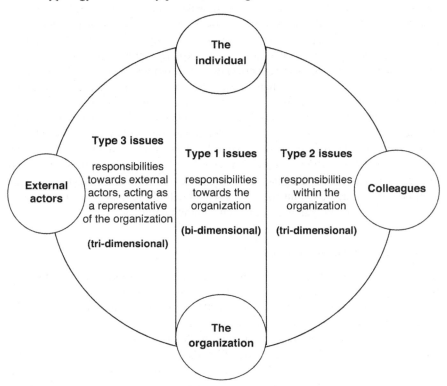

Figure 3.1 Types of ethics issues

It is important to note that in practice, ethics cases can spawn across the types presented above. Therefore, this typology should be understood not as a reductionist framework, but rather as a compass for navigating the variety of subjects which give substance to ethical dilemmas. It is used here to map the ethics environment of the European Commission and eventually to isolate the issues which, in this context, appear to be particularly salient or "tricky". In the following pages, I review the regulatory arrangements and official guidance in relation to these issues, as well as any memorable events or scandals that might have rendered these subjects "tricky" in the first place.

3.2.2 Type 1 issues: conflict of interests, outside activities and the limits of individual freedom of expression

In the area of type 1 issues, outside activities and independent publishing were indicated, by ethics correspondents, as the subjects which can become particularly sensitive. This is in line with internal statistics regarding authorization requests directed to the Appointing Authorities. Thus, outside activities – undertaken either in active service or during leave on personal grounds – make up for the largest share of such requests (on average 37 per cent and 20 per cent, respectively, between 2010 and 2014), while the files concerning publications and speeches usually represent on average 22.5 per cent (also for the period 2010–2014).[6]

Generally speaking, the activities performed by officials outside of their employment with the Commission can become ethically problematic if they entail a (perceived) conflict of interest. The jobs taken up by officials after leaving the Commission pose a very similar problem. Essentially, determining whether or not an outside activity (or a post-Commission job) is allowed implies balancing the probability of a conflict of interests against legitimate rights of the individual, namely to pursue alternative passions and interests, or, more fundamentally, the right to work. Given the wide variety of occupations individuals can undertake (while employed by the Commission or afterwards), decisions in this area will be highly contingent on the specific circumstances of a case, which means that ambiguities are likely to appear in practice.

Different provisions apply for officials who are in active service, for those who take leave on personal grounds and for those who have left the employment of the European Commission. Generally speaking, the regime which applies to the latter two categories is somewhat more flexible, in the sense that activities are permitted as long as they don't give rise to a conflict of interest or are otherwise detrimental to the interest of the Commission. As explained by internal experts, the Commission's approach has always been to find solutions so that the individual right to work could be exercised: in problematic cases certain substantive and/or time restrictions would be imposed, while outright refusals have been very rare (Ethics officials #26, #27). By contrast to the stance taken on former officials and those on CCP, the practice is particularly strict regarding extra-work occupations while officials are in active service. The SR obligation to request authorization is interpreted to cover just about anything, including low-risk situations such as volunteer work, symbolic membership in any organization, even refereeing academic papers (Ethics official #11) or participating in street demonstrations (Ethics official #6).

In internal communication, the emphasis is on reminding officials of the obligation to ask for permission before engaging in ancillary/post-employment activities and assignments. For those in active service, the activity in question must not be so time-consuming as to negatively impact on their work in the Commission or "give rise to any possible appearance of a conflict of interest or be in some other way discreditable" (Commission n.d.: 18). This effectively excludes any work carried out in a "profession" (architect, lawyer, etc.) and any commercial activities, but voluntary and charitable work, as well as limited teaching activities, are in principle permitted. For post-employment situations, the *Practical Guide to Staff Ethics and Conduct* also outlines that the obligations to "behave with integrity and discretion" (Art. 16 SR) and to "refrain from any unauthorized disclosure of information" (Art. 17 SR) continue to apply after the officials leave the service of the Commission.

It is interesting that post-employment restrictions are not addressed with any sense of urgency internally, because the Commission has received a lot of public criticism on this topic, much of it connected to a more general dissatisfaction over its relationship with the Brussels lobby (see below). As shown in the previous chapter, the growing concern and public campaigns over "revolving door" issues have had an important part to play in ushering in a stricter regime with the new *Staff Regulations*, with explicit interdictions regarding advocacy and lobbying activities undertaken by former senior officials and officials on CCP.

As regards the numerous authorization requests regarding publications and speeches, this seems to be a reflection of the fact that overall, Commission officials are a highly educated and rather independent-minded group, who seek alternative avenues for discussing and expressing their opinions. To be sure, many interviewees (Ethics officials #1, #2, #3, #4, #7, #9, #10, #11, #14, #15, #16, #17) mentioned that the external activities for which staff members request AA approval involve some kind of independent intellectual work (participation in conferences and public speeches, publications and teaching activities), and one ethics official even identified the amount of these private-time intellectual endeavours as a peculiarity of the Commission (Ethics official #21). In this context, the way individual freedom of expression is reconciled with organizational loyalty becomes very important. As with outside activities, this too is a question of finding the middle ground between exercising an individual right and upholding the interests of a public institution. Interestingly, these tensions are clearly signalled by the wording of official regulations in the Commission – Art. 17(a) of the *Staff Regulations* states that "an official has the right to freedom of expression, *with due respect to the principles of loyalty and impartiality*" (Commission 2004b: 10, added emphasis). Generally speaking, the official line is to cultivate a very guarded attitude towards expressing personal views in public (whether orally or in writing). Officials are advised to use circumspection and discretion regarding public appearances, even after they leave the organization (Commission 2006b). The general rule is that they should refrain from tackling professional issues linked to their attributions outside of their working environment, but if they do publicly express views on such matters, officials are required to make a clear disclaimer that these are their personal opinions and do not reflect the views of the Commission (Commission n.d.: 21). This also applies to social media (Twitter, Facebook, YouTube, etc.), which Commission officials can use only explicitly in a personal capacity. The general regime regarding publications applies to blogs as well, meaning that they require prior notification (Commission 2011b).

This cautiousness is justified by the fact that in the public's eye, the officials' association with the Commission is a permanent one. For example, the *Code of Ethics and Integrity of DG COMP Staff* warns that "even when you are expressing opinions as a private individual, it is worth considering in this regard that those views carry a certain weight with those hearing them, who will probably see you as a Commission official as well as a private individual" (Commission 2010b: 21). Cautiousness is particularly emphasized in connection with media relations – here, officials are advised to avoid handling journalists on their own and to refer them to the spokesperson's office – or, if that is not an option, to agree on a line to take with the hierarchy (Commission 2010b). In a nutshell, the message is simply that one can never be too careful. In the European Commission, expressing personal views (towards the outside world) is not encouraged, although, being a fundamental right, freedom of expression certainly cannot be denied.

The fact that internal communication advises prudence regarding public appearances and the expression of personal views should not come as a surprise – not only are these situations widespread (as discussed above), but they have also been at the root of problems for the Commission in the past. As Cini (2007a: 125) notes, at the time when the *Staff Regulations* were being revised during Kinnock's term, senior officials still vividly remembered the public embarrassment caused by Bernard Connolly's book *The Rotten Heart of Europe: The Dirty War for Europe's Money*, which dealt with the rationale and preparations leading up to the EMU and was extremely critical of the Commission. Connolly had written the book while on an extended leave of absence, and his employment with the Commission was terminated after it came out.

3.2.3 Type 2 issues: whistleblowing

As regards type 2 ethics issues, the internal guidance materials focus on relations with the hierarchy (the obligation to assist and tender advice to superiors, dealing with instructions that are manifestly illegal), relations among colleagues (mutual respect, tolerance), sexual and psychological harassment and the proper use of Commission means of communication (telephone, Internet access, e-mail, etc.). Although the IDOC annual reports regularly feature disciplinary cases relating to these matters, internal ethics experts have not indicated any of them as topics on which they receive questions from staff members or which might prove particularly problematic in practice. What was frequently mentioned, however, among type 2 issues, was whistleblowing. To be sure, many ethics correspondents (Ethics officials #1, #3, #4, #6, #10, #12, #17, #18) indicated whistleblowing as a principal means of monitoring standards of conduct in the organization. Its centrality to the Commission's ethics system was recently highlighted in 2012, when specialized guidelines were issued in the form of a Communication from Vice-President Šefčovič. Furthermore, as shown in the previous chapter, whistleblowing has been a subject of constant interest and criticism from the European Parliament.

Generally speaking, whistleblowing represents a delicate issue in organizational ethics management. All organizations face integrity risks, and it is the insiders who are best positioned to observe wrongdoing and signalize it. However, insiders are also the people who face the strongest incentives not to speak up (because of risks of retaliation), which makes the protection of whistleblowers a must for an effective ethics policy. Although the Commission is certainly no stranger to these dilemmas, explicit provisions on whistleblowing (i.e., Art. 22a and 22b) were introduced in the *Staff Regulations* only in 2004. The reporting of possible illegal activities and irregularities is formulated as an obligation,[7] with the disclosure procedure closely following the official hierarchy. Thus, reporting channels internal to the institution are prioritized over external ones –officials should inform first their immediate superiors, the Director General, and, "if he considers it useful", the Secretariat General or the OLAF. Only afterwards can officials go to the Court of Auditors, the Council, the European Parliament or the Ombudsman, and only after they have allowed the Commission (and OLAF) a reasonable period of time to take appropriate action. Any other possible recipients (e.g., press, NGOs) are excluded, which – as Cini (2007a) observes – puts the Commission's interpretation of whistleblowing completely at odds with the popular understanding of such acts, which imply an individual stepping beyond formal hierarchies and "going public" to report wrongdoing. The *Staff Regulations* require that whistleblowers transmit any evidence supporting their claims, and protection is offered only for *bona fide* disclosures (i.e., provided that the whistleblower "acted reasonably and honestly").

The *Guidelines on Whistleblowing* portray an effective whistleblower regime as "simply a question of good management" (Commission 2012a: 2), meaning that it is in the Commission's own interest to encourage people to speak up when they see wrongdoing. Indeed, some steps were taken to reassure would-be whistleblowers – for instance, the document explains clearly the kind of protection they can expect, as well as the guidance and support mechanisms which are at their disposal. Thus, whistleblowers are presumed to be of good faith (*bona fide*) until proven otherwise, their identity is kept confidential (i.e., known only to the recipient[s] of the disclosures) and several safeguards are in place in the event of hostile reactions from their immediate work environment (for instance, whistleblowers can request to be moved to a different Commission department). Those who consider making a disclosure can consult with their local ethics correspondent, with OLAF investigators (through an anonymous service linked to the web-based Fraud Notification System) or with other specialized ethics services in DG HR, IDOC or the Secretariat General. This being said, it is also repeatedly emphasized, throughout the *Guidelines*, that whistleblowing represents an exceptional measure and should be used as such. Only "serious irregularities"[8] can be reported through this procedure, and only if an official becomes aware of them in the performance of his/

her professional duties. Protection can be lost if staff members cannot show that the allegations made are honest and reasonable – which is why they are advised to "let the facts speak for themselves" when contemplating to make a disclosure (Commission 2012a: 8). The *Guidelines* reiterate the hierarchy of reporting channels presented above, stating that external whistleblowing must be an option of the last resort by virtue of the duties of discretion and loyalty that bind officials to the Commission.

Although these restrictions are justifiable to protect the system from malicious and frivolous reporting and to allow the Commission the chance to first solve problems internally, it cannot be said that in this regime people are encouraged to speak up. Rather, the message sent internally seems to be that one should think long and hard before taking this step. It is relevant, in this regard, that while ethics correspondents acknowledge they can provide advice to people who are considering blowing the whistle (Ethics officials #6, #10), none of them mentioned they would actually actively encourage such acts. Whistleblowing was described as an individual decision (Ethics officials #1, #6, #10, #18), rather than an obligation (as prescribed in the SR). In this optic, disclosures are acts of individual conscience, which means that the role of the organization is limited to offering some level of protection and guidance to those who, *of their own accord*, decide to step forward.

This reserved attitude makes sense considering the Commission has had a complicated and painful experience with whistleblowers. Two cases are worth mentioning here – Paul van Buitenen, in 1998/9, and Marta Andreasen, in 2003/4.[9] In both instances, the disclosures were public, which caused not only heated debates that put the Commission in a difficult position, but also led (indirectly) to policy changes.

Paul van Buitenen is probably the most well-known case. In 1998, Mr. van Buitenen worked as auditor in the Financial Control Directorate and, from this position, disclosed to the European Parliament evidence of irregularities and fraud regarding mainly the Leonardo da Vinci programs, which dealt with vocational training. His intervention was important in prompting the Parliament to open the inquiries which eventually led to the resignation of the Santer Commission in March 1999.[10] Mr. van Buitenen was suspended from his job at the Commission and later on embarked on a political career: he founded the party "Europa Transparant", ran with it in the 2004 elections in the Netherlands and won an MEP seat, serving as member of the Committee on Budgetary Control. The other prominent case was Marta Andreasen, who served as Chief Accountant in DG Budget. In the course of 2002, Andreasen raised concerns that the EU's accounting system was exposed to fraud, going first to her superior, then to the responsible Commissioner and the President of the Commission, and finally to the European Parliament, and later the press.[11] She was suspended from her job at the Commission – at the time, Kinnock publicly justified the decision pointing out that Andreasen was not suspended for whistleblowing, but for not following the Commission's whistleblowing provisions, as she had not waited for feedback on her internal complaints and revealed publicly confidential information (Cini 2007a). Similarly to van Buitenen, Andreasen started a political career in the European Parliament and has served as a member of the same Committee on Budgetary Control.

Both van Buitenen and Andreasen have eventually taken their disclosures outside the European Commission, causing important distress and embarrassment for their employer. Furthermore, both have later become involved in politics, and, as MEPs, they were in a position to attack the Commission on ethics questions. For these reasons, they are likely to be controversial characters – at least for those working in the Commission – and whether they are portrayed as heroes or villains, iconic cases such as these may prove crucial for shaping internal attitudes to whistleblowing.

3.2.4 Type 3 issues: exchanges with private interests

Finally, as to type 3 issues, the interaction with private interest representatives is acknowledged as being particularly delicate by Commission ethics experts, and the internal ethics literature generally stresses circumspection in these aspects. Contacts with stakeholders are not to be handled on individual bases, but rather officials should inform their hierarchy about forthcoming meetings, ask for instructions, and debrief on the outcome. Sometimes officials are advised to have another colleague present at such meetings (e.g., in DG TRADE) and, whenever possible, to meet on Commission premises (Commission n.d.: 12). They are also counselled to check if their interlocutors are registered the *Transparency Register*, and, if not, to suggest to them that they be so. The *Guidelines for Staff Regarding Contacts with Interest Representatives* succinctly present the code of conduct associated with the *Transparency Register*, so that Commission staff members know what kind of behaviour they can expect from those whom they meet (Commission 2008c). Two issues are particularly stressed in internal communication – what officials can communicate to interest representatives and what they can legitimately receive from them in terms of gifts, honours and various forms of hospitality. This makes sense, since both kinds of decisions require some degree of flexibility from staff members, and therefore the exercise of individual discretion.

With regard to the flow of information between Commission officials and external actors, the *Practical Guide to Staff Ethics and Conduct* makes it clear that while interest groups can provide valuable input in policy development, a risk also exists that staff may "be exploited for the purposes of a specific interest group with possible detrimental effects for the general interest of the Union" (Commission n.d.: 12). Officials are advised to be careful about what they share, especially when the information in question is confidential or otherwise sensitive. For instance, the DG MARKT ethics guidelines state: "remember that information that may seem of little relevance to you may be of value to others. It is therefore sensible to be discreet about your work at all times" (Commission 2010c: 11). This being said, according to the *Code of Good Administrative Behaviour*, as well as legislation regarding access to documents, the Commission operates in conditions of openness and transparency – meaning that as a matter of principle, its documents are accessible to the public unless one of several narrow and predefined exemptions apply (relating to protection of personal data, commercially sensitive information, court, arbitration and dispute settlement proceedings, etc.). But the *Staff Regulations* seem to imply the opposite (i.e., that public access is the exception), since Art. 17 states: "an official shall refrain from any unauthorized disclosure of information received in the line of duty, *unless that information has already been made public or is accessible to the public*" (Commission 2004b: 10, emphasis added). As hinted above, this article leaves officials more room for manoeuvre than it might initially appear, but it is nonetheless significant that here, as well as in internal guidance documents, the duty of confidentiality is emphasized over transparency.

With regard to the handling of gifts, invitations for meals and other forms of hospitality[12] from third parties, the general line, in internal ethics guidelines, is to advocate precaution and the avoidance of unnecessary risks. Officials are told that, as a rule, they should decline any such offers but, at the same time, it is also acknowledged that there are circumstances where acceptance can be considered, on a case-by-case basis. As pointed out by ethics experts, refusals can be seen as impolite (especially when cultural differences are involved) or sometimes are simply impractical.[13] Consultation and reporting are often recommended in this context. For instance, the codes of DG COMP and DG TRADE advise officials to seek guidance from their hierarchy or the local ethics correspondent, and if that is not possible, to do their best to decline diplomatically (Commission 2008b, 2010b).

Reflecting the need for flexibility, the *Guidelines on Gifts and Hospitality*, adopted in 2012, set out a number of criteria to guide decisions of whether or not to accept a gift/hospitality offer, i.e., the nature of the entity making the offer (public or private actor), the apparent motive behind the offer and the link between the entity and the Commission, the nature and estimated value of the gift/hospitality, etc. (Commission 2012b: 5). The basic advice is to always consider "whether the gift could compromise your autonomy" (Commission 2010c: 5) and to ask oneself: "is my behaviour risking the Commission's position?" (Commission 2006b: 10). When risks are assessed as minimal and acceptance is dictated by social, courtesy or diplomatic usage, the AA permission is assumed to be granted for gifts under 50 EUR, gifts of a symbolic value (such as diaries, calendars, small desk items, etc.) and simple meals, refreshments, lunches and dinners where the official participates strictly in the interests of the service and with the knowledge of his/her hierarchy. Explicit permission should be sought for gifts between 50 and 150 EUR, and anything over 150 EUR should be refused (it is assumed that AA permission will not be granted in such situations). However, as ethics officials point out, these financial thresholds are not always useful, because the value of some gifts may be difficult to assess on the spot so as to decide whether acceptance would be allowed or not (Ethics officials #2, #3, #9, #12, #24, #23).

The emphasis on cautiousness in dealing with lobbyists is in line with the sharp external criticism received by the Commission over its relationship with private interests. The controversy regarding former Commissioner John Dalli, who resigned in 2012 over improper dealings with tobacco lobbyists, may be a most high-profile case, but, considered from a longer-time perspective, it represents only a recent example in a string of public embarrassments suffered over similar issues by the Commission. The handling of gifts and hospitality has often been at the root of such episodes. One example is the case of Fritz-Harald Wenig in

2008, discussed in the previous chapter. Around that time, the European Ombudsman was notified of a smaller incident, regarding two officials from the same DG TRADE who had accepted VIP tickets to the Rugby World Cup in Paris, offered by Nike (*European Voice*, 29.10.2009). These cases were interpreted as accidents rather than a symptom of systemic weakness, but they did lead DG TRADE to significantly beef up its internal ethics arsenal, a fact which transformed it into somewhat of a forerunner in ethics management among Commission DGs.[14] It also bears mention that earlier, in 2005, Barroso himself came under fire over similar issues, specifically for spending a holiday on the yacht of Spiros Latsis, a magnate in the shipping industry, who had received EU funds from the Commission in previous years (*EU Observer*, 21.04.2005).

On a more general note, the Commission's relationship with private interests was thrown into the public spotlight with the launch of the *European Transparency Initiative* in 2008, which aimed at regulating the EU lobby by setting up a registration system and a code of conduct for interest representatives. The *Transparency Register*, now a joint enterprise of the Commission and the European Parliament, represents an acknowledgement, on the part of these institutions, of the need to open up and control the rapidly growing Brussels lobby scene. In their own words:

> Citizens can, and indeed should, expect the EU decision-making process to be as transparent and open as possible. The more open the process is, the easier it is to ensure balanced representation and avoid undue pressure and illegitimate or privileged access to information or to decision-makers.
>
> (European Union 2015b)

The *Register* currently numbers more than 8,200 registrants and represents obvious progress compared with the earlier days.[15] However, it continues to be widely criticized particularly for its voluntary nature and the lack of effective sanctions and enforcement, the not-so-subtle implication being that in upholding this system, the Commission refuses to do what it takes to render its decision-making process truly transparent, balanced and free from undue influence. The *Transparency Register* offered a platform for a critical debate on lobbying in the EU, where the long-existing claims of non-governmental organizations (NGOs) that the Commission was partial to corporate interests gained increased visibility. In fact, corporate lobby capture is probably the single most important criticism levelled against the Commission in the ethics area, and it is no coincidence that ALTER-EU, the principal watchdog coalition in Brussels, has been formed precisely around this agenda. As argued in one of its publications (Dinan and Wesselius 2010), on the Brussels scene corporate lobbyists outnumber citizens' groups and public-interest lobbies by a factor of five to one. The situation is described as a "David versus Goliath" confrontation, since it is not just the bigger numbers which favour the former, but also the larger financial resources mobilized to influence EU decision-making. Anti-corruption activists illustrate the point on preferential access emphatically, by, for example, reviewing the composition of many Commission expert groups (particularly in areas such as financial services, internal market, enterprise and climate change), which are dominated by industry (see for instance Vassalos 2010). In this context of astute (and uneven) competition for access to decision makers, and accusations of bias, how Commission officials handle contacts with interest representatives, and especially what they communicate and what they receive from them, becomes very important.

***

In conclusion, the internal guidance on sensitive subjects (such as outside activities, expressing private opinions, or dealing with gifts and hospitality from third parties) recommends an attitude of circumspection and prudence. The avoidance of (perceived) conflicts of interests seems to be key here. Wherever decisions need to be made on a case-by-case basis (hence blanket recommendations are unworkable), Commission officials are advised to think carefully before they act, consult with their hierarchy (and/or the ethics correspondent) and always ask when in doubt. With regard to whistleblowing, the Commission acknowledges the importance of this type of reporting but also cautions officials to use it carefully, as a measure of last resort, and never go outside the European institutions. In sum, the message is to play it safe.

3.3 Conclusion

This chapter presented the messages which pervaded the Commission's internal communication regarding ethics. This analysis was informed by the points made in Chapter 1 on using the theoretical lenses of organizational socialization. It has been argued that in an organizational setting, individuals engage in a process of social learning, whereby they gain an appreciation of the roles they occupy. Ethics is "learned" in this way, and the organizational ethics policy is one of the different sources which might feed the process. Much of the analysis has drawn on the *Ethics Communication*, which is essential here because it led the Commission to engage in an unprecedented effort to communicate internally about ethics.

Essentially, ethics was presented to employees as a means towards keeping the Commission's good institutional reputation. This meant that they had to display exemplary conduct, and the best way to do that was to exercise an attitude of prudence towards ethics questions and, importantly, to be aware of the Commission's regulations in this area and to stick to them. This is particularly visible in guidance on issues considered as particularly "tricky", where officials are advised to consult internally and to be careful about the kind of message they transmit to the outside world and how their behaviour impacts the Commission.

All of this makes sense given the environment in which the Commission carries out its activity. With the rise of investigative journalism and watchdog groups in the Brussels sphere, the organization became the subject of increased monitoring, as evidenced by the sleaze stories which have periodically made the headlines. Such episodes were politically charged, as the Parliament had a growing interest in pushing the Commission on ethics – therefore ethics slippages were liable to lose the Commission points in this inter-institutional confrontation. Thus, external and political pressures influenced not only the evolution of the system of ethics management in the Commission services (in particular, adoption of a hard-line approach in the aftermath of the Santer resignation, and the stilted transition to a "softer" value-based model after 2008), but also what the Commission chose to transmit internally about ethics. Its internal communication is essentially a transparent and honest account of these pressures and what they meant for staff members.

Chapter 5, which explores the ways in which organizational ethics policy shapes officials' views towards ethics, will build on the findings presented here. Namely, it will analyze how officials experience directly the Commission's ethics management system (e.g., by participating in professional events dedicated to ethics, such as training, workshops, etc., or reading documents on this subject – code of conduct, brochures, etc.). Moreover, it will trace whether and how the twin messages of rule compliance and care for the Commission's public image are reflected in the positions taken by officials on ethics.

Notes

1 The specialized literature makes a conceptual distinction between "codes of ethics" (which are relatively abstract, use aspirational language and aim at encouraging exemplary behaviour) and "codes of conduct" (which spell out more concretely behavioural expectations and aim at maintaining lawful, acceptable behaviour). For a detailed discussion, see Van Wart (2003).
2 The latter number corresponds not only to the staff of the Commission, but also to that of the European External Action Service and the European executive agencies, which IDOC has serviced on the basis of a service-level agreement since 2011.
3 These data were compiled on the basis of the annual activity reports of IDOC from 2004 to 2014, which I obtained through a public information request lodged with the European Commission. Some of the IDOC reports are available online at: www.asktheeu.org/.
4 In 2008 the Internal Audit Service did perform an audit on the Commission's ethics framework, covering two horizontal and four operational DGs – however, the document was not publicly accessible. Some DGs have used ethics quizzes as an evaluation tool (e.g., DG REGIO), but the instrument is not applied by everyone. Finally, the IDOC annual reports, discussed above, are not particularly helpful, as they do not systematically include statistics on the type of offences handled, therefore making it difficult to say whether some misbehaviors occur more frequently or with more severity than others.
5 The specialized literature has little to offer in what regards typologies of ethical dilemmas, with many authors (e.g., Wark and Krebs 2000, Kidder 2009) taking the dilemma content as the criterion for classification. Kidder (2009), for instance, states that most dilemmas are centred on four paradigms: truth vs. loyalty, individual vs. community, short term vs. long term, and justice vs. mercy. This kind of classification, however, tends to be reductionist – potentially, there could be far more combinations of conflicting values and imperatives. Focusing on relational dimensions rather than dilemma content has a better potential to capture the complexity of the ethical environment in organizations.
6 The analysis is based on data from the online one-stop shop authorization system of the European Commission, presented in its annual human resources reports for 2012, 2013 and 2014, available online at: http://bookshop.europa.eu/.

7 Article 22(a) states that "any official who, in the course of, or in connection with the performance of his duties, becomes aware of facts which give rise to a presumption of the existence of possible illegal activity [. . .] *shall without delay inform* [. . .]" (Commission 2004b: 11–12).
8 Defined as "illegal activities, including fraud and corruption, and serious professional wrongdoing" (Commission 2012a: 3).
9 More cases of whistleblowers in the Commission are documented in detail in a recent report commissioned by the European Parliament – PricewaterhouseCoopers Belgium and iForce (2011).
10 Mr. van Buitenen used internal channels to voice his concerns before addressing the Parliament. More information can be found in his book – van Buitenen (2000).
11 The events are described in detail in Andreasen (2009).
12 Hospitality is defined as "an offer of food, drink, accommodation and/or entertainment from any source outside the institution" (Commission 2012b: 4).
13 Some examples provided by ethics experts are: a lunch provided at the cafeteria of the company where EU officials carry out an inspection, in the absence of any viable alternatives, or a complimentary airport pick-up car sent by the company, again when no alternatives are available.
14 Apart from the usual range of policy instruments, DG TRADE is singular in introducing an internal gifts register for staff, and a far stronger institutional muscle behind ethics, in the form of a steering committee on ethics and the protection of sensitive information. The steering committee is composed of two directors, two heads of unit, the TRADE ethics correspondent and several other members. It meets four times a year to develop an ethics action plan and review its implementation (Ethics official #14).
15 The predecessor of the *Transparency Register* was the Commission's database for European civil society organizations (CONECCS). The broad definition of "civil society organizations" arguably made it possible to interpret CONECCS as a database of European interest (lobby) groups (Commission 2006a: 7).

4 Individual views towards ethics in the European Commission

This chapter presents an in-depth and nuanced account of how Commission officials think about ethics in public office. It is an exploratory exercise, meant to bring to light the patterns which pervade processes of ethical reasoning and map the lines of convergence and divergence. In short, this chapter offers a picture of ethics as it is represented on the work-floor at the European Commission. It is based on the views and experiences of employees who are not ethics experts but work for the organization in various other capacities. These are the people who now have to operate in the confines of the ethics regime produced by the administrative reforms of the last decade.

The chapter uses the empirical data yielded by the thirty semi-structured interviews conducted with Commission officials. The respondents' characteristics as well as the method of recruitment are covered at length in Chapter 1. As a condition of confidentiality, participants' names were replaced with randomly assigned numbers, and in some quotes, their nationality was obscured. Furthermore, the data are generally presented without indicating the DGs (their titles were replaced with letters), except for the few instances when this piece of information was considered relevant for the analysis.

The chapter is divided into three parts. The first one offers a number of preliminary methodological observations on the vignette technique and its use in this book. The second section presents the officials' responses to the three vignettes included in the interview guide. It shows how they judged the acceptability of the behaviour described in the vignettes and what the most frequently evoked arguments were. The third part of the chapter takes an overall view of the findings in order to identify the common line in EU officials' thinking about public ethics, as well as the points of divergence. Given that the latter do exist, the analysis subsequently covers the possible determining factors for these elements of internal divergence in the Commission.

4.1 Methodological observations

The interviews followed a topic guide which contained open questions and three vignettes. Essentially, this represents a multi-method approach, where the two techniques were used in complementary fashion to tap various aspects of "ethics in practice" within the European Commission. On the one hand, the open questions revealed how officials view their socialization experiences in the EU administration, their experience with and perception of ethics management instruments and the ethical challenges in their jobs. On the other hand, the vignettes revealed the individuals' positions and reasoning regarding ethics, and offered a concrete benchmark for comparison. Due to their centrality in the research project, in what follows I offer an extensive discussion of vignettes, covering first the main characteristics of this methodological instrument and afterwards its deployment in the book.

4.1.1 *General observations on the vignette technique*

Vignettes have been extensively used in sociological research to elicit data on group beliefs and values (Finch 1987, Hughes 1998, Jenkins *et al.* 2010), and particularly in studies dealing with sensitive issues or vulnerable groups.[1] One of the key advantages of this technique is that it minimizes social desirability bias, as respondents find commenting on fictional situations to be less threatening than answering direct questions, and thus they are less likely to dissimulate their attitudes (Finch 1987, Renold 2002). So, vignettes offer a non-intrusive and fruitful way of exploring issues which would otherwise be troublesome – an advantage which, unsurprisingly, made them particularly popular in ethics research.[2] Moreover, vignettes elicit attitudes in a much contextualized manner, thus avoiding answers which are overly generalizing and impossible to interpret (Finch 1987). Finally, by comparison with other methods, they can be more interesting and enjoyable for informants and stimulate their creativity (Schoenberg and Ravdal 2000).

Discussions around the limitations and challenges of the vignette method generally highlight two aspects. Firstly, vignettes are most productive when they appear authentic and relevant to participants, and thus they should be developed based on a thorough knowledge of the environment facing the target group. Secondly, vignettes are effective in revealing attitudes, beliefs or decision-making patterns but have limited value in predicting actual behaviour. As Jenkins *et al.* (2010: 178) caution, the aim "should not be to arrive at an accurate prediction of an interviewee's behaviour, but instead to achieve insight into the social components of the participant's interpretative framework and perceptual processes".

In empirical ethics research, vignettes are usually employed in quantitative studies, where participants are presented with a scenario and asked to choose from a list of predetermined answers. The work of Stewart and Sprinthall on moral development (Stewart and Sprinthall 1991, 1993, Stewart *et al.* 1997, Stewart *et al.* 2002) represents a relevant illustration. In opposition to this general trend, vignettes are used here in a qualitative fashion. This approach has the advantage of leaving "space for participants to define the situation in their own terms" (Renold 2002: 3), thus yielding richer data, which taps into the complex interpretative frameworks which are applied in ethical decisions. Vignettes can generate this type of data because, as Jenkins *et al.* (2010) point out, they lead respondents to engage in acts of perceptual orientation. Specifically, respondents associate with the character portrayed in the vignette and, in doing so, "assume that the protagonist is exposed to the same group norms as themselves, and so explicate those norms in their responses to the vignettes" (Jenkins *et al.* 2010: 180–181). In other words, responses, even if pertaining to a fictional character, will reflect the respondents' own experiences, memories and understandings of similar situations.

4.1.2 The use of vignettes in this research project

Each of the three vignettes included in the interview guide corresponds to a different type of ethics issue, according to the typology presented in Chapter 3. They were also constructed so as to reflect the ethics "hotspots" of the European Commission, discussed in the previous chapter. Focusing on these subjects, which were identified as delicate by the internal ethics experts, makes it more likely that scenarios will appear as dilemmatic to interviewees. On the other hand, the scenarios are also likely to have increased relevance in officials' work-lives, since these topics have not only been prioritized in internal communication, but also earned the Commission public criticism, including from the European Parliament.

As noted in Chapter 1, ethical dilemmas represent a fertile ground to elicit Commission officials' views, because such situations lead individuals into a process of ethical reasoning through which their views are articulated. Therefore, the vignettes all portray ambiguous situations. To achieve this, they were placed in the "grey" spaces of the Commission's ethics regulations. Namely, while none of the scenarios presents an outright transgression of the rules, the conduct of the central character in these stories – "John" – can raise some eyebrows, and there are reasons to both criticize and justify it. The coverage of the legal framework was defined through my own analysis and confirmed by several senior ethics experts in the Commission whom I asked for input. In addition to sparking ethical reasoning, the dilemmatic character of the scenarios represents an additional protection against social desirability bias. Namely, it is expected that interviewees would not answer in a biased way simply because there is no predetermined "right" answer to the vignettes, or at least not one which is immediately visible.

The vignettes were tested before large-scale use in seven pilot interviews with volunteers who had worked or were working at the time in the European Commission, in various positions and DGs.[3] This preparatory work served to ascertain whether vignettes seemed "real" to insiders and adequately reflected the specific working environment of the Commission. It also served to check whether they indeed appeared dilemmatic – which, in this context, meant evidence of genuine reasoning (i.e., slowness in responding, false starts, etc.) and, most importantly, a variation between responses. The stories were gradually improved based on the feedback gathered in the pilot interviews.

The vignettes featured two successive stages, where the second stage adds a layer of complexity and makes it less straightforward to judge the acceptability of the behaviour. They were presented to interviewees on separate sheets of paper, the second stage after they had already read through and commented on the first one.

Because the vignettes were used as a stimulus for discussing ethics (rather than a test of how "ethical" EU officials were), participants were allowed to more or less freely comment on them, being asked only whether they found the situations to be acceptable and why (not).[4] Follow-up and probing questions were used only to clarify, or expand further on certain points, collect examples or encourage the less forthcoming respondents. This approach allowed respondents to engage extensively in a process of ethical reasoning and explain the reasons why they judged certain types of behaviour to be (un)acceptable. Moreover, it encouraged them to go beyond the narrow scope of the vignettes and explain what could be a reasonable solution to the dilemma presented therein, or draw parallels to similar real situations which they have encountered throughout their career. Hence, the vignettes generated long and relatively unstructured answers, which pertained not only to ethical reasoning per se, but more broadly to the participants' rhetorical positions, the repertoire of organizational practices connected to ethics.

The main purpose of this open-ended approach was to capture ethics as perceived and experienced by participants themselves. For the same rationale, the data were analyzed in an inductive way, with the aid of specialized software (ATLASti). The data were coded to offer an overview of the recurrent topics and patterns in them, and based on this, certain general *types* of answers were gradually defined in bottom-up fashion. The process of fitting the data to these analytical categories inevitably meant sacrificing some of the data's richness. Thus, some of the more exotic responses had to be left aside, and some of the more sophisticated and rich responses were "analyzed down" to fit the existing types.

4.2 Individual positions on public ethics

In this section I analyze responses to the three vignettes incorporated in the interview guide. This is an exploratory analytical exercise and as such represents a first step in understanding how ethics is framed on the work-floor of the Commission. Each vignette is introduced with a brief consideration of the aspects that render the scenario therein an ethical dilemma; afterwards, the detailed results are presented. Officials' answers to vignettes were analyzed along two central lines. The first was whether the behaviour described in the scenario was judged to be acceptable or not. The vignettes were introduced with this question, which naturally drove the replies, as respondents engaged in reflection, ending with their taking a stand on the acceptability of the story. The second line referred more broadly to officials' reasoning around the vignettes. Their fuzziness triggered many "it depends" answers, which, as Hughes (1998) observes, are useful for exploring the main influencing factors. In this case, the "it depends" answers revealed the main considerations evoked by officials when assessing an ethically charged situation.

4.2.1 Vignette 1: the organization and the individual

The first vignette pertains to the relation between the individual and the organization, which is an ethical issue of type 1, according to the classification presented in Chapter 3. Here, problems arise when there is a conflict between the personal (private) interests of the official and the interests of the organization. Appraising conduct implies a consideration of the content and limits of an employees' responsibilities vis-à-vis their employer. Specifically, vignette 1 probes the quandary of individual freedom of expression vs. organizational loyalty while also touching on the subject of the "revolving door", both of which are presently very salient for the Commission.

84 *Individual views towards ethics*

> **Box 4.1   Vignette 1 "The Conference"**
>
> **Stage 1**
>
> John has been working in the DG _____ for almost two years. He recently participated, in a private capacity, at a scientific conference, where he presented a research article discussing the public health dangers of genetically modified organisms (a topic he intensively deals with in his job at the Commission). John wrote the article in his spare time; he asked and obtained his superiors' permission to make it public over three months ago. However, just before the conference, the Commissioner released a press statement indicating a different position from what John advocated in his article. John figured it was too late to change anything and went ahead with his presentation as planned.
>
> **Stage 2**
>
> Suppose now that John is working in the Commission as a contractual agent. His contract is about to expire and he suspects it may not be renewed – so he is thinking about future career prospects. Not long before his presentation, he had been discussing a job offer with the organizers of the conference.

In the vignette presented above, the central character – John – publicly expresses a viewpoint which is different from the official Commission stance, although, arguably, he has taken appropriate precautions by previously asking – and receiving – authorization for his article, as per the relevant provisions in the *Staff Regulations*. The situation raises dilemmas as to the limits and ways in which freedom of expression (in this case, scientific autonomy) can be reconciled with organizational loyalty (see Table 4.1). The situation is further complicated by the fact that the possible "revolving door" situation introduced in Stage 2 applies to a contractual agent. Temporary contracts are widely used in the European Commission (about a quarter of total staff) – this creates a sizeable population facing a different time horizon, and incentive structure, compared with the main body of *fonctionnaires*, who are tenured for life in their respective jobs. Although both groups are subject to the same ethics regulations, it seems fair to wonder whether they should be judged on exactly the same exigencies regarding their loyalty to the European Commission. The contacts and experience gained within the Commission are likely to be key for securing a future job, but how and to what extent is the use of these competitive advantages legitimate?

Results for the first stage of the vignette show little divergence: the large majority of officials believe it is not acceptable to publicly present a stance which is radically different from that of their institution. The key argument here is that when

Table 4.1 Positions on freedom of expression

	Acceptability (Stage 1)	Windows for individual freedom of expression	Position on professional situation
DG "A"	No	–	Strict
	Yes	√	Flexible
	Yes	–	Strict
	Yes	–	Strict
	No	√	Strict
	No	√	Flexible
	No	–	Strict
	No	–	Strict
	No	√	Strict
	No	√	Flexible
	No	√	Flexible
	No	√	Strict
DG "B"	No	√	Flexible
	No	√	Strict
	No	–	Flexible
DG "C"	Yes	√	Flexible
	No	–	Flexible
	No	–	Strict
	No	√	Strict
	Yes	√	Flexible
	Yes	–	Strict
	Yes	√	Flexible
DG "D"	No	√	Strict
	No	–	Strict
	No	–	Flexible
	No	–	Strict
	No	√	Strict
	No	√	Strict

in public, it is impossible to credibly distance oneself from one's organizational affiliation. A disclaimer can be useful from a legal perspective, but its practical effectiveness is sorely doubted. As one official explains:

> [Y]ou can put as many disclaimers as you want, as soon as people know that you are a Commission official (and they will always find out – I mean, just put it into Google, and there you have it), it would always say 'said by a Commission official', so it would always hamper the Commission.
>
> (Official #7)

86   *Individual views towards ethics*

In this context, some respondents made it clear that public criticism – expressed in whatever capacity – is a breach of loyalty:

> [No] matter if you're in your private or official capacity, we are the European Commission. And wherever the European Commission goes, it should be one team.
>
> (Official #26)

> [T]here comes some price with [this job], and you are always seen as an official of this institution, and if you go out in a private capacity, and you state things that are in contradiction to what is the official position of the Commission, then it is a problem.
>
> (Official #13)

This being said, a minority of respondents (in all DGs) believed that an official could legitimately exercise her/his freedom of expression, as long as it is clear that they are acting in a personal capacity. Some of them (Officials #8, #4, #14, #34) believe that an obvious disclaimer and the previous approval of the hierarchy are enough. What also seems to matter here is the scientific quality of the debate (Officials #4, #8, #12, #30, #3), implying that more legitimacy is attached to dissenting opinions if based on scientific "truths":

> If he has his research to ground his opinion, he should go on and do it – especially as he's not representing, in this case, the Commission as an institution, he can say whatever he wants, and hopefully he will be allowed.
>
> (Official #3)

The general caution over public appearances does not mean that individual freedom of expression is completely barred – but, rather, that it should be exercised under certain conditions. Subjects on which the Commission has not taken a (clear) public stance are often indicated as windows which can allow the expression of more personal views (Officials #32, #5, #9, #30, #7, #27). For example:

> I think it's boring if you just go to a conference [. . .] and you just trot out the line that has been agreed upon. And also, there's not a line that's been agreed on everything, so you can interpret certain lines, or you can push certain lines in certain ways.
>
> (Official #9)

Additionally, it helps if the divergence with the official line is but a marginal one (Officials #20, #10, #9, #30, #23), and if the official demonstrates some sense of equilibrium by mentioning it along with her own stance (Officials #8, #12, #10, #30, #3, #2):

> Fine, go ahead, but I suggest that you draw your attention to the fact that the Commissioner said such-and-such, and that this is your own personal view,

and I think you should also explain why the difference, and where you think that comes from.

(Official #2)

There was much more divergence over the second stage of the vignette, with positions roughly split in two camps – a flexible and a strict one.

Officials in the **flexible** camp perceive the behaviour depicted in the story as being acceptable, albeit to some degree ethically uncomfortable. Some (Officials #20, #18, #14, #30, #3, #15) appreciate that given a limited contract, it is justifiable to look for the next job and use the affiliation with the European Commission as an advantage in this process. One official described it as "normal" professional networking:

> This is for me normal life. I wouldn't be so shocked about that, a contractual agent is not an official, I think it's normal networking. [. . .] [It's] the professional context, you have a professional relationship, and when you look for a job you use first your professional contacts.
>
> (Official #3)

Others (Officials #6, #13) find that the imminent departure clears some of the burden of being permanently perceived as a representative of the Commission. For example:

> I can see that a lot of people would see it as justifiable, because he's finishing his job, he needs to make it clear that he is talking in his private capacity and that very soon he will not be working for the Commission, and if he makes it very very clear, then yes, it is acceptable.
>
> (Official #13)

On the other hand, those in the **strict** camp find the behaviour unacceptable – but there are several nuances to this. Many of the radicals (Officials #1, #8, #28, #32, #22, #7, #23, #27) show a fair amount of appreciation for the precariousness of the professional situation but feel that, in this equation, loyalty to the organization should prevail. For example:

> It's even sadder for him, but as long as he's a contractual agent, he's bound by the obligations under the Staff Regulations. [. . .] If he had already left, then that would not be a problem, but as long as he's there – no.
>
> (Official #7)

And elsewhere:

> Being a civil servant is a career choice, being a contractual agent is anything but a career choice. Probably what he does can be justified more, but it's still a problem.
>
> (Official #23)

On the other hand, there were some who did not express such sympathetic views but, on the contrary, interpreted the situation as a conflict of interests: "this is not acceptable; there must be a way that these kind of interests can be announced inside" (Official #24). Others found that it casts doubt on the intellectual honesty of the person:

> It makes it more negative. [. . .] [O]ne can imagine that the intention of going ahead was not motivated by the objectivity of the information, or the principle, but because there is a vested interest in getting a job further down the line.
> (Official #16)

Part of this strict discourse is a conviction that disagreements are legitimately voiced only through internal channels (Officials #6, #28, #26, #9). In cases of extreme divergence, the honourable solution is to simply exit the organization:

> [D]efinitely going against your employer, whoever it is, is not fine. I wouldn't do it. If there is a point of disagreement, I just quit the job; I go somewhere else where I can pursue it – but not here. You lose credibility.
> (Official #26)

***

Responses to this vignette show that, in general, officials attach more importance to organizational loyalty than to individual interests – even when the latter can easily be considered legitimate. As regards freedom of expression, the cautiousness advocated by official policy is certainly reflected in officials' attitudes, most of whom look unfavourably towards expressing private views in public. The EU officials espouse a strong sense of representation, and being highly conscious of their official role often translates into a blurring of the boundary between the public and the private life. Own voices are not completely muted by the occupation of public office, but the "safe" spaces left for their expression are rather narrow and do not include (strong) criticism of the Commission. More divergence was revealed in the second stage of the vignette, with responses condensed around a strict discourse and a flexible one. Most respondents showed an appreciation for the challenges of a short-term contract, but it is only a minority (i.e., those expressing flexible positions) who believe this merits a relaxation of the high bar at which organizational loyalty seems to be set.

4.2.2 Vignette 2: officials within the organization

The second vignette pertains to the relations among the individuals within an organization, which is an ethical issue of type 2, according to the classification presented in Chapter 3. Here, problems arise when employees face conflicting incentives or the "greater good" slips between the employees' individual duties. Specifically, the vignette dwells on the issue of reporting misconduct witnessed at the workplace.

Box 4.2   Vignette 2 "The Missing Files"

Stage 1

John has been recently appointed to DG _____ as a program officer. He is responsible for overseeing the execution of projects funded by EU grants. While preparing a report, he comes across a project execution file from a few years back, which is missing some important financial documents usually required from grant beneficiaries. John concludes there is some cause for concern (especially as there are large amounts of euros involved), but, being new on the job, he's not sure how rigorous the reporting requirements were in the past. He takes up the matter with his colleague, who had dealt with the file before him, but the colleague replies that there are only some minor procedural problems and advises John not to pursue it any further. John puts the file away.

Stage 2

Some time after, John accidentally finds out that before joining the Commission, his colleague used to work for the beneficiary who did not submit the full financial documentation. However, by now John has developed a good working relationship with his colleague and genuinely has a great professional esteem for him. He decides it is for the best not to pursue the issue of the missing files.

In this vignette, it is difficult to say – judging strictly on the regulatory framework – whether the character (John) is breaking the rules. Although reasons for concern do increase as the story progresses, ultimately it remains unclear whether an irregularity has been actually discovered, or even whether John's suspicions are strong enough to warrant further action. This kind of uncertainty and conflicting incentives are typical of whistleblowing decisions, which involve a balancing act between one's own interests and moral values on the one hand and the duty of loyalty towards colleagues and the organization as a whole on the other. Moreover, peer reporting (i.e., disclosing wrongdoing which involves an immediate colleague) is particularly sensitive because it entails sacrificing relationships with co-workers, who can be friends or mentors of the whistleblower (Table 4.2). In this particular scenario, things are further complicated because the possible irregularity pertains to financial management, for which the Commission has been severely criticized in the context of the Santer resignation and afterwards with the Eurostat affair.

Results for the second vignette revealed virtually no divergence in appraising the acceptability of the behaviour displayed. With one exception, all respondents found the character's actions to be ethically questionable, for both stages of the

90 Individual views towards ethics

Table 4.2 Positions on whistleblowing

	Acceptability	Reasons		Report/consult with ...		
		Orientation to others	Orientation to self	Another colleague	Superior	Other bodies
DG "A"	No	–	–	√	–	–
	No	–	–	–	–	√
	No	–	–	√	–	–
	No	√	–	–	√	–
	No	√	–	–	√	–
	No	√	–	–	–	–
	No	√	–	–	√	–
	No	√	–	–	√	–
	No	√	–	–	√	–
	No	–	–	√	√	–
	No	√	√	√	–	–
DG "B"	No	–	√	–	√	–
	No	√	–	√	√	–
	No	√	–	√	–	–
DG "C"	No	–	–	–	√	√
	No	–	√	–	–	√
	No	–	√	–	√	–
	No	√	–	–	√	–
	No	–	√	–	√	–
	No	√	√	–	–	–
	No	–	√	–	–	–
DG "D"	No	√	–	–	√	–
	Yes	–	–	–	–	–
	No	–	–	–	√	–
	No	–	√	–	√	√
	No	–	–	–	√	–

story.[5] The oft-made point here is that when confronted with possible wrongdoing, it does not suffice to consult just the colleague involved. Officials find necessary a due diligence of sorts, which goes beyond what is described in the scenario:

> I could imagine going first off to the person who used to deal with the file and ask [her] about it, but I don't think he can leave it there – unless the colleague explained in more detail, and explained why. I think at the very least he should go and speak to someone else about it, and if necessary he puts a note in the file, copied to his immediate superiors, to say: this all seems to me

Individual views towards ethics 91

> OK, but I want to draw your attention to this problem, I spoke about it to so-and-so, and she said it was OK for the following reasons. That would be the safest thing to do.
>
> (Official #2)

The need for a second opinion is evident to everyone, but there are different options as to who else should be involved. Some interviewees indicated a discussion with another (more experienced) colleague, others indicated OLAF (or other competent audit) as a last resort; however, most people believe that their superior is the appropriate interlocutor (but sometimes after consulting lower in the hierarchy). As one official explains, possible problems should be quickly passed up to the superior:

> [Y]ou have to tell your superior that you think there might be a problem, even if it is a stupid thing. If your superior says that's nonsense and you should not be worried, then it's fine – but otherwise this is the only way to proceed in this kind of case.
>
> (Official #27)

With this vignette, divergence was apparent at the level of argumentation. There were two (not mutually exclusive) discourses used to explain the ethical lapses in the story.

The first discourse is characterized by an **orientation to others**, as it stresses the larger interests that are at stake, be it those of the Commission as a whole or the interests of the team. Essentially, the message is that in a situation of this type, one needs to consider the broader picture and not simply his/her own position, or that of their colleague. For example:

> If the guy's alright, there will be explanations for the papers; on the other hand, if you let it go, and there's something going on, then I think it's a disaster for all concerned. If anybody does find out in an audit or whatever, then John and his colleague, and everybody else, are going to be in deep trouble.
>
> (Official #20)

Part of this discourse is a requirement to consider the pros and cons of taking the matter further. In other words, in itself reporting has no value, and one should engage in such action only if the stakes are high enough. As one official explained:

> [If] the file was somehow still going on, and due to this lack of documents there are still costs arising from this file, so that you could say: 'OK, now we realized there is something missing in this file, that there is something wrong with it, we should stop making these payments', then I would say there's a reason to look into it, but if the thing is closed . . .
>
> (Official #7)

92 *Individual views towards ethics*

The second discourse is characterized by an **orientation to self**, as it stresses personal interest, or personal professional responsibility, as the reason for reporting. Some officials have depicted the choice in rather stark, self-interested terms, as the easiest way of shifting, or sharing the burden, and staying "safe":

> John has to cover his back, and whatever he finds that is suspicious, he has to at least discuss it with his superiors – because he may be accused at the end himself, that he neglected, or he did not do this, or that.
>
> (Official #30)

And elsewhere:

> [To] say 'no' to something which may afterwards be put out as a big scandal . . . [Y]ou don't want this responsibility, so I would go to the Head of Unit and he would decide what to do.
>
> (Official #22)

For others, it is not so much about protecting one's own interests, but rather about taking ownership of the public role and assuming the responsibility which comes with it:

> For me, the ethical point, in terms of behaviour, is that because it's your file, you're responsible for that. Even if it's after the fact, you can cross-check with the predecessor and various interlocutors, and at some point you need to have your opinions, even if 90 per cent comes from others.
>
> (Official #34)

Moving on, it is important to note that among Commission officials, the responsibility to report is understood as being strictly limited to one's area of competence and to problems which are discovered by chance. In other words, nobody is under an obligation to monitor his colleagues, or be so zealous as to conduct private investigations (Officials #32, #7, #18):

> [F]or me there is a limit between proactively seeking to dig out dirt in the system, including outside your competence area, and then to give it to a third party, [. . .] and being confronted yourself with a problem of conscience that you're not willing to overlook. And it's not the same thing; I don't feel that civil service here has a mandate to nose around in all our files.
>
> (Official #18)

This interpretation is certainly in line with the SR provisions (Art. 22a), which indicate that an official should make a disclosure if "in the course of, or in connection with the performance of his duties, he becomes aware of facts which give rise to a presumption of the existence of possible illegal activity" (Commission 2004b: 11, emphasis added). Nonetheless, it suggests that whistleblowing is legitimate only as an exceptional solution – that is, for those cases where breaches are severe, and evidence is easily available (which, in real life, is not likely to be the case).

***

In conclusion, at a general level officials believe that where suspicions of wrongdoing exist, one should take action – this mostly implies reporting the matter to a superior, sometimes after or in parallel to consulting another colleague. There are two distinct sets of justifications for reporting (i.e., discourses oriented to others or to self); however, these are not mutually exclusive. Not addressing a possible problem could be detrimental to both the organization and the employee, and there were several officials mentioning both sets of reasons. The unifying theme in all of this is the logic of consequentiality. Reporting is rarely considered as the ethical response by default – rather, it seems to be a means to an end, and as such it has merit when based on a calculation of consequences for either oneself, or one's group, or, indeed, both.

4.2.3 Vignette 3: the official, the organization and external actors

The third vignette pertains to the relation between the organization and the outside world, which is an ethical issue of type 3, according to the classification presented in Chapter 3. Here, problems arise when the interests and/or expectations of external actors clash with each other or with those of the organization. Appraising conduct implies a consideration of the content, and limits of an official's responsibilities, seen as a representative of his/her organization, towards stakeholders. Concretely, the vignette explores the relationship between Commission officials and lobbyists, and, in that context, how gifts and information flows are handled.

Box 4.3   Vignette 3 "The Lobbyist"

Stage 1

John works in DG _____. He is currently heading a team tasked with writing the Impact Assessment for a future important directive. He meets over lunch with a lobbyist who represents a large labour union association and who offers John a report containing much needed information for the Impact Assessment, which is due soon. The lobbyist tells John that he hopes to be kept informed of the developments made with the new directive proposal. John takes the report, thanks him for the information, and says he'll "see what he can do". The lobbyist insists to pay for lunch, and John accepts.

Stage 2

A week before the proposal reaches the College of Commissioners, the lobbyist gives John a phone call, asking for updates. John explains that at this stage,

> the document is not public. In response, the lobbyist insists and reminds John of their excellent collaboration so far. Knowing that the labour union is indeed a key stakeholder for his DG, John gives the lobbyist a general description of what the text looks like over the phone, but says he cannot help him further.

Vignette 3 presents a fairly common occurrence: a Commission official meeting with a lobbyist over lunch, receiving a report and keeping communication as the legislative proposal develops further. The first problematic point here is the lunch, which is paid for by the lobbyist. As discussed in Chapter 3, regulations allow officials a degree of leeway whenever gifts, invitations for meals and other forms of hospitality are involved, because these essentially represent forms of social courtesy, which, in and of themselves, do not pose a challenge from a public integrity standpoint. However, if the value is too high or if the context in which these gifts and invitations occur is somehow improper, they can easily (be perceived to) jeopardize officials' impartiality. Therefore, in this area the lines of demarcation between being polite and – to put it bluntly – corrupt are quite sensitive and can only be drawn on a case-by-case basis.

The other problematic aspect in the vignette is the communication between the lobbyist and the Commission official. Generally speaking, meeting with interest representatives and exchanging policy-relevant information are encouraged under the principles of transparency and open consultation. On the other hand, however, officials are bound by a duty of confidentiality, as Art. 17 *SR* stipulates that they should not disclose information received in the line of duty "unless that information has already been made public or is accessible to the public". As discussed already in the previous chapter, this provision is not as restrictive as it may sound: no Commission document is excluded *a priori* from the right of public access, and this is true even for documents which have either not been finalized or are not intended for publication (such as preliminary drafts, interim reports, draft legislative proposals or decisions).[6] However, overall, the inherent tensions between the principles of transparency and confidentiality create a situation of imbalance between the amount and extent of information received by the Commission from interest representatives and what it can communicate back to them. Although some leeway exists, this state of affairs is likely to be particularly challenging for the Commission, given its traditional dependence on external policy expertise (see, for instance, Mazey and Richardson 1993, Bouwen 2002, Chalmers 2012).

Results for the first stage of the vignette unsurprisingly show that meeting with stakeholders and receiving policy-relevant information is virtually not called into question. Respondents view such contacts as useful, even necessary, and entirely part of their job. As one official aptly put it:

> [As] an EU representative, you must interact with lobbyists, and you must interact with companies. I feel very strongly that people who are afraid of that have not understood their job. We're not here to be afraid of outsiders.
> (Official #18)

This being said, there is clear divergence in appreciating the way in which the meeting with the lobbyist proceeds, with positions split into two roughly equal camps: a "strict" one (14 officials), and a "flexible" one (16 officials) (Table 4.3). The central dividing issue here is the lobbyist picking up the bill for lunch – on this everybody commented, and it was oftentimes the first subject to be approached.

Strict officials point out that it is never justified to allow a lobbyist to cover the bill, as it entails serious risks for one's independence and reputation. This is basically a risk-averse discourse, where accepting lunch is seen as compromising an official, or at least putting him/her in an awkward situation. Although it is allowed,

Table 4.3 Positions on meeting a lobbyist

	Receipt of report	Position on lunch
DG "A"	Acceptable	Flexible
	–	Strict
	Acceptable	Flexible
	–	Strict
	Acceptable	Strict
	Acceptable	Strict
	Acceptable	Strict
	Acceptable	Flexible
	Acceptable	Flexible
	Acceptable	Strict
	Acceptable	Flexible
	Acceptable	Flexible
DG "B"	Acceptable	Strict
	Acceptable	Strict
	Acceptable	Strict
DG "C"	–	Strict
	Acceptable	Strict
	Acceptable	Flexible
	Acceptable	Strict
	Acceptable	Strict
	Acceptable	Flexible
	Acceptable	Strict
DG "D"	Acceptable	Strict
	Acceptable	Strict
	Unacceptable	Flexible
	Acceptable	Flexible
	Acceptable	Strict
	Acceptable	Flexible

it is preferable to play it safe and avoid these circumstances altogether. One official explains his stance in the following terms:

> Commission officials' salaries are big enough to be able to pay for lunch, or dinner, and a good bottle of wine or champagne. It's not worth it, this bloody 30 EUR are not worth to get in trouble later. I like to sleep well.
>
> (Official #14)

Along similar lines, another interviewee describes a prudent attitude in his interaction with lobbyists:

> Unfortunately, I'm on the list for some of these lobby firms, and so they sometimes phone me up and ask me to go for lunch, or ask me to go for coffee. [. . .] And I tend to go to just that coffee place around the corner from here – so I don't want there to be any doubt, oh, someone sees me and says: 'he was seen speaking to Jacques the other day in the coffee bar and there is a problem'. I'll always make sure it's covered here, I don't want there to be any sort of perception that they're paying for lunch, or even coffees and stuff – I don't like it.
>
> (Official #2)

Some officials taking a strict position also point to the fact that the payment could be interpreted as a transaction of sorts, by which John remains indebted to the lobbyist (Officials #20, #2, #14, #26, #7, #11, #23). Moreover, others question whether a lunch meeting is a proper format for interacting with stakeholders (Officials #12, #20, #24, #2, #6, #18, #26, #30, #7).

On the other hand, **flexible** respondents argue that in itself, the lunch is not a problem. It is a form of professional interaction, which can be practiced so long as the official makes it clear that it does not imply any preferential treatment:

> It always depends on what message you send, whether the lobbyist can really have hopes that, if he paid for lunch, he's going to get something or not. Otherwise it's not a big deal. [. . .] You could consider it kind of a business [meeting], and it's OK as long as you're clear on where you stand.
>
> (Official #10)

There are even some who find ludicrous the notion that the lunch could "buy" the lobbyist special attention: "here it would be ridiculous to refuse. Some of my colleagues do, but personally I would not do it. [. . .] I know that it will not influence afterwards in any way what I'm saying" (Official #34). Overall, the payment for lunch may be acceptable if it is done on the basis of reciprocity (Officials #1, #28, #27), if the partner is well known and trusted (Officials #1) and if the lunch is not overly expensive (Officials #1, #38, #19). From a "flexible" perspective, the entire issue is considered a form of courtesy, with a cultural undertone:

This is really a cultural issue, and people would be shocked by an invitation to a pizzeria, whereas I find it of a symbolic nature. Of course, you do not accept invitations to a three-star Michelin restaurant to meet somebody you do not know. But it happens. What I always say is that if somebody wants to invite me, sometimes if I know the guy sufficiently, I pay, so he can invite me the next time, and there is no . . . nobody feels embarrassed, if it's done on this basis.

(Official #1)

The second stage of the story was specified in very general terms, and thus did not support respondents directly judging the situation presented. In other words, the answer was often "it depends", reflecting the point frequently made in the interviews that disclosing information to external parties is done on a case-by-case assessment. As one official explained: "this is not something you can learn in a book, when to give and when not [. . .] because it depends on the information, and it also depends on the person. It's certainly one of the most difficult things" (Official #1).

The purpose, therefore, was not so much to capture how positively or negatively officials appreciate the disclosure of information to the outside, but rather to spark a discussion on the conditions under which they would (not) do it, and the aspects considered when making this call. At this point, a conflict between public values was visible: on the one hand, the duties of confidentiality, and loyalty to the Commission, and on the other hand, the value of transparency, which dictates that the Commission be an open and accessible institution. Table 4.4 provides an overview of the issues mentioned in the course of responses.

Table 4.4 includes only the arguments which were most frequently used by officials as they discussed the vignette. Before presenting the results, it is important to mention that there were also other subjects which were brought up, but less often – first, the need to assess whether disclosing information to the lobbyist would grant him/her an unfair advantage over other stakeholders, and, second, the opportunity of consulting with a hierarchical superior, or referring the lobbyist to one.

Overall, officials proved to be open for communication, unless the information in question was "confidential", "sensitive", "political" or otherwise contentious. More often than not, what this meant was that giving a "general description of the text" is fine so long as it contains only information which is already public or well known from previous consultations. Of course, many realize that this would not carry too much value for the stakeholder:

You don't say what exactly was decided, but you say that a number of options were considered, and it's OK. Usually, these things don't come out of the blue – they have been discussed in various forums, so people really know. For me, it would be more of a window-dressing exercise, where you just take five minutes to speak to this stakeholder, to have a general talk with him, without revealing anything – that's perfectly fine.

(Official #10)

98 *Individual views towards ethics*

Table 4.4 Positions on the disclosure of information

	Provide already public information	Protect Commission decision-making	Keep stakeholder relations
DG "A"	√	√	–
	–	√	–
	√	√	–
	√	√	–
	–	√	–
	–	√	–
	–	–	√
	–	–	–
	√	√	–
	√	√	√
	√	–	–
	√	–	–
DG "B"	–	√	–
	–	–	√
	–	–	√
DG "C"	√	–	–
	–	–	√
	–	√	√
	–	–	–
	–	–	√
	√	√	–
	√	–	√
DG "D"	–	√	–
	–	√	√
	–	√	–
	√	√	–
	√	√	√
	√	√	–

This, among other things, shows that officials are well aware of the applicable regulations (see Art. 17 SR discussed above) – roughly half of interviewees brought up the argument of information already in the public domain. It also shows a preference for staying well within the safety zone installed by these regulations. It is true that there were officials in all four DGs who were willing to go beyond this minimum threshold, but overall, they were a minority. Just to illustrate this other trend, this is how one interviewee justifies his choice for a more forthcoming approach:

> I would say if somebody gives information, it's not unnatural to give some of that information back, it's important how that information is handled. [. . .] [If] it is not really confidential, but just sort of something that should not be brought to the attention of the public, I feel that he can adequately say a few things about where it is going. If he doesn't do that, he will create a situation where this lobby group will later on come after him, and probably criticize the Commission for not doing a diligent job in consultation.
>
> (Official #18)

If it could jeopardize the internal decision-making process of the Commission, officials are exceedingly cautious about transmitting (any) information to external actors. This was the argument most frequently mentioned in discussing the story, and it speaks of an overall preference for loyalty to the employer over transparency. Of course, the argument does take on different meanings in different parts of the Commission. In DG MARKT it shows an appreciation for the hard negotiation work behind legislative proposals and for the fragility of the compromise reached – which officials feel obliged to shield from last-minute pressures. This is how an official in DG MARKT describes her own portfolio:

> In that particular field, I probably wouldn't say anything, because it's so sensitive and with everything you say you are likely to cause a last-minute thunderstorm, which risks messing up the decision taken in the College, because you have people running to the cabinets, so it's in your own interest to shut up. But if you have things that are less sensitive, less contentious, then, yes, I say: "these are the subjects, and this is kind of the direction we are going in".
>
> (Official #7)

In DG COMP, the stress on prudence and confidentiality is directly related to the rigours of interacting within a litigation framework, with legal professionals:

> There's a difference between a legislative proposal and a [case] decision. If you are in a competition framework, I don't think I, or my colleagues, would have a one-to-one meeting with a party, be it a complainant, or a party investigated, because it's far too tricky, in the sense that people can later on say: Mrs. X said so-and-so, or Mr. Y said so-and-so, and that can be very dangerous for the case, or even for the appeal against the case.
>
> (Official #32)

By comparison, the number of officials who discussed the need to keep good working relations with stakeholders is rather low. This is interesting, because everybody agreed that receiving information from the outside is a legitimate and necessary process – but one which, apparently, does not entail any obligation to (try to) reciprocate, or at least not to the same extent.

Finally, it is important to point out that consulting over draft papers, or sending out an internal document is labelled a "leak" and condemned in stark terms by everyone. This being said, leaks are a fact of life in the Commission, and the vignette triggered recollections of such occurrences in all DGs.

***

In conclusion, at a general level everyone agrees that meetings with stakeholders are legitimate and necessary; however, the way these should be handled sparks disagreement. The analysis of interview data has highlighted two types of discourses – a strict and a flexible one. While the former holds that it is never justified to allow a lobbyist to cover the lunch bill, because this can discredit an official, in the latter the lunch is not a problem as long as the right message is being sent. Regarding the appropriateness of releasing information while decisions are still in internal cooking, the first and most important consideration is loyalty to the Commission. However, this is interpreted and related in different ways to the contact with external actors.

4.3 Ethics on the work-floor: commonalities, divergence and determinants

This section presents an overall discussion of the findings. It dwells on the common line in EU officials' thinking about public ethics, as well as the points of divergence, and further explores possible determining factors for the latter.

4.3.1 Commonalities and divergence

The analysis of the vignettes has revealed a mixture of commonalities and divergences in the way EU officials relate to public ethics. Broadly speaking, the common line is defined by a pronounced sense of loyalty to the Commission, which appears to be the core value in the moral system of the EU civil service. In the first vignette, loyalty translates into a general reticence towards expressing private views in public. The public office is interpreted as putting a reserve on one's private life, and although most officials do see spaces where individual freedom of expression can still be enacted, these are rather limited. In the second vignette, loyalty means an understanding that some measure of due diligence is necessary when confronted with possible wrongdoing, which goes beyond discussing the matter with those directly involved. Finally, in the third vignette, organizational loyalty translates into a guarded approach in communicating with stakeholders. The preference is to stay well within a safe zone, by limiting communication to information that is already public or known from previous consultations. The most important consideration in deciding on the release of information is its potential impact on the decision-making process of the Commission.

Beyond this common line, there is, however, some significant divergence. This occurs at a secondary level, indicating that certain details and nuances situated somewhat at the margins of an ethical quandary can elicit different reactions from staff.

The divergence is mostly expressed in the form of strict vs. flexible stances. Broadly speaking, with the first position, ethics is portrayed in absolute, categorical terms, while with the second one there is more emphasis on the value of finding the middle ground. Essentially, what drives the strict/ flexible split is a difference in the officials' orientation towards compromise, when faced with conflicting public values. Those in the strict group would prefer to choose unequivocally one value over others, while the "flexible" officials would rather find a way of accommodating them.

The different appreciations of compromise hide, on a deeper level, different preferences for handling risk. The "strict" discourse can be interpreted as a risk-averse one, because in this optic, avoiding compromises is a way of staying safe, and being safe is, in turn, the way to be "ethical". The converse is not necessarily true – i.e., that the "flexible" discourse is risk loving – however, here being "ethical" is not threatened by accommodating different values and imperatives. Risk avoidance is most visible with the third vignette, where the strict solution holds that it is never justified to allow a lobbyist to cover the lunch bill because of the risk of compromising the official's position; consequently, it is best to avoid such circumstances altogether. On the other hand, those taking a flexible perspective dismiss this risk – for them, lunch in itself is not a problem as long as the right message is being sent. In the first vignette, risk pertains not so much to the individual official, but to the organization, which might be damaged by an employee who (is forced to) look for a new job. In the "strict" discourse, the absolute primacy of organizational loyalty represents a way of containing this risk, while for the "flexible" camp, some (minimal) risk can be tolerated, given the challenges of working on a short-term contract and the value of freedom of expression.

In the second vignette, differences are visible in the way officials justify decisions to report (possible) wrongdoing. While one discourse lays more emphasis on the larger issues that are at stake (be they those of the Commission as a whole or, more restrictedly, those of the team where the official works), the other stresses self-interest (here, reporting is presented as the wise thing to do for the one who has come across a possible problem). Importantly, the two sets of motivations are not mutually exclusive. In the following chapter it will be shown that officials frame their discussion of (any) ethically sensitive issues in the same way – talking through a problem is the right approach because, on the one hand, dialogue leads to better solutions, but, on the other hand, it covers the one who is involved. Therefore, this mix of altruistic and self-centred motivations is the other axis – besides the strict/flexible divide – around which differences in ethics thinking are structured. It is important to note that the risk plays a role here as well – basically, reporting a (potential) problem is understood, by Commission officials, as the safe (i.e., risk-minimizing) and therefore desirable option.

4.3.2 Exploring the divergence

Given the existence of obvious divergence in the way EU officials think about ethics, it is important to consider the possible determining factors. Why is it that some people seem more bent on compromise, while others are not, and why would some more readily evoke self-regarding reasons, while others focus on altruistic ones? At this point, some of the observations made with regard to sampling in Chapter 1 should be restated. Namely, the book uses a maximum variation sample, which illustrates, in a balanced way and within some predefined limits, a wide range of the characteristics of the staff who populate the Commission services (i.e., different nationalities, professional backgrounds, organizational posts and types of employment contracts). In this way, the findings presented above, regarding EU officials' thinking about ethical questions, can be extrapolated to other (significant) parts of the Commission, despite being drawn from a small sample of thirty interviewees. However, due to its size, this sample is not appropriate for determining which factors are behind the differences in patterns of thinking described above. In quantitative language, the problem is one of overdetermination.

Having said this, the data can nevertheless be used as an exploratory probe, to suggest hypotheses which would be tested in future research. Therefore, the arguments made in this section should be understood as promising pointers, which could be explored in the future using different types of samples and methods. In what follows I will discuss two variables – nationality and organizational position – which, as argued in Chapter 1, might determine differences in ethics thinking among Commission employees. The focus is on these two because they are the most widely discussed in the literature. Nationality is a central variable in EU socialization research and the "usual suspect" on which diverging standards of conduct in the Commission have been pinned. On the other hand, individuals' organizational positions appear to be the most significant counterweight to national orientations.

4.3.2.1 Nationality

As argued elsewhere in the book, officials' nationalities matter insofar as ethics is concerned because EU countries vary significantly in their politico-administrative cultures and levels of corruption. Thus, individuals socialized in these different national environments would not have common understandings of ethical behaviour. The Commission becomes the site of a "clash of cultures" between the "clean" North and the "corrupt" South, and an East which is possibly "corrupt" as well, given its communist past and weak institutions during the post-communist transition.

That these are overgeneralizations is clear enough. It is also evident, from the research carried out here, that the Commission is not experiencing a "clash of cultures" with regard to ethics. On the contrary, officials are basically in agreement on where to draw the line between what is acceptable and what is not, and, considered in the bigger picture, the differences which do occur are marginal.

Individual views towards ethics 103

The vignette analysis suggests that the strict/flexible divide, described at length in the previous section, comes down to individual-level factors, as there is no clustering of answers following DG lines. Table 4.5 shows the divergence between strict and flexible stances in vignettes 1 and 3, together with officials' nationality, which is represented in terms of geographical blocks (North/ South/East[7]).

Overall, the distribution of answers is the following. For vignette 1, the "South" group contains four strict and five flexible positions; the "North" group has five strict and three flexible, while the "East" group has eight strict and three flexible.

Table 4.5 Strict/flexible positions and nationality

		Position on professional situation	Position on lunch
DG "A"	S	Strict	Flexible
	E	Flexible	Strict
	N	Strict	Flexible
	E	Strict	Strict
	S	Strict	Strict
	N	Flexible	Strict
	E	Strict	Strict
	S	Strict	Flexible
	N	Strict	Flexible
	N	Flexible	Strict
	S	Flexible	Flexible
	E	Strict	Flexible
DG "B"	S	Flexible	Strict
	N	Strict	Strict
	E	Flexible	Strict
DG "C"	E	Flexible	Strict
	N	Flexible	Strict
	E	Strict	Flexible
	E	Strict	Strict
	S	Flexible	Strict
	S	Strict	Flexible
	S	Flexible	Strict
DG "D"	N	Strict	Strict
	N	Strict	Strict
	S	Flexible	Flexible
	E	Strict	Flexible
	E	Strict	Strict
	E	Strict	Flexible

With vignette 3, in the "South" group there are four strict and five flexible positions, in the "North" group there are six strict and two flexible, while in the "East" group we have seven strict and four flexible. This distribution hardly suggests any patterns, with one possible exception – in the group of old Member States (i.e., "North" and "South" considered together) there is a more even mix of strict and flexible stances, while with the new (post-2004) Member States (i.e., the "East" cluster) there is a clear predominance of the strict discourse.

The national culture hypothesis, sketched above, would actually suggest the opposite, i.e., a predominance of "flexible" stances in the "East" group (if, by a stretched interpretation, such a stance would denote a certain comfort with more ambiguous, questionable behaviours). The situation, then, may have less to do with nationality, and more with the circumstances in which staff from new Member States joined and experienced the European Commission. The majority of these interviewees were relatively young, at the beginning of their careers and, with one exception, occupied non-managerial positions. It is possible that the more strict outlooks would be due to the lower hierarchical positions and lower work experience, which would render these employees more prone to risk avoidance. On the other hand, however, officials from new Member States have joined the Commission at a point when the Kinnock reforms had been well under way, and the organization had largely left behind the days of very debilitating public scandals, such as the Santer resignation and the Eurostat affair. The predominance of strict positions may, therefore, also be due to their entering the Commission at a time when ethics was already an issue. Considering all this, perhaps a more fruitful hypothesis, worth investigating in future research, would concern generational differences in the Commission – namely, whether the more seasoned staff members, who had been there before the major administrative reforms were implemented, have different views on ethics compared with newer staff, who had joined in the post-Kinnock era.

This being said, the possibility that the strict/flexible divide comes down to individual psychological traits should not be dismissed. Although this group of factors is outside the research parameters of the book, it is worth mentioning here (as an illustration more than anything else) the concept of tolerance of ambiguity, defined as "the tendency to perceive ambiguous situations as desirable" (Budner 1962: 29). Essentially, this concept, employed in organizational psychology among other fields, pertains to individual reactions (from attraction to rejection) towards situations which are unfamiliar, complex or susceptible to multiple conflicting interpretations (see Furnham and Ribchester 1995 for a review). The different appreciations of compromise, which makes the difference between flexible and strict stances, may be explained by different levels of tolerance of ambiguity in individuals.

Before moving on, one other aspect is worth mentioning, namely that many interviewees expressed a strict view with regard to the possible "revolving door" situation, but a flexible one on the lobby lunch, and vice versa. To give just one example, this is how one official expressed flexibility on vignette 1, but a strict stance on vignette 3:

Individual views towards ethics 105

I probably wouldn't do it, but it is easy to say being a *fonctionnaire*, and having to look for a different job right after. . ... I think that if he is really just about to finish his job in the Commission, and he makes it very clear that this is a private capacity, and he will no longer be working for the Commission – it's acceptable.

(Official #13)

I personally, as a rule, never accept anybody to pay for my lunch, even though it goes within the scope of what we are allowed to do. [. . .] But for the clear conscience, I always insist to pay for my own lunch, and my own coffee, and whatever.

(Official #13)

This variation suggests that the topic in regard to which ethical judgement is made matters, since individual officials displayed different sensitivities for the two vignettes. One's own personal experience can also play a role here. The variation also suggests a certain degree of indecisiveness on behalf of officials (which is not surprising given the ambiguity of the scenarios). Being on the fence, it is possible that they would opt for a strict answer in one instance, but a flexible one in another. As mentioned earlier in the book, these two types were inductively constructed to be relatively accommodating, and as such they cover answers which vary in their intensity. The fact that an official may switch between a strict and a flexible position in different scenarios does not invalidate that this is, indeed, the line of difference for ethics judgements. It does mean, however, that more research would be needed to understand whether there is an ambiguity threshold above which individuals are likely to become more volatile in their ethical judgements, and where that may be situated.

4.3.2.2 Organizational position

To restate a point made in Chapter 1, there is a good deal of empirical evidence in the EU literature which suggests that individuals' organizational positions within the Commission represent an important influence on their decision behaviour and, ultimately, on their identity. Egeberg (2012) suggests that this "portfolio logic" acts as a counterbalance to national orientations. Therefore, it matters where in the Commission one works. Insofar as ethics is concerned, this aspect is relevant because the Commission's functions entail different ethics problems, which, in turn, could influence differently officials' views towards ethics.

With interviewees recruited from four DGs, the data allow for an exploration of this possibility. And there are, indeed, two points where answers to vignettes are clustered along DG lines. However, given the small number of respondents, it is difficult to say whether these clusters are indeed patterns or just coincidence.

Firstly, in the vignette dealing with whistleblowing, the other-oriented discourse appears slightly predominant overall, and certainly more frequent among case handlers, both in DG COMP and in DG ENV (see Table 4.2, DGs "A" and "B", respectively). This could be a result of the function performed by these two DGs. Being involved in legal work and thus constantly in the position of defending the interests of the Communities, perhaps referring to those interests (as opposed to self-preservation) is a more natural language for case handlers.

Secondly, in the discussion on disclosure of internal information in vignette 3, officials in DG COMP have mentioned far less frequently (compared with those in other DGs) arguments relating to the need for keeping good relations with stakeholders (see Table 4.4). Judging from the answers offered by COMP officials, it seems that this decreased sensitivity towards a two-way dialogue is linked to an awareness of the power imbalance between the Commission and its stakeholders, which puts the former in the driver's seat:

> The truth is that a good working relationship is always there, because the lobbyist lives off what trickles down from the Commission. He will never walk away. And if he walks away because I'm very strict with the rules, then so be it. If it's not this lobbyist providing me with the information, there would be another one, because there is always somebody having an interest that their info gets passed on to us.
>
> (Official #8)

Knowing they can afford to stop communicating at any point that might raise problems creates a certain feeling of relaxation:

> We are the ones in charge and in control, and you are always in a position to say that now I stop talking about this, I cannot tell you anything more, that's it, and if you don't want to answer, you don't have to – always.
>
> (Official #10)

By comparison, in other DGs, officials are more inclined to support a two-way dialogue with stakeholders and to find ways of achieving it within the confines and the limits of the institutional framework. This quote from a REGIO official illustrates well the difference of perspective:

> When you're dealing with stakeholders, be they NGOs, or business groups, or whatever, if you want to have a functional relationship, you cannot act like it's fixed when they turn up and say: "here, we give you all the information, Commission, what do you think?" – "We think nothing". Many of my colleagues would say: "no, no, don't say anything!" ... For me, that is dysfunctional. You can very often say something without violating any specific secrets, without giving anybody any tool to take you to court or anything else. That's an ad-hoc judgement.
>
> (Official #18)

In what follows, I will propose that this difference of perspective is due to the functional specialization of DG COMP, which is linked to a number of internal cultural specificities, but also to a tighter regulatory framework.

COMP is the only DG entirely dedicated to enforcement.[8] This presumes that as a rule, the relationship with external actors is from the start an adversarial one. Generally speaking, national governments or companies do not engage with this part of the Commission unless they are (or are suspected of being) in breach of competition rules. Consequently, COMP case handlers see themselves as "fighting" – although it is important to note that the three instruments of competition policy[9] differ in this regard. Namely, anti-trust is far more confrontational than the other two, which is a natural consequence of the purely punitive nature of the work carried out in this part of DG COMP. As one official explains:

> Anti-trust is always conflictual, we are always fighting with the companies, there is nothing they can gain from us (in state aid, they can get the money, in mergers, they can go ahead with the mergers). With us, they face nothing but bad news – we're not popular, we always have to fight for everything.
> (Official #2)

What is more, COMP officials are aware that they have the upper hand in this fight – which is not surprising, given that DG COMP is, objectively speaking, endowed with far-reaching investigative prerogatives unparalleled elsewhere in the Commission.[10] Simply put, they are the DG with the power, and they know it. The following quotes are illustrative:

> [T]hen it's our discretion, and if they don't provide us with the information, then we say: alright, our purely factual information leads us to the conclusion that this is the case . . . and it might be totally opposite to what they need, or want, or have hoped for. This normally helps to get factual information. We have also legal possibilities, but in such a situation I'm very relaxed.
> (Official #8)

> [P]recisely because you are addressing something in the future, companies may be willing to make concessions in order to get clearance. And viewing that timing is also very short for them, they don't want to go on an in-depth investigation, maybe you can "extort" from them a number of concessions that you wouldn't [otherwise].
> (Official #16)

It seems fair to assume that the powers of DG COMP and its culture of adversity would lead officials who work here to place more emphasis on defending the Commission's position, rather than cooperating with external actors. A contributing factor is that DG COMP is placed somewhat outside the regular inter-institutional interactions in the EU arena. The average case handler has little to no contact with other European institutions, or even with other parts of the Commission. One

108 *Individual views towards ethics*

interviewee, who had been transferred from DG COMP to DG MARKT, explains the relative seclusion very well:

> [W]hen you are in DG MARKT, or specifically in policy, it's a very EU-specific kind of job. I learned much more about the institutions and how they function probably in six months here than I ever did in DG COMP, because DG COMP is very much. . ... They are the DG with the power, they do what they do, they take the decisions, and that's it.
>
> (Official #27)

The situation is different for DG MARKT, DG REGIO and DG ENV, whose activities put them much more in the broader EU institutional framework, in the web of interests around them and therefore in a position where the need to exchange information, negotiate and compromise is more evident. From this perspective, it is interesting to note that DG MARKT appears almost as the opposite of DG COMP, because here lobbyists and other interest representatives are natural partners (in a way that they are not for the others), and the regular contact creates long-standing relationships and possibly more space for trust:

> Our main stakeholders are industry associations. These are the people who are very often consulted, and very much listened to. We have numerous meetings all the time, and if there is something new, we always consult with them and we always see what their thinking is.
>
> (Official #27)

By comparison, sometimes, in DG COMP, a lobbyist becomes someone to be "resisted":

> Resisting lobbyists is sometimes the best way to protect ourselves, and if they are too intrusive, I can be rude, and I've already been rude in some instances, because, as I said, there are files about which you can say things, and others where you can't.
>
> (Official #1)

But this is only part of the explanation. Some elements of the internal regulatory framework of DG COMP can also explain why officials who work here seem to be less sensitive about the necessity of a two-way dialogue with external actors. Within the Commission, DG COMP is peculiar in that it operates with a high volume of market-sensitive, confidential information. To prevent misuse of this information, the local ethics regulations are stricter here than in other parts of the Commission, with the key issue being the avoidance of (the perception of) conflicts of interests. For instance, the internal ethics code of DG COMP introduces three types of in-house conflicts of interest declarations, additionally to what is generally required for Commission officials – a general annual declaration, a case-specific declaration (completed by staff when they are assigned to a case) and an inspection declaration (for participants in anti-trust and mergers inspections). Leakage of confidential information is another risk, against which enhanced security measures have been introduced. To give just one example, case managers are required to keep a "who knew what and when" document, which would allow tracing back information flows in case of allegations of insider dealing (Commission 2010b). At the individual level, this amplified security environment translates into things such as a "clean desk" policy, locking one's office while away or destroying hardcopies of secret documents.

Therefore, overall, DG COMP appears to be, by comparison with other parts of the Commission, a very procedure-heavy setting. This, too, affects interaction with external actors – as COMP officials work within a litigation framework and interact mostly with legal professionals, they are more careful about their meetings, and more guarded about what they say. This is how one official who had previously worked in DG MARKT described the enhanced rigours of her new position in DG COMP:

> [DG COMP] is very rules based, very procedural, where for every single step you have a procedure, and if you don't follow it, you are sure that the lawyers will be on your back – for sure. So, of course, you have to be more reserved, and somehow more cautions. Not that you don't have to be cautious when you're making policy, but there the framework within which you're operating is much looser. You meet with people, and it's not like they will come back and say: "my rights of defence were violated".
> (Official #10)

Therefore, this tighter regulatory framework may lead COMP staff to be more concerned about protecting sensitive information from leaking out, rather than promoting a two-way dialogue. Here information flows are highly controlled, as clearly shown in this comment by a COMP official on the casual receipt of a policy report over lunch:

> [W]e have a completely different system, and anything we take – if we want to use it – it must be registered, and the source must be known, and also the way it got here. I find it very strange just to take something like that.
> (Official #6)

By comparison, other DGs handle less confidential (explosive) information, and their procedural constraints do not appear to be as taxing. To give just one example, in DG REGIO there is room for a more pragmatic approach in case the Member States' annual implementation reports prove inadequate: "sometimes you just need some information that has not reached you. And you just immediately pick up the phone and say: 'hello, where's the file?'" (Official #26).

In conclusion, DG COMP appears to be an outlier within the Commission. It has the powers and acts as an almost full-blown independent regulatory agency. This status shapes differently officials' judgements regarding the appropriateness of disclosing internal information to external parties. To be sure, like everyone else, COMP officials consider whether releasing information might damage the Commission's position and its internal decision-making. They are also fully opposed to leaks. However, unlike officials in other parts of the Commission, COMP case handlers seem to place more value on confidentiality and are less inclined to balance it out against the requirements of openness and transparency. This situation could be investigated further in future research, perhaps through a comparison that would include one or several European administrative agencies.

4.4 Conclusion

This chapter offered a detailed account of how Commission officials think about ethics in public office. It has been shown that they share much common ground in the way they relate to public ethics. The convergence is around a pronounced sense of loyalty to the Commission, which appears to be the core value in the moral system of the EU civil service. Beyond this, however, at a secondary level, there is space to express divergent opinions. There are two axes around which difference in ethics thinking is structured. The first refers to orientation towards compromise in the face of conflicting public values – while with the "strict" position the preference is to choose univocally one value over others, with the "flexible" one it is to find a way of accommodating them. The second axis refers to justifications for discussing (potential) ethical problems – while one discourse stresses self-interest (i.e., reporting is the safe thing to do for the one who has come across a potential problem), the other stresses the larger issues at stake (i.e., be it the interests of the official's team, or those of the Commission or the fact that consultation achieves better solutions). The unifying theme in all this is the handling of risk. With the strict/flexible divide, the different orientation towards compromise is based on an appraisal of the risk entailed. With the second divide, reporting itself is seen as a way of avoiding risk – the difference being whether this risk is seen as affecting primarily oneself or others.

Given the existence of obvious divergence in the way EU officials think about ethics, the possible determining factors were considered in the second part of the chapter. Considering the limitations of the sample, the analysis went no further than suggesting hypotheses which might be tested in future research. It was shown that nationality, the traditional "usual suspect" for different understandings of ethics within the Commission, is not particularly helpful in explaining the second-order differences revealed by the data. An alternative and more useful hypothesis relates to generational differences in the Commission – namely, more seasoned staff members, who had joined the Commission before the Kinnock reforms, may have different views on ethics compared with newer staff, who came in the post-Kinnock era.

On the other hand, there are elements to suggest that officials' organizational positions matter for their views on ethics, but perhaps not in a systematic way. What the data have revealed is the special case of DG COMP, which, unlike other DGs, handles vast amounts of confidential data and is subject to a stricter procedural framework. Also unlike other places in the Commission, DG COMP has a culture of adversity vis-à-vis its counterparts (case handlers see themselves as "fighting"), which is unsurprising, since it is dedicated entirely to enforcement and enjoys very substantial powers. All these factors shape COMP officials' perception over external actors, and the boundaries of appropriate communication with them. Specifically, they proved to be (by comparison with officials in other DGs) more sensitive to the need to control and protect internal information and less inclined to consider the need to keep good relations with stakeholders.

The existence of commonalities in officials' thinking about ethics – which this chapter has revealed – can be interpreted as a sign that the Commission's ethics management system is having an impact on the work-floor. Of course, this statement invites caution. To the extent that the commonalities have emerged within the Commission, they are surely due to more complex processes of influence. Furthermore, Chapter 1 has warned against overstating heterogeneity in the Commission's recruitment pool. Regarding specifically the sample used in this thesis, it is fair to assume that the interviewees entered with some pre-existing notions of what ethics in the civil service presumed, given that many of them had previously worked in public administration, or in a (private sector) position which put them in contact with public bodies and/or the EU institutions. This being said, the convergence is significant, because one of the purposes of having an ethics management system is precisely to bring everyone in the organization on the same page about what is acceptable and what not. Moreover, as Chapter 3 has demonstrated, the Commission has had this aim when it engaged in vigorous awareness-raising and guidance actions after 2008. Therefore, the following chapter will take this as a starting point, as it seeks to determine the mechanisms by which the ethics policy of the European Commission influences its employees' views towards ethics.

Notes

1 See, for example, Hughes (1998), Barter and Renold (2000).
2 For instance, O'Fallon and Butterfield (2005) find in their review that scenarios are the most widely used method for probing ethical decision making in the business ethics field. With regard to the administrative ethics literature, Frederickson and Walling (2001) argue that vignettes are often used in studies which take an experimental approach.
3 The institutional membership of the interviewees is the following: the Secretariat General (SG), DG Enterprise and Industry (DG ENTR), DG Humanitarian Aid (DG ECHO), DG Trade (DG TRADE), DG Enlargement (DG ELARG), DG Information Society and Media (DG INFSO), DG Mobility and Transport (DG MOVE).
4 The standard approach is to ask participants what they themselves would do or what a third person would do, sometimes both (Finch 1987, Renold 2002). The slightly different approach taken here was judged to be more effective to get respondents to evaluate the scenarios and thus express their ethical reasoning.
5 Which is why the data presentation does not make any distinction between the two stages of the vignette.
6 Importantly, such preparatory documents can only be released after the act to which they contributed (a legislative and non-legislative act, some communication or report, etc.) has been adopted. See Commission 2005, and the *Commission Decision of*

5 *December 2001 Amending Its Rules of Procedure (notified under document number C(2001) 3714)*.

7 The split was done on geographical considerations, as follows: North (Austria, Belgium, Luxembourg, Denmark, Finland, Germany, Ireland, the Netherlands, Sweden, UK); South (Italy, Greece, Cyprus, France, Portugal, Spain); and East (Bulgaria, Romania, the Czech Republic, Hungary, Estonia, Lithuania, Latvia, Poland, Slovakia, Slovenia). Scores for 2011 in Transparency International's Corruption Perception Index (the most well-known corruption measurement instrument to date) indeed correlate with these geographical blocks, showing higher values for countries in the North, compared with those in the South, or East. For more on this, see: www.transparency.org/research/cpi/cpi_2011.

8 Seven out of its nine Directorates perform this function. Out of the remaining two, one is dedicated to competition policy and strategy, and the other has management support functions – human and financial resources, document management, ethics, security and IT (Commission 2010a).

9 DG COMP takes action against several types of anti-competitive behaviour, and for each there is a correspondent "instrument" in its arsenal. Firstly, there are anti-competitive agreements, such as cartels and market-sharing, as well as the abuse of dominant market position – this instrument is commonly referred to as "anti-trust". The second instrument – "mergers" – deals with mergers and acquisitions which may distort competition in the EU. Finally, the third instrument – "state aid" – deals with potentially distorting governmental aid. A notification system applies to mergers and state aid – the Commission must be notified of, and approve, future concentrations with a Community dimension, or planned state aid respectively. In anti-trust, however, cases are opened *ex officio* by the Commission, or following complaints or (for cartels) following leniency requests.

10 The Commission makes use of several investigative tools unavailable in other policy fields: written requests for information (backed by fines in case of no or late answers), taking interviews and statements from relevant natural or legal persons, and, finally, the notorious ad-hoc inspections on the company premises (in cooperation with national competition authorities and local law enforcement).

5 Discussing "common sense"
How ethics management shapes individual views towards ethics

This chapter seeks to determine the mechanisms by which the organizational ethics system of the European Commission influences its employees' views towards ethics. In order to do this, it is first necessary to determine whether the influence actually exists – in other words, whether Commission's ethics management framework feeds employees' learning about the ethics of their organizational roles. This so-called socialization outcome was defined, in Chapter 1, by two aspects – first, that officials think about ethics in similar ways, and, secondly, that there is an overlap between official messages regarding ethics and the comments and positions expressed by employees on the subject.

The previous chapter, where the vignettes were analyzed at length, has covered the first of these points and demonstrated that officials indeed share substantial common ground in their appreciation of ethics. This chapter takes the analysis further, by tackling the second point above. Namely, it starts by inquiring whether there are any matches between the Commission's official communication on ethics and the arguments expressed by interviewees as they reasoned through the vignettes. The second section covers officials' direct experience with and perception of ethics policy instruments in the Commission. These additional elements make it possible to determine with more confidence whether the Commission's ethics management system is indeed being "felt" on the work-floor. Based on these data, the third and final section of the chapter pieces together the causal mechanism by which it influences officials' views towards public ethics.

5.1 Official communication and views from the work-floor

In Chapter 3, it was established that the Commission's internal communication on ethics revolved around two messages: one of compliance (or, more specifically, rule awareness) and another of care towards the organization's public image. This section explores whether these messages are reflected in the way officials think about ethics.

The most visible point of convergence, between the official policy line and the ethics reasoning of employees, is the preoccupation with the Commission's public image. In official communication, ethics was justified as a way of keeping a good institutional standing: the people who worked for the Commission represented its "human face", and, as such, they had to display exemplary conduct; mistakes in this area came with high reputational costs, as the organization was monitored with increasing aggressiveness by the press, watchdog groups and the Parliament. There is a clear connection between this background and the general reticence, in vignette 1, towards expressing publicly divergent personal opinions. Doing this is seen, by some officials, as a breach of loyalty simply because it makes the Commission look bad. Being careful about public appearances, then, has much to do with being mindful of public image and is fuelled by an understanding of the high level of public exposure and scrutiny to which the Commission is subject:

> The Commission is watched from all sides in Europe, and [. . .] if anything comes out of the Commission, in a way it is carved in stone. That is why decision-making needs to be carefully prepared, and that is also why the people working at the Commission need to be extremely aware that what they say is not just taken for granted as their private opinion.
>
> (Official #32)

In vignette 2 we also see public image arguments playing a role in the way Commission officials think about whistleblowing. It is significant that none of the interviewees mentioned external receptors (e.g., the press) as a feasible option for making disclosures. In fact, most officials expressed a preference for a "local" solution to the problem presented in the vignette (i.e., consulting the superior or a colleague). These answers may be expected, since the scenario does not depict an explosive issue, and, as explained before, the *SR* encourage following the hierarchical line in reporting wrongdoing and exclude the possibility of external whistleblowing. However, if we look closer at the way reporting is justified, it is clear that officials would not go outside the Commission (or the sphere of the EU institutions) even if the wrongdoing were very grave. This kind of move would be counter-intuitive for those who see reporting as the right thing to do *for* their organization and team (see the "other"-oriented discourse described in Chapter 4), while for officials who stressed self-interest, going against the organization at their own expense would not make sense. All of this suggests that disclosures, even well-founded, are problematic if they publicly damage the Commission. As one official explained: "you owe allegiance and solidarity to your system. You're not supposed to – in the first place – try to damage your system" (Official #18). This is important, because in the extreme – where problems are systemic and resistance to change is high – whistleblowers have little choice but to step outside official channels. Also, oftentimes, it is this kind of disclosure that is the most effective – as proven even by the Commission's own experience with whistleblowers.

The other central feature in the Commission's internal communication about ethics was the focus on explaining the relevant regulations, and their correct interpretation. From this perspective, it is significant that many regular officials brought up this subject. Thus, with vignette 3, a little over half of the interviewees mentioned rules on accepting gifts and such from external parties – in most cases, this was the 50 EUR threshold. Also in vignette 3, many interviewees explicitly mentioned that they would consider whether the information they release to external actors is already in the public domain – which is exactly what Art. 17 *SR* stipulates. The important point here is that the reference to regulation was not prompted by the interviewer – in these conditions, its appearance means that rules genuinely enter the officials' reasoning around an ethically ambiguous situation.

Finally, and perhaps surprisingly, the officials' divergent positions on the vignettes are also indicative of the influence of organizational ethics policy. This is the case because the element of risk is so centrally featured in these divisions. To recapitulate some of the points previously made, the strict and flexible positions differ in the appreciation of risk – while the former portrays compromise (i.e., accommodating different values) as risky, the latter does not. With the second divide (between self-/other-oriented positions), reporting itself is seen as a way of avoiding risk – the difference being whether this risk is seen as affecting primarily oneself or others. Therefore, the important point is not so much that Commission officials have different views on ethics but that it is on (certain aspects of) risks that they disagree about. This means that, overall, being ethical has a lot to do with staying safe – even though individual preferences vary on where and how to draw the line. The centrality of risk proves that on the Commission work-floor, ethics is framed in line with the compliance-based logic, where ethical behaviour is largely equated with staying out of trouble. And this, in turn, is a reflection of organizational communication, which focused on avoiding mistakes (by paying attention to rules, and for the sake of the Commission's institutional reputation).

5.2 Ethics as "common sense"

Most interviewees reported that they had participated, at some point in their careers, in a work event dedicated to ethics – in most cases, this turned out to be either a specialized training, or a session in a more general-purpose training, or simply a presentation held by ethics experts. Other respondents remember having used internal literature on the subject – be it an ethics guide/brochure or the Intranet pages dedicated to ethics. All of this is a clear indication that ethics has gained a more consistent organizational profile in the Commission, and that the large-scale awareness-raising efforts started with the *Ethics Communication* have indeed reached the work-floor level.

This being said, many officials believe that ethics policy instruments have limited usefulness for their work. More often than not, the content of these training sessions, presentations and guidelines is labelled "common sense" – with the implication that content-wise they are at least partially redundant. As some officials have aptly explained:

> These things are good, because they make you aware of the environment that you're in, but from what I recall it didn't alert me to anything I wouldn't naturally know or naturally do.
>
> (Official #32)

116　*Discussing "common sense"*

> In the beginning, I received a short booklet on that, and then I remember I read it, and there were no surprises, everything was for me logical.
>
> (Official #14)

On the other hand, those who have not participated in ethics events do not feel they have missed much. Again, ethics is about common sense – and if that somehow is not enough, one can easily get an idea of what goes and what does not by observing colleagues:

> But I feel clean in the way that I approach my job and the way I do things, even if I've never read this code, but I should. [. . .] I've never read the codes because I think there are things that are simple, just a good sense of behaviour.
>
> (Official #3)

> Somehow, being in this environment, with time you develop a sensitivity to this, and I simply follow that. I don't think I ever went to a course, maybe I did, but I don't remember.
>
> (Official #22)

Moreover, in some cases there is frustration with the bureaucracy created by new ethics regulations, which seems superfluous, if not insulting. As one official explained:

> We are now asked to make a declaration of possible conflict of interest for very small amounts of money or shares we may have. So, they think I'm going to be not loyal and to risk my career because I have 500 EUR of shares in this company, which I never look at. OK, I have to declare them; it's good to declare them. But the problem is that all this generates red tape.
>
> (Official #1)

Ethics is described as "common sense" even by internal experts (Ethics officials #7, #10, #8, #17), and the point is made also in official ethics literature. For example, an ethics brochure in DG COMP opens with a forward by the Director General, stating that "in most cases, dealing correctly with ethics is above all a question of common sense and open communication" (Commission 2011a: 3).

Given the frequent appeal to ethics as a commonsense matter, it is useful to further unpack the concept. As a wrap-up to the interview, all regular officials were asked to succinctly define what being an "ethical" official meant for them. Broadly speaking, answers may be grouped around two positions. One group described ethics as a personal, almost organic attribute. For these officials, ethics represents a "personal feeling" (Official #10), an intuition (Official #4), a sensitivity (Official #14), something which comes naturally (Official #30), something one gets from home (Official #13) or simply good character (Official #27). Here are a couple of illustrative statements:

> I think in the end it depends on a person's character. For me – I have a very simple and intuitive method: if I manage to sleep OK at night, it means my conscience is clear.
>
> (Official #4)

> To me it's really a personal thing, it's something that . . . if a person has the ethics, or the morality in him, then he would have it whether he is a Commission official, or somebody else.
>
> (Official #27)

> For me, ethics is something that you cannot gain by working here or there. Ethics is something that you get from home, and if you don't have that background, from home, then it's very difficult to absorb a different culture.
>
> (Official #13)

In this optic, ethics is conflated with, or at least draws heavily on, one's own personal (private) morality. The other group of officials offered definitions of ethics which had at their core the avoidance of conflicts of interests. Here, ethics is construed in terms of public role responsibilities, as it has much to do with putting the public interest above your own (Officials #2, #24, #12), and being loyal to your organization (Officials #22, #26, #19), being mindful of a higher mission (Official #9) and guarding one's independence (Official #31). For instance:

> It comes down to looking at the higher mission and aim that you have. [. . .] [If] you're going to work here for the EU, you should have a view that it is not just about you, not just about your country, or a particular directive, or interest, that you're here for a particular reason.
>
> (Official #9)

> [M]aking sure that you are independent in your work. That's the condition to be respected by the public. If you want to deliver a good service, you need to be independent and above any suspicion.
>
> (Official #31)

These differences are interesting, because they demonstrate – as the vignettes have also done – that there are nuances and diversity in the way Commission officials think about ethics. But whether it is seen as a matter of intuition and personal conscience or as the golden rule of forswearing personal interests, ethics seems to be something rather basic. And this is, indeed, the main idea behind the "common sense" label – that ethics is easy and accessible and that people somehow already know which behaviour is acceptable and which is not.

Is ethics really something so obvious as to reduce it to common sense? Objectively, there is some truth to this description, if one looks at ethics as designating the core values of civil service – independence, objectivity, loyalty, transparency, and the like. These notions are fundamental to modern day democratic order, and it would be hard to imagine that anybody who has come to be employed in the European Commission would not know or accept them. From this perspective ethics is indeed common sense. This book, however, has examined ethics in ambiguous contexts, where it is more difficult to judge what constitutes ethical behaviour. As the vignette analysis has shown, in these contexts Commission officials do sometimes take divergent positions on where to draw the line between what is acceptable and what is not. Here ethics ceases to be obvious and commonsensical, otherwise there wouldn't be any variation.

Therefore, the point to take away from this discussion is that ethics is *perceived* as common sense, which means that there is an assumption, within the Commission, that staff share the same basic values. From this perspective, the Commission's ethics policies appear to be at least partially redundant and are not *perceived* as affecting officials' thinking about ethics – although, as demonstrated before, there are clear indications that this is, in fact, happening. Whatever influence exists, it is rather surreptitious. An investigation of causal mechanisms can reveal why this is the case.

5.3 Discussing ethics

It is useful to start the discussion on causal mechanisms by observing that Commission officials have a certain disposition to talk about ethics. Almost all respondents remarked that if confronted with a dilemma, their first reaction would be to turn to their superiors and/ or colleagues. In these circumstances, consulting the regulations, or the ethics specialists is seen as the less convenient option: "if I have any doubts, I will ask the colleagues, because I don't have time to read 100 pages, I'll just ask somebody who knows, it's faster" (Official #4). On closer inspection, it appears that these discussions about ethics are framed in two very different ways, revealing a mixed bag of motivations.

On the one hand, there are officials who make the point that discussing ethically ambiguous issues is conducive to better solutions:

> I believe that by shaking things, by moving them, by asking people around what do they think, that I will find a solution. So I would go and ask, or discuss the issue with someone that I think has confidentiality, trust, as well as knowledge.
>
> (Official #30)

In this context, it is important to have a good relationship with the interlocutor. Indeed, many officials (Officials #16, #20, #32, #2, #6, #26, #30, #23, #27, #9, #13) believe that within their units there are people who could be approached, because they "understand" and can be trusted. For example, this is how a DG ENV official describes one of her superiors:

> I am in a very privileged position, that we have a very experienced deputy with a top-notch moral stance – at least that is how I see him. He's someone I have a lot of trust in, and he's somebody you can rely on that it would not go any further, it would stay with him.
>
> (Official #13)

The remarks of a Head of Unit in DG COMP go along similar lines:

> I think we, in this Directorate, have excellent relationships with the hierarchy, and perhaps if there's a small-scale dilemma, I would talk to my Deputy Head of Unit, and ask for his opinion, and see whether we can solve it among our unit, or among the persons involved, him and me. If it is of a more general interest, I would always talk to my immediate superior, who's the Director, with whom I have a very good personal relationship, so that means that I can really openly discuss these things, reveal when I have doubts and look at her for guidance, so I would not need to fear that I am overruled in a way that I would not agree with or I could not understand.
>
> (Official #32)

On the other hand, there are also those who find that bringing up an ethically charged issue is the prudent and safe thing to do. In this logic, the issue is not so much negotiating a good solution, but passing along (or at least sharing) the responsibility of making a decision. This kind of approach appears often in discussions around the vignettes. Thus, on vignette 1, many (Officials #8, #16, #24, #28, #32, #2, #10, #30, #5) believe that the character (John) should double check with the hierarchy before attending a conference in a private capacity. This is framed as prudence:

> [S]ince he knows that the Commissioner made a press statement, then he has to be proactive and ask: "what do I do?" Because it's also in his best interests. He has to go and ask: "do I still go on with this, do I change the message, do I cut to the part on which we can agree?"
>
> (Official #5)

The same is true of vignette 3, where officials have often indicated that they would consult a superior before releasing internal information, or simply refer stakeholders to a superior (Officials #1, #8, #12, #2, #26, #34, #11, #15, #19, #23). The reason is also prudence:

> There can be situations where you can give some level of info, but not all. It really depends. Sometimes you do it, and when you give info, it's always best to have the backing of your hierarchy, so you are sure.
>
> (Official #1)

120 *Discussing "common sense"*

In other words, talking about ethics takes the edge off the individual and makes it everybody's problem. As one official has aptly explained: "sometimes, it's very comfortable being in an organization, you just go to your boss, and then it's their problem" (Official #2). Along similar lines, another official looks back on a difficult case he handled at the beginning of his career and concludes that the best advice he ever got was to "shout" when things got tough:

> [I]t was at that point that I got the best advice from [my boss]. She said to me: "when you're in trouble here, shout! Because then it's not only you who's struggling with this problem, it's everybody else".
>
> (Official #20)

These observations clearly show that Commission officials have a certain predilection for discussing ethically sensitive issues, particularly within their units. In the absence of a more consistent recourse to the instruments in the ethics policy arsenal, it would seem that shared understandings of ethical behaviour are forged in these kinds of interactions. Officials "learn" their ethics by discussing problems with their peers and superiors. Talking about ethics, however, is supported by a double set of motivations – on the one hand, finding an optimal solution, and, on the other, diffusing responsibility. These motivations are mutually reinforcing (i.e., an official might be interested to talk about an ethically charged situation to both solve it in an acceptable way and get him/herself covered); however, the quality of the interaction may vary depending on which type is prevalent.

This being said, for the research question pursued in this book, it would be important to establish whether these discussions about ethics are linked in any way to organizational factors and in particular to the Commission's ethics policy framework. This seems to be, indeed, the case. On the one hand, interviews have shown that the dialogue between unit members, and with superiors, is a standard approach for problem-solving in the European Commission. This is evident in the way officials recollect the beginning of their careers in the European Commission and the process of becoming accommodated within the organization. Looking back, the majority feel that their colleagues were the most useful resource in understanding how things are done in the Commission. Newcomers seem to enjoy an open-door policy, deemed as key to becoming an operational member of the team:

> [T]he colleagues here are very open, very nice, a productive and informal friendly working environment. Would I change? I would really think twice about that. It's no problem at all to walk into anybody's office and say: "I have this-and-this problem". For newcomers, especially for newcomers – when I arrived, they said: "come and ask me, no problem about that", if they're busy, they tell you anyway, saying "don't come now, come in two hours, or come tomorrow, or let's have lunch together" – something like that.
>
> (Official #8)

From this perspective, the discussions about ethics seem to fit a broader norm of how things are done in the Commission. If officials turn to their immediate work circle for solving problems and "learning the ropes", it makes sense that they would proceed in the same way when confronted with a potential ethical problem.

But it is not just this cultural feature of Commission life which supports discussions on ethics. The influence of policy interventions is also visible. Namely, the Commission's increased preoccupation with ethics and in particular the large-scale awareness-raising actions implemented over the last years under the banner of the *Ethics Communication* have rendered ethics into a more visible and salient topic in everyday work-life – which was not the case before. The novelty of this increased attention to ethics is confirmed by the Commission's experts. They list awareness among staff members as one of the most important achievements of ethics reforms (Ethics officials #8, #9, #10, #14, #20, #21, #22, #24, #25), and ethics correspondents consider it the most significant change in their respective DGs (Ethics officials #6, # 7, #9, #18, #19). Some took the increased number of questions they receive from staff (even on immaterial aspects) as an indication of this transformation (Ethics officials #7, #18, #16). Certainly, these testimonies coming from ethics experts are of limited value, given that they are largely based on subjective perception and limited experience. However, the internal statistics do lend some support to the view that there is more ethics awareness, as the total number of AA authorization requests has increased constantly over time, from 2,095 in 2007, to over 3,100 in 2013 (Commission 2013c). Furthermore, the assessments of ethics experts are in line with the experiences of regular Commission officials, who, as shown above, have participated in ethics events and used internal ethics guidelines – which means that they have indeed experienced more ethics "talk" in recent years.

But more awareness is only part of the story. Going more into specifics, there are certain features of the Commission's ethics regime which encourage discussions about ethics. As shown before, the *Staff Regulations* impose numerous restrictions and an obligation to ask for authorization on a good deal of issues. For officials on the work-floor, this means that it is better to check before doing something which may turn out to be problematic. This, in fact, is exactly the message coming from the Commission's ethics bureaucracy and internal guidelines: to apply prudence and circumspection and always consult when in doubt. In these new circumstances, ethics is red-flagged. For employees it simply becomes unwise to sit on ethically sensitive issues, and they will share them with superiors and/or colleagues, whether driven by self-interested or more altruistic motives.

To state the argument more concisely, the Commission's ethics policy arsenal does impact on officials' thinking about ethics, but largely in an indirect way. Content-wise, it does not bring much new to the table, as demonstrated by the frequent reference to ethics as common sense. From the perspective of regular Commission officials, ethics appears to be obvious enough, whether they think of it as a matter of intuition and personal conscience or as the golden rule of forswearing personal interests (by putting first the public interest, a "higher mission", or loyalty to the Commission). Judged from this angle, ethics is not something which should (or could) be taught as such. The Commission's ethics bureaucracy seems to acquiesce on this point, since they themselves often describe ethics in terms of common sense.

However, ethics policy interventions and, in particular, the wave of awareness-raising and guidance activities prompted by the *Ethics Communication* did succeed in problematizing ethics, i.e., making an issue out of it. As such, it gets picked up in internal discussions. Interviews have shown that Commission officials have a certain disposition to talk through ethically sensitive or unclear issues and that they would do so most likely with their colleagues and/or superiors. This is an important point, namely that when in need, Commission officials seek ethics guidance not from official sources, but from other people, preferably the ones next to them. Trust plays a role here, as do self-protection and, simply put, convenience. These dynamics demonstrate that whatever influence organizational ethics system may have, it will be mediated by the human environment in which officials are placed. This also largely explains why ethics policy instruments are not seen, by Commission officials, to be particularly relevant, or useful for their work.

The most immediate evidence that ethics policy gets filtered through the "human factor" is the fact that officials frame differently their discussions about ethics – on the one hand, an altruist type (i.e., common solution-seeking), and on the other, a self-interested one (i.e., diffusing responsibility). One may speculate that the outcomes of these discussions will differ depending on the relative prevalence of these two motivations, as it is likely that only the first type can really sustain genuine debates (and common sense-making) about what being ethical means and where the boundaries are drawn. However, the exact mix of motivations will be determined by the personalities of those involved, the quality of the relationship between them and, more generally, the work atmosphere in their units. It is largely not influenced by the Commission's ethics policies.

5.4 Conclusion

This chapter was dedicated to exploring the impact of ethics management efforts on the work-floor of the Commission. It has been shown that there is an indirect impact on officials' views about ethics. That some influence occurs is evident given that employees have largely the same notions about ethics and, more than that, because there is an overlap between messages coming from the official framework, and the positions that they express. The fact that risk appears so often in the interpretation of the vignettes is also significant. Even though the officials disagree over it, it is clear that the terms of the discussion are set in accordance with the Commission's compliance-based ethics system, where being ethical has much to do with staying safe.

However, ethics is frequently described as a matter of common sense. This suggests an interesting situation, where ethics management instruments – without being ineffective – are not perceived as particularly relevant in everyday work-life. This lack of perception is explained by the rather subtle influence of policy. Namely, the Commission's ethics management efforts have an impact because they put ethics on the map, and so the topic gets picked up in internal discussions. Commission officials prefer to seek ethics guidance from their colleagues and/ or superiors, and not from official sources. This means that ethics management works somehow through the back door, and its influence is mediated by the human environment in which officials are placed.

This finding is consistent with the point made in organizational socialization literature (elaborated at length in Chapter 1) that individuals prefer to seek information from peers and superiors, rather than official channels. What we see in the Commission's case is actually the interplay between formal and informal learning sources – more specifically, the formal sources trigger appeal to the informal ones. Commission officials experience official communication on ethics, and they do glean something from it. However, when actually confronted with an ethically sensitive situation, the preference is to turn to their immediate circle. And it is probably those situations, when information is sought out proactively by employees, which are the most fruitful as an exercise in learning ethics. Significantly, the preference to seek counsel from the immediate work circle is actually supported by rather strong incentives. To officials, this solution is simply more convenient, but also safer (because reporting a potential problem provides "cover", but also because employees are more likely to find trustworthy people among close colleagues). Since it is hard to imagine that these incentives are a peculiarity of the Commission, the preference towards informal learning sources is likely to be found in other organizations as well.

On the other hand, these findings show that middle managers are the main go-to points for the resolution of all sorts of problems, including those with an ethical content. Interviewees hardly mentioned consulting with an ethics correspondent on an ethical dilemma (at least not as a first option), although, reading the *Ethics Communication*, one gets the impression that this is precisely the purpose for which the post was set up. Instead, the predilection to talk to immediate superiors proves that, in fact, the highest demand for ethics guidance, as well as authority to speak on ethics, is located at the level of middle management. Moreover, this is a role that incumbents accept – for instance, one Head of Unit I interviewed remarked that "the boss should make clear that whenever there is a problem, he is there to protect his staff. I think that, fundamentally, the nature of the boss is to allow his staff to work in a bubble of serenity" (Official #16).

These findings are in line with the importance attached, in empirical ethics literature, to leaders and with widespread warnings that ethics regulation will fail without leadership commitment and the right "tone at the top" (see, for instance, the review by Heres and Lasthuizen 2012). Significantly, ethical leadership is constructed as a bidimensional concept, i.e., the ethical leader is at once a "moral person" (a dimension pertaining to the leader's personal traits and character) and a "moral manager" (a dimension pertaining to the leader's efforts to influence ethics among his/her staff) (Brown and Treviño 2006). The case of the Commission highlights the importance of having ethics management strategies that will develop the "moral manager" perspective, because people in leadership positions are likely to be at the front lines when it comes to offering ethical guidance and detecting possible problems.

Before concluding, a disclaimer made in Chapter 1 should be restated. Namely, owing to the fact that all those who participated in interviews had volunteered to do so, there is a possibility of bias in the sample. It may contain only officials who have a certain interest in ethics or are convinced of its importance, and only units with good work relations and a clean history. This means that the ethics discussions reported so widely here may not necessarily be the rule everywhere in the Commission and would certainly be less likely in units with a more tensed atmosphere. Therefore, it would be more correct to conclude that the causal mechanism described in this chapter applies only in the presence of supporting conditions.

Another limitation of the sample is that it covers only a certain hierarchical level in the Commission – mid-management (Head of Unit) and below. Things may be different at the higher echelons – arguably, for those in senior positions, it may not be acceptable, or possible to consult/ report in the same way as those in the lower ranks do. After all, they are the ones expected to make decisions (authoritatively), rather than pass them up the hierarchical chain of command. Moreover, the senior officials can afford to rely more on their own experience when drawing the line between the ethical and the non-ethical.

Conclusion

This book has taken stock of reforms in the area of public ethics implemented at the European Commission since the Santer resignation in 1999. The analysis presented the Commission as a case study in ethics management and focused on uncovering whether and how the reforms have shaped Commission officials' views regarding appropriate behaviour in public office. In what follows, the main findings of the book will be reviewed, and I will elaborate on contributions made to research in the fields of administrative ethics and EU integration.

Summary of findings

Chapter 1 presented the analytical framework of the book. It was established that "ethics" has a situational character, referring to appropriate behaviour in public office. As such, it may be equated with public role morality. The parameters of "ethics" are defined by reference to the core values and standards of behaviour which ground the operation of the civil service (i.e., objectivity, impartiality, loyalty, etc.). From the perspective of the individual civil servant, ethics becomes significant in those situations of choice where the values and standards mentioned above are likely to be jeopardized. The ethical dilemma is one such choice situation, which is particularly interesting because it features two (or more) values which are in conflict, thus making it difficult to judge what the ethical course of action is. Commission officials' views were elicited in the context of ethical dilemmas – namely, three dilemmas were included in the interview guide, in the form of written vignettes.

Taking a holistic view, the ethics policies of the European Commission were analyzed not as discrete measures, but as part of a so-called ethics infrastructure – an umbrella term which covers a range of institutional structures and procedures that, taken together, sustain ethical conduct and prevent (and punish) integrity violations and corruption. An ethics infrastructure is the expression of "a systematic and conscious effort to promote organizational integrity" (Menzel 2005: 29), referred to as ethics management. Organizational socialization was taken up as a theoretical perspective. OS is understood as a process of social learning through which an individual comes to appreciate the knowledge, values and expected behaviours associated with an organizational role. In this perspective, ethics becomes something that – like other parts of the (public) role/job – can be learnt. An organization's ethics system is one of several sources which can be used in this endeavour – therefore, the aim, for the following chapters, was to uncover the messages which the organization sent internally, to its staff, regarding the type of behaviour that is (or is not) acceptable, and what will be (or not be) punished.

Chapter 1 also introduced the reader to the European Commission, and explained choices of research design which tailored the project to the specificities of this organization. Overall, the book is based on qualitative research methodology, relying on a combination of document analysis and in-depth interviews with internal ethics experts in the Commission, as well as – for lack of a better term – "regular" officials (i.e., employees without ethics expertise, who work for the organization in various other capacities). This latter group was selected from the "policy" DGs, which are more interesting from an ethics perspective, because they display the full range of issues confronting the organization. Four other selection criteria were defined – nationality, organizational position, type of employment and professional background – deemed to make a difference in the process of organizational socialization, specifically with regard to the subject of ethics. The group of respondents displays variation along all these coordinates, thus it can be considered a maximum variation sample, which reflects, in a balanced way and within some predefined limits, the heterogeneous nature of the European Commission staff.

Chapter 2 provided an empirical account of the ethics management system which applies to the European Commission services. Findings show that a comprehensive ethics infrastructure is in place nowadays, which has been built up incrementally. Designed to clean up and revitalize the organization in the aftermath of the Santer resignation, the Kinnock reforms installed the building blocks of the system and in doing so engendered a compliance-based ethics regime, where tightening controls was seen as the main mechanism to ensure ethical behaviour. Convinced that "common sense and values are often a more efficient guide than long rulebooks" (Kallas 2007: 10), Kinnock's successor attempted a switch to a "modern" system based on guidance and shared values. This has materialized in a dramatic increase of awareness-raising and guidance instruments throughout the Commission (e.g., codes of conduct, ethics training, lunchtime debates, workshops). The momentum was maintained after 2010 with similar activities and the creation of guidelines on topical issues, such as the handling of gifts and hospitality offers from third parties and whistleblowing.

What the Kallas package achieved was a diversification of ethics management instruments, rather than a more fundamental change of the philosophy behind the system, as suggested by the official discourse. To be sure, the literature suggests that a compliance-based system relies on adherence to administrative procedures and the policing of bad behaviour, while an integrity-based one is concerned with the promotion of aspirational values and the encouragement of good behaviour. Elements of both styles are present within the Commission nowadays – however, the heavy regulatory framework, as well as the fact that internal communication was focused squarely on familiarizing staff with this framework, shows that, ultimately, ethics is viewed in a compliance logic as avoiding mistakes and staying safe. This outcome is explained by the changing external environment of the Commission, in particular the increased scrutiny exercised by both media and anti-corruption NGOs, as well as the eagerness of the European Parliament to hold the Commission accountable on ethics matters.

Chapter 3 offered an overview of what and how the Commission chose to communicate internally to its employees on the subject of public ethics. Findings show that internal communication featured two central, interrelated messages – rule awareness and care for the Commission's public image. Namely, ethics was justified to officials as a means of keeping a good institutional reputation – which meant that they, as representatives of the Commission, were expected to conduct themselves beyond reproach. The best way to do that was to exercise an attitude of prudence towards ethics questions and, importantly, to be aware of the relevant regulations in this area, and to stick to them. These messages are in line with the compliance-based approach which characterizes the ethics system in the Commission services, and reflect the external constraints and more intensive public surveillance to which the organization was subject, as discussed in the previous chapter.

Following up on these points, the remainder of the chapter showed how these central messages materialized with regard to specific subjects which were considered, by internal experts, as being more likely to give rise to ambiguities in practice. Firstly, officials were advised to be very vigilant regarding the (perception of) conflicts of interests. In this context, a lot of emphasis was placed on the obligation to ask for prior permission in a variety of circumstances (engaging in external activities, publishing, accepting honours and other positions, even unpaid, etc.), as stipulated in the *Staff Regulations*, and on being very careful about how personal views are expressed in public settings. Reporting misconduct witnessed at work was another sensitive area. The Commission has a whistleblower protection system in place but, importantly, the official line was to recommend that this channel be used only for severe wrongdoing and as a measure of last resort, and to never go public with such disclosures. Finally, the relationship with external parties, in particular interest representatives, was also highlighted in internal communication. Apart from recommending a general attitude of circumspection, officials were advised to be particularly careful about information communicated to the outside and, as a rule, to refuse any gifts and hospitality offers, as these can (be perceived to) jeopardize impartiality.

Chapter 4 offered an account of how Commission officials think about ethics in public office. Findings show that they share much common ground in the ethics area. The consensus is around a pronounced sense of loyalty to the Commission, which appears to be the core value in the moral system of the EU civil service. Beyond this, however, at a secondary level, there is space to express divergent opinions. There are two axes around which differences are structured. The first of these is represented by the orientation towards compromise in the face of conflicting public values – here, there are two positions: a "strict" one, where the preference is to choose univocally one value over others, and a "flexible" one, where the preference is to find a way of accommodating the values. The second axis refers to justifications for discussing (potential) ethical problems – here, again, there are two positions, one where self-interest is stressed (i.e., reporting as a safe thing to do for the one who has come across a potential problem), and another which emphasizes the larger issues at stake (be they the interests of the official's team or those of the Commission, or the fact that consultation achieves better solutions).

The type of sample used here makes it difficult to determine which factors are behind these (second-order) differences. However, it is plausible that they have a lot to do with personal preferences and sensitivities regarding the handling of risk, which is the central element in the divisions discussed above. A tentative exploration on the role of nationality showed that it does not seem a useful explanation for the observed differences – what might matter instead is the time when officials joined the Commission (specifically before or after the Kinnock reforms). On the other hand, officials' organizational positions seem to be important, but hardly in a systematic way. Rather, what the data suggest is that DG COMP is an outlier within the Commission. Its sharp functional specialization on enforcement, the outstanding powers it enjoys, and its procedural framework, which is exceptionally strict, are all factors which shape differently officials' perception regarding external actors. Unlike interviewees from other DGs, those who work in DG COMP seemed to be more concerned about protecting the Commission's position and controlling information flows, and mentioned less frequently the need to have a two-way dialogue with external stakeholders.

This being said, what should be emphasized about Chapter 4 is that it revealed a great deal of convergence in the way Commission officials think about public ethics. One of the reasons the European Commission was considered a significant case study was precisely the fact that the heterogeneous nature of its staff would have predicted such a convergence to be less likely. The Commission, it was argued, was a *hard case* in ethics management. The existence of common ground, therefore, is significant. Certainly, the commonalities – to the extent that they have emerged within the organization – are the product of a more complex process of organizational influence. But it is reasonable to conclude that as part of this process, the Commission's ethics policy has, to some degree, shaped its employees' views on the subject.

In fact, if a closer look is cast on the divergent stances mapped above, they are telling of the influence of the system of ethics management. This is so because the disagreement relates to certain aspects of risk – which demonstrates that overall in the Commission, being ethical has a lot to do with staying safe (even though individual preferences vary on where and how to draw the line). The centrality of risk proves that on the Commission work-floor, ethics is framed in line with the compliance-based logic, where ethical behaviour is largely equated with staying out of trouble. This, in turn, is a reflection of organizational communication, which focused on avoiding mistakes (by paying attention to rules, and for the sake of the Commission's institutional reputation). In fact, the twin messages of rule awareness and care for public image were explicitly reflected in the officials' comments around the vignettes.

Building on these findings, Chapter 5 has explored the mechanisms by which ethics policy comes to influence Commission officials' views. These are not straightforward. Most interviewees have directly experienced ethics training, codes and the like, and they do glean something from them, in the sense of adopting the "spirit" of what is being communicated. Nonetheless, the frequent characterization of ethics as a matter of "common sense" shows that these policy instruments are not perceived as particularly relevant in everyday work. They transmit something which is, somehow, already known. Furthermore, when ambiguous situations occur, officials report a preference to seek ethics guidance from their colleagues and/or superiors, and not from official sources.

All of this shows that, ultimately, the Commission's efforts in this area have an impact because they put ethics on the map in internal organizational life. What is actually being achieved is the problematization of ethics – by setting up organizational structures and instruments which are expressly dedicated to it, by enhancing communication about it, by preaching an attitude of cautiousness towards it. This red-flagging – staking out ethics as an "issue" – causes ethics questions to get picked up in discussions within administrative units, which represent the standard approach for problem-solving in the European Commission (at least for the hierarchical levels covered in this research). Thus, one may speak of an indirect influence of organizational ethics policy, which is heavily mediated by the human environment in which officials are placed.

The limits of ethics management

This book began by noting that nowadays ethics management represents an international best practice standard – and yet, despite this popularity, little is known about the impact of ethics policies on organizations and on the individuals working therein. A lot of empirical research is dedicated to mapping the policy instruments and approaches associated with it, but this tells us more about what ethics management *is* – rather than *how* it works. The book, therefore, made a contribution to this less researched aspect by analyzing the case of the European Commission.

The findings, briefly summarized before, demonstrate the limits of what can be achieved through ethics management. To be clear, there are developments in the Commission which are very likely effects of ethics reforms. The topic nowadays has salience and visibility in organizational life, and employees do demonstrate ethics awareness, combined with a predilection for sorting out ethically sensitive issues through internal discussions/reporting. But in the complex ethical landscape of the European Commission, ethics policies represent just one of several factors which shape officials' thinking on ethics.

On the one hand, individual-level attributes matter. Even though, as March and Simon (1993: 22) note, organizational roles are, by their nature, highly constrained (and ethics certainly is heavily regulated in the European Commission), a space of autonomy still exists, which allows individuals to appraise certain details and nuances of a quandary based on their personal sensitivities. On the other hand, the group matters. Commission officials' preference for turning to the immediate work circle for advice means that individuals "learn" their ethics (at least partially) from the people around them – not only by talking to them, but also (presumably) by observing their example. And finally, the cultural features of the organization also matter. Officials' attention towards ethics is closely connected to a pre-existing ethos of loyalty to the Commission. To be clear, the idea that strong ethics is crucial for institutional reputation and that mistakes in this area hurt the Commission resonated well with civil servants who had traditionally exhibited strong attachment to their "House".[1] Along similar lines, there would probably not be (so much) internal "talk" about ethics if it weren't for the pre-existing cultural norm which held that problems (of various sorts) should be reported/discussed, preferably with one's superior.

Of course, these observations are not necessarily surprising – the key role of work peers and especially leaders is broadly recognized in the specialized literature (as indicated in Chapter 1), as is the importance of organizational culture (see, for instance, Victor and Cullen 1987, 1988, Maesschalck 2004b, Erakovich and Wyman 2009). Nonetheless, how these factors *interact* with ethics policy is generally poorly understood (but see Cowell *et al.* 2011 and Loyens 2013 as two noteworthy exceptions). The example of the European Commission has demonstrated that such interactions do exist, and this is a crucial aspect to be taken on board in ethics policy design. Therefore, there is a need for more sophisticated theoretical tools in the field, which could better inform us on what an ethics management system responsive to local organizational conditions might imply.[2]

Moving on, another important finding of this book, which deserves further consideration, is that ethics reforms have a profoundly political character. The characteristics of the ethics system in place at the Commission services level were determined, to a large extent, by the political confrontation with the European Parliament. Namely, as shown in the analysis, the CIE reports which preceded the Santer resignation allowed the Parliament to (indirectly) set the agenda for ethics reform in the Commission. Built in the aftermath of a most debilitating public scandal, the system featured a hard-line approach, widely understood as a check against such disasters ever re-occurring. This initial framing of ethics as a cure for corruption, buttressed in later years by episodes of scandal of varying scale and alongside a European Parliament that became more and more invested in watching and punishing the Commission for ethics failures, led to a path-dependent pattern which made it impossible to relax controls even after the storm had passed. Largely in response to this context, for the Commission, ethics management became tightly connected to public image considerations. Operating in conditions of increasingly sharp scrutiny, the organization used ethics measures as a way of managing not only the conduct of its own staff, but also – perhaps more importantly – public perceptions. The internal awareness-raising efforts, which were meant to sensitize employees regarding ethics rules and their importance for institutional reputation, represented a strategy to minimize the risk of (perceived) corruption and, implicitly, the negative publicity associated with it.

These findings again highlight the need for more refined theoretical tools in the literature dealing with ethics management. Although not without its critics (see particularly Maesschalck 2005), the compliance-integrity continuum still represents the principal reference point, and as such it frames both theory and practice around the polarizing concepts of "low road" and "high road" ethics. Future research would gain from bypassing this perennial opposition to focus more on the influence of contextual factors, such as the history and the politics behind ethics reforms, as well as the accompanying public image games, which, as illustrated here, can prove hugely important for determining the character of ethics management systems.

Apart from these theoretical implications, the path-dependent character of ethics management (as illustrated by the case of the European Commission) also contains lessons of general value for other organizations engaged in public ethics reforms. As mentioned in the Introduction, the Commission is far from unique in adopting a hard-line approach to ethics management in the aftermath of corruption scandals. As Roberts (2009) explains, reformers usually prefer the compliance model because it reduces organizational penalties for the illegal behaviour of their employees and encourages internal conformity while satisfying public demands that something be done about ethical standards. It's simply easier. A clear danger in taking this route is to end up with an overly complicated regulatory system, which is difficult to understand for employees, and ultimately ineffective. This is well known, which is why there is a tendency in the practitioner literature to praise the merits of "high-road" ethics. As Jeremy Pope explains:

> A compliance-based approach – 'The Low Road', looking for a precedent or a rule to govern every possible circumstance – is never going to get us there. Individuals need to be able to judge competently for themselves what is right, or the best of the available options, and likewise what is wrong, or unjustifiable – and to have the courage to act accordingly.
> (Pope 2008: 80–81)

The other danger, less visible and which the experience of the European Commission has highlighted, is that a hard-line regime borne out of scandal can be very difficult to change afterwards. This is important, because the type of transition proposed by Kallas (i.e., from compliance-based to softer, value-based approaches) is common in the Western world. It seems, however, that if ethics policies are introduced in situations of crisis, as a form of damage control, this can firmly set the tone for the future, by diminishing the political profitability of moving to a high-road style later on.

On a more optimistic note, another lesson to draw from the experience of the European Commission is that a highly diverse staff body does not represent an insurmountable obstacle in organizational ethics management. As detailed in Chapter 4, Commission officials think about public ethics largely along the same lines. This is significant especially for international bureaucracies, because it demonstrates that differences of nationality, previous professional background, organizational position and so on are not overbearing, and apparently can be ironed out with time spent in the organization and with strong ethics awareness-raising actions. In fact, the findings of this book suggest that the Commission, contrary to popular beliefs, is not likely to be the home of a "clash of cultures" in terms of ethics standards between officials coming from northern, southern and central/eastern European states. And contrary to widespread clichés, the Commission bureaucracy is not a caste of self-serving Eurocrats, detached from Europe's citizens and unaccountable for their decisions. Quite the contrary, the Commission is subject to intense public scrutiny and has taken ethics seriously since the Santer resignation. In highlighting these aspects, the book adds to recent literature which shows that the contemporary European Commission is different from both popular stereotypes and its portrayal in previous studies (Kassim *et al.* 2013) and has come to resemble a "normalized" executive (Wille 2013).

Finally, the themes analyzed in this book are relevant for a broader debate in public administration, on the use of control and trust mechanisms in organizational management and on the motivation of public sector employees. Our assumptions of what motivates public servants – whether they act out of altruistic considerations or self-interest or, to use Julian Le Grand's (2003) famous terminology, whether they are "knights" or "knaves" – have concrete implications on managerial choices: knights can be trusted, while knaves have to be controlled. However, the task of marrying control and trust in organizational management is challenging, not only because organizations should cater simultaneously to the knights and knaves in their ranks, but also because at a conceptual level the relationship between the two mechanisms is poorly understood (for a review, see Das and Teng 1998, Bijlsma-Frankema and Costa 2005). The relevance of this debate for choices in ethics management is clear: a compliance-based system relies on control, while an integrity-based one relies on trust.

This book did not analyze the Commission's ethics system to show how different trust and control elements affected officials' motivation to act ethically. It did, however, highlight the difficulties inherent in the transition to a system which more closely resembles the integrity-based model, as proposed by Siim Kallas, and in this it has demonstrated that at the level of ethics policy *design*, combining trust and control is a taxing exercise. The concepts of "high road" and "low road" ethics reflect fundamentally different notions of how individuals can be motivated to behave ethically, and, ultimately, what organizational ethics is about. These notions do not naturally sit together, although the idea of a policy *continuum* suggests that they should. Blanket recommendations in the literature that a good balance should be achieved (e.g., Gilman 1999, Menzel 2005) do no more than obscure the practical intricacies involved in the task. It is these inconsistencies that explain, in part, why the Commission came into a situation where instruments specific to a value-based approach were coupled awkwardly with a system whose fundamental philosophy remained steeped in control. Of course, the task was also significantly complicated by the politicization of the reform process, as discussed above.

To be clear, the argument advanced here is not that one should not combine trust and control elements in ethics management, but that the terms in which the debate is currently framed are not very helpful. Room exists to develop more supportive conceptual frameworks, which would account in a more nuanced way for the relationship between the two mechanisms, and especially the conditions under which they are complementary or contradictory. Steps have been taken in this direction, with some authors (Greasley *et al.* 2006, Cowell *et al.* 2011) applying the lens of responsive regulation theory (see Ayres and Braithwaite 1992). In this optic, a relationship of hierarchy exists between ethics management instruments – i.e., an "enforcement pyramid", which has informal, cultural mechanisms at the bottom and formal, compliance ones at the top. This predicts that the existence of powerful sanctions will enable regulators to appeal first (and with more success) to informal mechanisms. The approach, however, is not without its critics – Six (2013), for instance, suggests that in responsive regulation theory, control/repression and trust/cooperation are too narrowly represented as substitutes (a tit-for-tat strategy) and suggests that social determination theory (see Deci and Ryan 2000, Ryan and Deci 2000) can offer insights for an improved model where the two may have complementary effects on target compliance. Six and Lawton (2013: 648–651) apply these arguments to ethics regulation and formulate tentative hypotheses.

It seems fitting to close this section by further reflecting on the portrayal of ethics as "common sense". It was surprising to find this reference so widely used in the Commission – an organization whose staff is culturally diverse and where, consequently, shared understandings cannot be taken for granted (particularly for a stretchy concept such as "common sense"). Therefore, analyzing its prevalence here may bring to light lessons with more general applicability.

In the book, I have argued that the widespread qualification of ethics as "common sense" denotes an assumption within the Commission that staff members already know which behaviour is acceptable and which is not. This, in turn, means that the organization's ethics policy is perceived to be (partially) redundant. Therefore, the problem is not that ethics management is superfluous (it is not), but that it is perceived as such.

While this interpretation holds, there are some additional details which make for a more nuanced and interesting picture. It is important to note that the Commission's communication about public ethics was not all just common sense. In fact, as shown in Chapter 3, a lot of effort went into popularizing and explaining regulations – which represent a type of knowledge that not everyone can be assumed to have, particularly when it comes to details. In fact, the Commission's ethics bureaucracy used the "common sense" label not to downplay the importance of the subject, but to make these regulations more palatable for staff. It was a way of normalizing and justifying them. For instance, a 50 EUR cap on gifts may come as a novelty, but it is justified because everyone understands that receiving gifts is not OK (that is just common sense). In this optic, the reference to "common sense" does not challenge the codification of ethics but validates it. It is a way of presenting ethics in a more friendly way, as something familiar. And, from this perspective, perhaps the fact that ethics management *seems* superfluous is not actually a problem.

But whether interpreted in a positive or negative light, the fact that ethics gets the "common sense" label proves that managing it is not – to paraphrase Menzel

(2001) – the same as managing budgets, policies or people. Common sense represents a set of basic norms – an intuition almost – which individuals acquire outside of organizational life. They are then expected to use it within the organization to distinguish between right and wrong. Ultimately, this means that public ethics flows from personal ethics – the two are so closely linked that the possibility of a separate sphere of public role morality is practically excluded. Of course, the *theoretical* possibility of such a construct is a philosophical question. What matters here is that in practice, in the Commission's case, it does not hold. The unspoken assumption seems to be that a good (moral) person will make a good official, and, in fact, *the organization counts on it*. And this proves that despite its popularity, managing ethics is still an odd notion, simply because ethics feels very – too – personal.

A cynical reading of this conclusion casts doubt on the very utility of ethics management. If it really represents the regulation of common sense (and we accept that everyone understands the same by "common sense"), then there hardly seems any point to it. Why commit significant organizational resources only to tell people something they already know? This book has documented a process by which organizational ethics policy influences individuals' views on ethics. It has demonstrated that it is not a useless exercise, but the fact that doubts can reasonably be raised in this regard is important. These doubts show that ethics management is a tool with a double purpose: it targets the organization's integrity, as well as its public image, but one would be misguided to think that these two are (always) complementary objectives.

The European Commission after ethics reforms

This book has explicitly steered clear of making any judgements on the ethical health of the Commission today, or determining whether the organization has "cleaned up", compared with the time before ethics reforms were implemented. It was, however, possible, without resorting to a diagnosis logic or a before/after comparison but simply based on the available data, to determine that these reforms have had an impact on how Commission employees think about and approach ethical problems at work. Based on these findings, several implications can be discerned as to the overall effectiveness of the Commission's ethics regime.

To begin with, this book has demonstrated that public ethics is nowadays a fundamental feature in the way the European Commission defines and practices democratic governance. What is more, the Commission's approach to ethics management has matured over time. During the Kinnock era, there was little evidence of systematic thinking over its ethics infrastructure (see Cini 2007a: 211–213), but afterwards things have changed. The *Ethics Communication* demonstrates a more careful consideration for internal organizational conditions, as shown in Chapter 2. Furthermore, in implementing this agenda, there was clear concern within the Commission's ethics bureaucracy for finding effective solutions (e.g., the discussions and best practice exchange in the network of ethics correspondents), learning from past experience (e.g., the guidelines on whistleblowing and gifts/hospitality, adopted in 2012, each with a two-year revision clause) and adapting to ad-hoc developments (e.g., issuing special guidelines on the 2014 European Parliament elections). These developments demonstrate that the Commission has evolved to a more complex and nuanced approach, which does bode well for the effectiveness of its ethics regime.

Another significant point is that ethics is being discussed among "regular" staff members – or, at the very least, that Commission employees demonstrate a predilection towards doing so. The increased awareness of ethical issues and willingness to seek advice represent desired outcomes in both compliance-based and value-based ethics systems (Huberts *et al.* 2014: 229). As argued before, in the Commission such discussions are not entirely due to policy interventions, but they would certainly not be there in their absence. This development can be considered a sign of deeper (and positive) cultural change within the organization, by comparison with the Santer era. Although more research would be needed to ascertain this point, a Commission where ethics is openly talked about is certainly very different from one where, as the CIE reports concluded, it was "difficult to find anyone who has even the slightest sense of responsibility" (CIE 1999a: 144).

Finally, it is noteworthy that in recent years the Commission did not experience corruption scandals on the scale of those that rocked it in the late 1990s and early 2000s. To be clear, it still got into trouble occasionally, but not for the sort of massive systemic failures which lay at the core of the Santer resignation and the Eurostat affair. Perhaps, with ethics being on the map, the organization is less likely to encounter problems nowadays – after all, staff members are trained to evaluate ethics within a risk framework, by weighing the likelihood that a certain course of action would cause a public scandal, or otherwise harm the Commission. This can be interpreted as a sign of successful reform if we accept that an ethics system is effective when integrity *risks* are properly contained (cf. Six and Lawton 2013: 644).

This being said, it is also important to highlight the negative implications associated with the fact that despite changing the policy repertoire, the philosophy behind the Commission's ethics system remained heavily focused on compliance. This configuration might produce perverse effects on the motivation of public actors. Frey (1997), Frey and Jegen (2001) and Le Grand (2003) show that management systems built on the assumption that individuals are utility-maximizing rational actors can lead to a loss of altruism in the civil service – or, to use Le Grand's terminology, they can leave "knights" to turn into "knaves". Greasley *et al.* (2005: 29–30) have argued along similar lines, showing that an overreliance on compliance mechanisms will reduce individuals' autonomous, intrinsic motivation to act ethically. This discussion relates to the difficulty of combining well trust and control in ethics management, explored above.

Since this analysis has not focused on Commission officials' behaviour, or their motivation, it is difficult to ascertain directly whether a "crowding out" effect (as described above) is present. However, it has been demonstrated that many officials remain unconvinced of the utility of ethics management instruments for their day-to-day work, and consider ethics a matter of "common sense". This means that such measures are indeed perceived as externally imposed, and, considering the scale of ethics activity in the Commission in the past years, there is a real chance that staff members might experience a sense of fatigue with ethics and ethics regulation. This possibility has been acknowledged by some internal ethics experts, who noted that overregulation can send the message that people are not trusted within the Commission (Ethics official #14) and may render them awkwardly strict and cautious in interactions with external actors (Ethics official #16). Another interviewee observed that they can't afford to "treat people like babies" (Ethics official #21). However, the possibility of cutting down on rules seems slim – if anything, the tendency in recent years has been the exact opposite, as evident with the recent amendments to the *Staff Regulations*.

These points should be balanced against the fact that the analysis conducted here has only focused on the Commission services. The management of ethics for the College of Commissioners is markedly different in its character, with a much stronger emphasis on soft law and guidance (Cini 2007a), and although important progress has been made by comparison with the Santer era, this system is more lax than the one in place for the services. It is significant, in this respect, that Transparency International's recent EU integrity system report found that "the generally good controls on the conduct of staff contrast starkly with the weak checks on the behaviour of Members of European Parliament (MEPs) and senior EU figures", Commissioners included (TI-EU 2014: 11). Overall, this situation may mean that the risk for slippages that result in reputational damage is nowadays higher as regards the political echelons of the Commission.

The observations above suggest that there is ground to hope that the ethics regime in the Commission services might be effective. However, it is important to note that ethics reforms as such have not helped the Commission's standing in inter-institutional relations at the EU level. In fact, they are part of a broader decline in power suffered by the organization since the Maastricht Treaty (see, e.g., Peterson 2008, Nugent 2010). On the one hand, the Kinnock reforms, in forcing the Commission to address its "management deficit" (Metcalfe 2000), have made it more difficult to accomplish its political vocation as the "motor of integration". Specifically, the reforms brought about an explosion of procedural constraints and bureaucratic red tape (particularly but not exclusively in financial management), which has affected mostly middle and senior managers by reducing their resource base for policy drafting (see, for instance, Wille 2007, Bauer 2008, 2009, Ellinas and Suleiman 2008, Kassim *et al.* 2013). Ethics reforms are very much part of this rising audit mentality in the Commission, and although the measures adopted during and after Kallas' mandate are likely to have curbed the worst excesses of the Kinnock years, ethics regulations still translate into time-consuming paperwork for Commission officials.

On the other hand, generally speaking, the European Parliament has not been shy to use its increasingly solid powers to hold the Commission to account, in an effort to consolidate its position as *the* democratic force in EU politics after the Maastricht Treaty (Corbett *et al.* 2003). In this respect, ethical failures in the Commission, or deficiencies in its ethics system have all been opportunities for the

Parliament to flex its muscles. Ever since the Santer resignation, the Parliament has proven very adept at identifying and fructifying various occasions to push the Commission on the ethics front – either by using the budgetary levers, less visibly through stimulating debate and coalition-building on specific ethics subjects or by amending relevant legislation. This analysis has emphasized the Commission services, but it is important to note that the Parliament has been equally insistent (perhaps even more so) with regard to the ethics of Commissioners. Suffice it to point out that during hearings for Commissioners-designate – arguably one of the points where the Parliament is at the height of its power vis-à-vis the Commission – MEPs have regularly screened candidates for behavioural standards and conflicts of interest. Neelie Kroes in 2004, Rumiana Jeleva in 2010 and Miguel Arias Cañete and Jonathan Hill in 2014 are all noteworthy examples. Significantly, it was the Parliament's resolve that eventually pushed the Bulgarian government to withdraw Jeleva's candidacy on account of irregularities in financial and interest declarations (*EurActiv*, 13.01.2010).

In a nutshell, pressure from the European Parliament, often coupled with the actions of pro-transparency NGOs and, in recent years, those of a more activist European Ombudsman, has kept the Commission in a defensive posture. In these conditions, despite its responsiveness, it was unable to claim any credit for implementing ethics reforms, and whatever initiative it did show in this area (i.e., most points in the *Ethics Communication*) has largely gone unnoticed in public. Because of the political environment, the Commission cannot bank on these reforms to enhance its reputation as an institution with high behavioural standards. This is somewhat ironic, because objectively speaking the Commission has done a lot in terms of ethics reform, and its systems are probably more advanced by comparison with both the Parliament and the Council (the fact that the Parliament introduced a Code of Conduct for MEPs only in 2012 speaks volumes in this regard).

Outlook

It seems fitting to end this reflection by discussing the more recent developments occasioned by the change of the College of Commissioners in September 2014. The Juncker Commission is the first one where a direct link exists between the results of the European Parliament elections and the nomination of the President of the Commission, in accordance with Art. 17(7) of the Treaty of Lisbon. This represents a significant boost for democratic legitimacy, at least in theory. This Commission certainly takes it seriously, as it presents itself openly and with pride as a "political" Commission. According to its Political Guidelines, this concept boils down, on the side of output legitimacy, to being "bigger and more ambitious on big things and smaller and more modest on small things" (Juncker 2014: 3), and, on the side of input legitimacy, to building a "special partnership" with the European Parliament (Juncker 2014: 11). Standards of behaviour are not explicitly mentioned, but the multiple commitments to enhance institutional transparency are relevant in this regard.

In particular, the Juncker Commission seems determined to dispel widespread notions regarding the excessive influence of narrow, moneyed interests on the EU policy process. It has, to this end, pledged to make the current lobby registration system (i.e., the Transparency Register) mandatory and to extend its coverage to the Council (Juncker 2014: 11). This marks a clear departure from the previous line – the Barroso II Commission had always defended the status-quo based on the increasing number of entries and other marginal incentives said to render the Transparency Register quasi-mandatory (see Šefčovič 2014). The changes proposed by the Juncker Commission represent a long-awaited but nonetheless ambitious move, as they are set to come up against significant legal and political obstacles. On the one hand, the only option to have a mandatory regime based on legislation is using Art. 352 TFEU, which requires unanimity on the Council and the consent of the Parliament (Commission 2015b: 3) – surely a time-consuming alternative with dubious chances of success. On the other hand, there is little appetite for change in the Council, which participates in the Transparency Register as an observer and never seemed keen to extend its role. According to initial consultations, the Council's participation, should it happen, would be restricted to its Secretariat and possibly the Presidency, with Permanent Representations being a firm red line (Ethics official #28).

In the meantime, the Commission has sought to demonstrate its conviction with two decisions issued in November 2014, whereby Commissioners, their *cabinets*, and Directors General were obliged to publish meetings held with interest representatives and self-employed individuals on their respective web pages. A further *Communication on the Working Methods of the European Commission 2014–19 (C(2014) 9004)* indicated that as a rule, Members of the Commission should not meet with unregistered actors. These changes were justified on the logic that more transparency will increase citizens' trust – in the words of President Juncker:

> We could do the best possible work but it will be worth nothing if we do not earn the support and trust of the citizens we are working for. So let us be more transparent, because in fact we have nothing to hide.
>
> (Commission 2014b: 1)

Internally, the implementation was very swift and generally smooth, although the decisions were clearly taken in a top-down manner with next to no internal consultation (Ethics official #28). The impact on the public scene in Brussels was immediate and significant, with the average number of registrations per month more than tripling in the first three months of operation of the new system (see JTRS 2015).

Overall, these measures demonstrate strong commitment on behalf of the Commission, since not being able to meet with high-level people in the organization is, for interest representatives, by far the most substantial registration incentive they have had to date.[3] On a different note, if these developments are correlated with the findings discussed in Chapter 4 regarding officials' attitudes towards meeting stakeholders, one might speculate as to a more fundamental change in the Commission's relationship with the Brussels lobby. To be clear, the Commission is reputed for initiating and welcoming contact with a wide variety of interests and for practicing open access as an "institutional ideology" (Mazey and Richardson

2006). However, the probity of exchanges between lobbyists and officials is being publicly contested. A variety of regulatory interventions have sprung up around the issue and the internal organizational discourse highlighted risks and public reputation concerns, the result of which is that Commission officials are clearly highly sensitized and cautious as to whom they meet, how, and what they communicate. This, together with the latest decisions of the Juncker Commission, discussed above, have rendered access to decision-makers more formalized and it is possible that the relationship will become more rigid in the future, despite the Commission's traditional (over-)reliance on external policy expertise.

It should be noted that although the Juncker Commission has earned some public praise for its new approach to lobbying transparency, it does not seem likely that it could, on this basis, "lead by example", as proposed in the Political Guidelines. It is telling, in this regard, that Vice-President Timmermans' call for the European Parliament to follow suit in declaring meetings with lobbyists has been countered with arguments regarding the (superior) legitimacy conferred on MEPs through popular vote (*EUObserver*, 23.04.2015), which indicates the Parliament's profound distaste for being told what to do in this area, particularly by the Commission. Beyond the inter-institutional confrontation, it is also important to consider that just like with ethics policies, the relationship between transparency (especially online transparency) and popular legitimacy is far from straightforward. As Curtin and Meijer (2006) note, only a limited number of people actually access information presented on EU websites, and, furthermore, many of those who do use it are European civil society organizations, whose representativeness and links to the grassroots levels are debatable. Moreover, the highly technical nature of the information provided, as well as its sheer quantity, can lead to overload and confusion. In the case of the Transparency Register, the problem is compounded by the poor quality of information – in 2013, for instance, 68.6 per cent of the entries subject to quality checks were found be non-compliant (see JTRS 2013). In conclusion, one should avoid naïve assumptions about the positive impact transparency can have in the larger scheme of things.

Finally, it is also noteworthy that the Juncker Commission is set to grapple with the same (if not a higher) level of incisiveness than the European Parliament has demonstrated in the past regarding ethics issues. The eighth parliamentary term has seen the formation of the *Intergroup on Integrity, Transparency, Corruption and Organised Crime* in January 2015, which represents the fructification of collaborative efforts between MEPs and civil society organizations. The latter used the electoral campaign of 2014 to convince candidates to formally commit to an agenda of greater transparency and integrity in European governance (if elected to the European Parliament), by signing anti-corruption pledges. Each of the seventy-six members of the *Intergroup* have signed at least two of the three pledges advanced by the Transparency International Brussels Office, ALTER-EU, and Restarting the Future, respectively (ITCO 2015a). Reuniting MEPs from different political groups, who have common interests in particular political topics, intergroups represent platforms for expertise sharing and cooperation. Owing to their informal setting, they are often key to building wider consensus and common understandings within the European Parliament around specific policy issues (Corbett *et al.* 2011). Furthermore, intergroups are very permeable to outside interests and regularly include non-state actors in their structure, although the degree of co-optation varies significantly (Nedergaard and Jensen 2014). Although it is too soon to tell what impact the *Intergroup* might eventually have, its very existence as well as the context in which it emerged suggest that the European Parliament has become the site of coagulation of a more substantial interest in ethics and anti-corruption policy, which includes but also goes beyond aspects of public life in Brussels (for instance, the *Intergroup* currently advocates for European legislation that would set uniform standards for whistleblower protection across the EU; see ITCO 2015b). If it is to stay true to its promise of building a "special partnership" with the EP – based on a political, not technocratic, dialogue – the Juncker Commission will have to engage seriously with these fledgling demands.

Final remarks

Before concluding, a word of caution is in order over the implications that ethics reforms might have for the legitimacy of the European Commission. It has been noted several times throughout this book that ethics policies serve a democratic legitimation function, whereby conditions are created for those in public office to act with integrity, a fact which, in turn, stimulates popular trust in government. However, the relationship between ethics measures and trust represents an assumption more than anything else, and it has rarely been empirically tested (but see Feldheim and Wang 2004, Downe *et al.* 2013 for exceptions). One should not be too enthusiastic about the potential, given that popular trust in government represents a complex phenomenon that has no straightforward links to either corruption (Van de Walle 2008), transparency (Grimmelikhuijsen 2009) or public service performance (Van de Walle and Bouckaert 2007). In the case of the EU, these realities are further complicated by the multilevel and highly heterogeneous nature of the political system, which prevents change in Brussels from filtering down to the level of the European citizenry. Furthermore, the actors which scrutinize the Commission, expose its failures and ask for change are themselves subject to powerful centre – periphery dynamics, to the effect that their activity will matter too little to affect the broader European mood. Significantly, Kohler-Koch (2010) notes that there is little evidence that European civil society organizations are successfully acting as "transmission belts" to inform and mobilize ordinary European citizens for political action, despite their vast potential to hold the European Commission accountable. Along similar lines, Wille (2013) argues that although the Commission has acquired strong "inward" accountability structures (making it a highly controlled executive), its lack of "outward" accountability by which to connect to European citizens means that its democratic legitimacy problems continue. In conclusion, the Commission's isolation in the "Brussels bubble" means that its preoccupation with public ethics and, more broadly, its commitment to a "good governance" agenda are not likely to matter much for offsetting popular feelings of disaffection vis-à-vis the European Union.

With this being said, public ethics is set to become an increasingly visible and relevant aspect of public life in the European Union. To some extent, the creation of the *Intergroup on Integrity, Transparency, Corruption and Organised Crime* in the European Parliament, and its agenda, reflects this dynamic. Ethics now constitutes a major aspect of the internal governance of all European institutions – as mentioned in the Introduction, many others apart from the Commission have introduced or revised their ethics policies in the past years. To give just a recent example, several European agencies (i.e., the European Environmental Agency, the European Medicines Agency, European Chemicals Agency, among others) have updated their conflict of interest and transparency policies after a program of onsite visits conducted by the European Ombudsman between 2011 and 2013 (European Ombudsman 2014b). In 2014, in light of its new role in the prudential supervision of credit institutions, the European Central Bank undertook an overhaul revision of its internal ethics framework, whereby it strengthened conflicts of interest rules, introduced a new code of conduct for members of the Supervisory Board, and set up a specialized compliance office to advise staff on ethics issues (European Central Bank 2014). Also importantly, the European Commission is not the only one to have suffered public scandals around integrity violations, which suggests that media and civil society scrutiny are becoming more diversified. The most obvious example here is the 2011 "cash for amendments" affair at the European Parliament, where three MEPs were proven to have accepted payment from journalists posing as lobbyists, in exchange for placing specific amendments in draft legislation (*EurActiv*, 21 March 2011). Taken together, these developments suggest that even though doubts may be raised as to the success of public ethics policies as democratic legitimization instruments, their popularity and use in the EU institutional system is on the rise, as is the attention that citizens pay to the behaviour displayed by European officials.

Notes

1 For instance, Shore (2000) has documented that EU civil servants demonstrate a marked sense of loyalty towards the Commission.
2 This argument goes along similar lines to Maesschalck's (2005) (unfortunately rather lonely) contribution. Demonstrating the poverty of the compliance-integrity continuum as a conceptual device, the author proposes to enrich it by including insights from anthropology – grid-group theory (Douglas 1978), more specifically. Thus, compared with the conventional approach, which tends to focus solely on the intensity of regulation (i.e., the "grid" dimension, in the language of grid-group theory), this new perspective is sensitive to the patterns of interaction between organizational members, and thus opens up spaces for more nuanced managerial strategies.
3 Other previous incentives included getting automatic alerts when public consultations opened in areas of interest indicated by registrants, and access to EP premises (badges were issued only for representatives of registered organizations).

References

Abélès, Marc, Irène Bellier, and Maryon McDonald. 1993. *Approche Anthropologique De La Commission Européenne*. Brussels: European Commission.
Alliance for Lobbying Transparency and Ethics Regulation (ALTER-EU). 2010. *Bursting the Brussels Bubble: The Battle to Expose Corporate Lobbying at the Heart of the EU*. Brussels. Available at: www.alter-eu.org/book/bursting-the-brussels-bubble.
———. 2011. *Block the Revolving Door: Why We Need to Stop EU Officials Becoming Lobbyists*. Brussels. Available at: www.alter-eu.org/sites/default/files/AlterEU_revolving_doors_report.pdf.
———. 2015. 'The European Transparency Initiative and ALTER-EU.' Available at: www.alter-eu.org/about/coalition [Accessed October 14, 2015].
Andreasen, Marta. 2009. *Brussels Laid Bare*. Plympton, Devon: St. Edwards Press.
Applbaum, Arthur Isak. 1999. *Ethics for Adversaries: The Morality of Roles in Public and Professional Life*. Princeton, NJ: Princeton University Press.
Ashforth, Blake E., David M. Sluss, and Alan M. Saks. 2007. "Socialization Tactics, Proactive Behavior, and Newcomer Learning: Integrating Socialization Models." *Journal of Vocational Behavior* 70 (3): 447–462.
Ayres, Ian, and John Braithwaite. 1992. *Responsive Regulation: Transcending the Deregulation Debate*. New York: Oxford University Press.
Balint, Tim, Michael W. Bauer, and Christoph Knill. 2008. "Bureaucratic Change in the European Administrative Space: The Case of the European Commission." *West European Politics* 31 (4): 677–700.
Ban, Carolyn. 2010. "Reforming the Staffing Process in the European Union Institutions: Moving the Sacred Cow Out of the Road." *International Review of Administrative Sciences* 76 (1): 5–24.
———. 2013. *Management and Culture in an Enlarged European Commission: From Diversity to Unity?* Houndmills, Basingstoke, Hampshire: Palgrave Macmillan.
Barter, Christine, and Emma Renold. 2000. "'I Wanna Tell You a Story': Exploring the Application of Vignettes in Qualitative Research with Children and Young People." *Social Research Methodology* 3 (4): 307–323.
Bauer, Michael W. 2008. "Diffuse Anxieties, Deprived Entrepreneurs: Commission Reform and Middle Management." *Journal of European Public Policy* 15 (5): 691–707.
———. 2009. "Impact of Administrative Reform of the European Commission: Results from a Survey of Heads of Unit in Policy-Making Directorates." *International Review of Administrative Sciences* 75 (3): 459–472.
———. 2012. "Tolerant, If Personal Goals Remain Unharmed: Explaining Supranational Bureaucrats' Attitudes to Organizational Change." *Governance* 25 (3): 485–510.

Behnke, Nathalie. 2002. "A Nolan Committee for the German Ethics Infrastructure?" *European Journal of Political Research* 41: 675–708.

Beyers, Jan. 2010. "Conceptual and Methodological Challenges in the Study of European Socialization." *Journal of European Public Policy* 17 (6): 909–920.

Bijlsma-Frankema, Katinka, and Ana Cristina Costa. 2005. "Understanding the Trust-Control Nexus." *International Sociology* 20 (3): 259–282.

Bommer, Michael, Clarence Gratto, Jerry Gravander, and Mark Tuttle. 1987. "A Behavioral Model of Ethical and Unethical Decision Making." *Journal of Business Ethics* 6 (4): 265–280.

Bossaert, Danielle, and Christoph Demmke. 2005. *Main Challenges in the Field of Ethics and Integrity in the EU Member States*. Maastricht: European Institute of Public Administration.

Bouwen, Pieter. 2002. "Corporate Lobbying in the European Union: The Logic of Access." *Journal of European Public Policy* 9 (3): 365–390. doi:10.1080/13501760210138796.

Brewer, Gene A., and Sally Coleman Selden. 1998. "Whistle Blowers in the Federal Civil Service: New Evidence of the Public Service Ethic." *Journal of Public Administration Research and Theory* 8 (3): 413–439.

Brown, Michael E., and Linda K. Treviño. 2006. "Ethical Leadership: A Review and Future Directions." *Leadership Quarterly* 17 (6): 595–616.

Brown, Michael E., Linda K. Treviño, and David A. Harrison. 2005. "Ethical Leadership: A Social Learning Perspective for Construct Development and Testing." *Organizational Behavior and Human Decision Processes* 97 (2): 117–134. doi:10.1016/j.obhdp.2005.03.002.

Budner, Stanley N. Y. 1962. "Intolerance of Ambiguity as a Personality Variable." *Journal of Personality* 30 (1): 29–50.

Chalmers, Adam William. 2012. "Trading Information for Access: Informational Lobbying Strategies and Interest Group Access to the European Union." *Journal of European Public Policy* 20 (1): 39–58. doi:10.1080/13501763.2012.693411.

Chao, Georgia T., Anne M. O'Leary-Kelly, Samantha Wolf, Howard J. Klein, and Philip D. Gardner. 1994. "Organizational Socialization: Its Content and Consequences." *Journal of Applied Psychology* 79 (5) (October): 730–743.

Checkel, Jeffrey T. 2005. "International Institutions and Socialization in Europe: Introduction and Framework." *International Organization* 59 (Fall): 801–826.

Christensen, Tom, and Per Lægreid. 2011. "Ethics and Administrative Reforms." *Public Management Review* 13 (3): 459–477.

Christiansen, Thomas. 1997. "Tensions of European Governance: Politicized Bureaucracy and Multiple Accountability in the European Commission." *Journal of European Public Policy* 4 (1): 73–90.

Cini, Michelle. 1996. *The European Commission: Leadership, Organization and Culture in the EU Administration*. Manchester, NY: Manchester University Press.

———. 1997. "Administrative Culture in the European Commission: The Cases of Competition and Environment." In *At the Heart of the Union: Studies of the European Commission*, ed. Neill Nugent, 71–88. Houndmills, Basingstoke, Hampshire: Palgrave Macmillan.

———. 2004. "The Reform of the European Commission: An Ethical Perspective." *Public Policy and Administration* 19 (3): 42–54.

———. 2007a. *From Integration to Integrity: Administrative Ethics and Reform in the European Commission*. Manchester: Manchester University Press.

———. 2007b. "Ethics Management in the European Commission." In *Institutional Dynamics and the Transformation of Executive Politics in Europe*, ed. Morten Egeberg, 119–148. Mannheim: Connex.

———. 2008. "European Commission Reform and the Origins of the European Transparency Initiative." *Journal of European Public Policy* 15 (5): 743–760.

———. 2010. "Éthique et Réforme Administrative de la Commission Européenne." *Revue Française D'administration Publique* 133: 45–60.

———. 2014. "Institutional Change and Ethics Management in the EU's College of Commissioners." *British Journal of Politics & International Relations* 16 (3): 479–494.

Commission. (n.d.). 'Practical Guide on Staff Ethics and Conduct.' [internal document].

———. 2000. 'Code of Good Administrative Behaviour – Relations with the Public.' Available at: http://ec.europa.eu/transparency/code/_docs/code_en.pdf [Accessed October 14, 2015].

———. 2004a. 'Competing the Reform Mandate: Progress Report and Measures to be Implemented in 2004 COM(2004) 93 Final.' Available at: http://eur-lex.europa.eu/LexUriServ/LexUriServ.do?uri=COM:2004:0093:FIN:EN:PDF [Accessed March 30, 2012].

———. 2004b. *Staff Regulations of Officials of the European Communities and Conditions of Employment of Other Servants of the European Communities [Compendium]*. Brussels. Available at: http://ec.europa.eu/civil_service/docs/ toc100_en.pdf [Accessed April 19, 2011].

———. 2005. *Access to European Commission Documents – A Citizens' Guide*. Brussels. Available at: http://ec.europa.eu/transparency/access_documents/docs/guide_citoyen/citizen_guide_en.pdf [Accessed August 20, 2012].

———. 2006a. 'Green Paper: The European Transparency Initiative COM(2006) 194 Final.' Available at: http://eur-lex.europa.eu/LexUriServ/LexUriServ.do?uri=COM:2006:0194:FIN:EN:PDF [Accessed March 31, 2012].

———. 2006b. 'Ethics and Integrity: Participant's Manual.' [internal document].

———. 2007. 'Note from VP Kallas to the College: Towards a Communication on Ethics in the Commission SEC(2007) 277.' [internal document].

———. 2008a. 'Communication from Vice-President Kallas to the Commission on Enhancing the Environment for Professional Ethics in the Commission SEC(2008) 301 Final.' Available at: http://ec.europa.eu/archives/commission_2004–2009/kallas/doc/com2008_0305_ethic_en.pdf [Accessed March 31, 2012].

———. 2008b. 'Code on Ethics and Integrity of DG TRADE Staff.' [internal document].

———. 2008c. Contacts with interest representatives – guidelines for staff. *Commission en plus* (17.10-23.10 2008), 2–3. Brussels.

———. 2009. 'Note to All DG SANCO Staff A5/2009/D/150255.' [internal document].

———. 2010a. *Annual Activity Report 2010: DG Competition*, Brussels. Available at: http://ec.europa.eu/atwork/synthesis/aar/doc/comp_aar.pdf [Accessed August 20, 2012].

———. 2010b. 'Code on Ethics and Integrity of DG COMP Staff.' [internal document].

———. 2010c. 'Ethics Guidelines for DG MARKT Staff: A User's Guide to the Existing Ethics Rules and Regulations.' [internal document].

———. 2010d. Impartiality beyond any doubt: ethics and integrity in the Secretariat General. [internal document]

———. 2011a. 'Impartiality, Integrity, Independence: Ethics and Good Behaviour in DG COMP.' [internal document].

———. 2011b. 'Social Media Guidelines for All Staff – Administrative Notice no 34/2011.' [internal document].

———. 2012a. 'Communication from Vice-President Šefčovič to the Commission on Guidelines on Whistleblowing – SEC(2012) 679.' Available at: www.coe.int/t/dghl/standardsetting/cdcj/Whistleblowers/EU%20guidelines%20-%20Whistleblowing.pdf [Accessed October 5, 2014].

———. 2012b. 'Communication from Vice-President Šefčovič to the Commission on Guidelines on Gifts and Hospitality for Staff Members – SEC(2012) 167.' Available at: http://ec.europa.eu/transparency/docs/sec_2012_0167_f_en_communication_to_commission_en.pdf [Accessed October 5, 2014].

———. 2012c. *Human Resources Report of the European Commission 2012*. Luxembourg: Publications Office of the European Union.

———. 2013a. 'Summary Document on Changes Related to Staff Regulations Review.' Available at: http://u4unity.eu/document2/SR_summary_20130705.pdf [Accessed October 14, 2015].

———. 2013b. 'Activity Report of the Investigation and Disciplinary Office of the Commission (IDOC) 2013.' [internal document].

———. 2013c. *Human Resources Report of the European Commission 2014*. Luxembourg: Publications Office of the European Union.

———. 2014a. *Human Resources Report of the European Commission 2014*. Luxembourg: Publications Office of the European Union.

———. 2014b. 'Opening the Windows: Commission Commits to Enhanced Transparency.' Available at: http://europa.eu/rapid/press-release_IP-14-2131_en.htm?locale=en [Accessed October 14, 2015].

———. 2014c. 'Practical Guide for Commission Staff on Procedures in Inquiries, Pre-Disciplinary and Disciplinary Proceedings.' [internal document].

———. 2015a. *Human Resources Report of the European Commission 2015*. Luxembourg: Publications Office of the European Union.

———. 2015b. *Roadmap for the Establishment of a Mandatory Transparency Register for Interest Representatives*. Brussels. Available at: http://ec.europa.eu/smart-regulation/impact/planned_ia/docs/2015_sg_010_transparencyr_04022015_updated_fvp_en.pdf [Accessed October 14, 2015].

Committee of Independent Experts (CIE). 1999a. *First Report on Allegations Regarding Fraud, Mismanagement and Nepotism in the European Commission*. Brussels. Available at: www.europarl.europa.eu/experts/pdf/reporten.pdf [Accessed March 31, 2012].

———. 1999b. *Second Report on Reform of the Commission: Analysis of Current Practice and Proposals for Tackling Mismanagement, Irregularities and Fraud*. Brussels. Available at: www.europarl.europa.eu/experts/pdf/rep2-1en.pdf and www.europarl.europa.eu/experts/pdf/rep2-2en.pdf [Accessed March 31, 2012].

Coombes, David. 1970. *Bureaucracy and Politics in the European Union – A Portrait of the Commission of the E.C.C.* London: George Allen & Unwin.

Cooper, Terry L. 1998. *The Responsible Administrator: An Approach to Ethics for the Administrative Role*. 4th ed. San Francisco: Jossey-Bass.

Cooper-Thomas, Helena D., and Neil Anderson. 2006. "Organizational Socialization: A New Theoretical Model and Recommendations for Future Research and HRM Practices in Organizations." *Journal of Managerial Psychology* 21 (5): 492–516.

Corbett, Richard, Francis Jacobs, and Michael Shackleton. 2003. "The European Parliament at Fifty: A View from the Inside." *JCMS: Journal of Common Market Studies* 41 (2): 353–373.

———. 2011. *The European Parliament*. 8th ed. London: John Harper Publishing.

Cowell, Richard, James Downe, and Karen Morgan. 2011. "The Ethical Framework for Local Government in England." *Public Management Review* 13 (3): 433–457.

Cox, Robert W. 1969. "The Executive Head: An Essay on Leadership in International Organization." *International Organization* 23: 205–230.

Cram, Laura. 1994. "The European Commission as a Multi-Organization: Social Policy and IT Policy in the EU." *Journal of European Public Policy* 1 (2): 195–217.

Curtin, Deirdre, and Albert J. Meijer. 2006. "Does Transparency Strengthen Legitimacy? A Critical Analysis of European Union Policy Documents." *Information Polity*. Available at: http://dx.doi.org/10.2139/ssrn.1434862 [Accessed July 10, 2015].

Das, T.K., and Bing-Sheng Teng. 1998. "Between Trust and Control: Developing Confidence in Partner Cooperation in Alliances." *Academy of Management Review* 23 (3): 491–512.

Deci, Edward L., and Richard M. Ryan. 2000. "The 'What' and 'Why' of Goal Pursuits: Human Needs and the Self-Determination of Behavior." *Psychological Inquiry* 11 (4): 227–268.

Dehousse, Renaud, and Andrew Thompson. 2012. "Intergovernmentalists in the Commission: Foxes in the Henhouse?" *Journal of European Integration* 34 (2): 113–132.

Demmke, Christoph, M. Bovens, T. Henokl, K. van Lierop, T. Moilanen, G. Pikker, and A. Salminen. 2007. *Regulating Conflicts of Interests for Holders of Public Office in the European Union: A Comparative Study of the Rules and Standards of Professional Ethics for the Holders of Public Office in the EU-27 and EU Institutions*. Maastricht: European Commission Bureau of European Policy Advisers.

Dercks, Lisa. 2001. "The European Commission's Business Ethics: A Critique of Proposed Reforms." *Business Ethics: A European Review* 10 (4): 346–359.

Dimitrakopoulos, Dionyssis G. (ed.). 2004. *The Changing European Commission*. Manchester: Manchester University Press.

Dinan, William, and Erik Wesselius. 2010. "Brussels: A Lobbying Paradise." In *Bursting the Brussels Bubble: The Battle to Expose Corporate Lobbying at the Heart of the EU*, 23–32. Brussels: Alliance for Lobbying Transparency and Ethics Regulation (ALTER-EU). Available at: www.alter-eu.org/sites/default/files/documents/bursting-the-brussels-bubble.pdf [Accessed August 20, 2012].

Dobel, J. Patrick. 1993. "The Realpolitik of Ethics Codes: An Implementation Approach to Public Ethics." In *Ethics and Public Administration*, ed. George H. Frederickson, 158–176. Armonk and London: M.E. Sharpe.

Douglas, Mary. 1978. *In the Active Voice*. London: Routledge.

Downe, James, Richard Cowell, Alex Chen, and Karen Morgan. 2013. "The Determinants of Public Trust in English Local Government: How Important Is the Ethical Behaviour of Elected Councillors?" *International Review of Administrative Sciences* 79 (4): 597–617.

Egeberg, Morten. 1999. "Transcending Intergovernmentalism? Identity and Role Perceptions of National Officials in EU Decision-Making." *Journal of European Public Policy* 6 (3): 456–474.

———. 2004. "An Organisational Approach to European Integration: Outline of a Complementary Perspective." *European Journal of Political Research* 43 (2): 199–219.

———. 2006. "Executive Politics as Usual: Role Behaviour and Conflict Dimensions in the College of European Commissioners." *Journal of European Public Policy* 13 (1): 1–15.

———. 2012. "Experiments in Supranational Institution-Building: The European Commission as a Laboratory." *Journal of European Public Policy* 19 (6): 939–950. doi:10.1080/13501763.2012.681456.

Eisenberg, Nancy. 2000. "Emotion, Regulation, and Moral Development." *Annual Review of Psychology* 51 (1): 665.

Ellinas, Antonis, and Ezra Suleiman. 2008. "Reforming the Commission: Between Modernization and Bureaucratization." *Journal of European Public Policy* 15 (5): 708–725.

———. 2011. "Supranationalism in a Transnational Bureaucracy: The Case of the European Commission." *Journal of Common Market Studies* 49 (5): 923–947.

Erakovich, Rodney, and Sherman Wyman. 2009. "Implications of Organizational Influence on Ethical Behaviour: An Analysis of the Perceptions of Public Managers." In *Ethics and*

Integrity in Public Administration: Concepts and Cases, ed. Raymond W. Cox III, 76–91. Armonk and London: M.E. Sharpe.

European Central Bank. 2014. 'Press Release: ECB Publishes Revised Ethics Framework and New Code of Conduct for Supervisory Board Members to Reflect Supervisory Tasks.' Available at: www.ecb.europa.eu/press/pr/date/2014/html/pr141222.en.html [Accessed February 28, 2016].

European Ombudsman. 2012. 'Public Service Principles for the EU Civil Service.' Available at: www.ombudsman.europa.eu/en/resources/publicserviceprinciples.faces [Accessed September 20, 2015].

———. 2013a. 'Decision of the European Ombudsman Closing Her Inquiry into Complaint 297/2013/(RA)FOR against the European Commission.' Available at: www.ombudsman.europa.eu/en/cases/decision.faces/en/52934/html.bookmark#hl6 [Accessed October 10, 2015].

———. 2013b. 'Annual Report 2013: Strasbourg.' Available at: www.ombudsman.europa.eu/en/activities/annualreports.faces [Accessed October 10, 2015].

———. 2014a. 'Annual Report 2014: Strasbourg.' Available at: www.ombudsman.europa.eu/en/activities/annualreports.faces [Accessed October 10, 2015].

———. 2014b. 'Report on Visits to Agencies: Strasbourg.' Available at: www.ombudsman.europa.eu/en/activities/visitreport.faces/en/59248/html.bookmark [Accessed October 14, 2015].

European Parliament. 2010. 'Decision of 5 May 2010 on Discharge in Respect of the Implementation of the European Union General Budget for the Financial Year 2008, Section III – Commission, P7_TA-PROV(2010)0134.' Available at: http://eur-lex.europa.eu/eli/dec/2010/494/oj [Accessed June 13, 2016]

———. 2011. 'Decision of 10 May 2011 on Discharge in Respect of the Implementation of the General Budget of the European Union for the Financial Year 2009, Section III – Commission, P7_TA(2011)0194.' Available at: http://data.europa.eu/eli/dec/2011/550/oj [Accessed June 13, 2016].

———. 2014. 'Resolution of 3 April 2014 on the Court of Auditors' Special Reports in the Context of the 2012 Commission Discharge, P7_TA-PROV(2014)0288.' Available at: http://eur-lex.europa.eu/legal-content/EN/TXT/?qid=1465841588522&uri=CELEX:52014BP0905(04) [Accessed June 13, 2016].

———. 2015. 'Decision of 29 April 2015 on Discharge in Respect of the Implementation of the General Budget of the European Union for the Financial Year 2013, Section III – Commission and Executive Agencies, P8_TA(2015)0118.' Available at: http://data.europa.eu/eli/dec/2015/1616/oj [Accessed June 13, 2016].

European Union. 2015a. 'European Commission Civil Service.' Available at: http://ec.europa.eu/civil_service/index_en.htm [Accessed October 14, 2015].

———. 2015b. 'Transparency Register – Transparency and the EU.' Available at: http://ec.europa.eu/transparencyregister/public/homePage.do [Accessed October 6, 2015].

Feldheim, Mary Ann, and Xiaohu Wang. 2004. "Ethics and Public Trust: Results from a National Survey." *Public Integrity* 6 (1): 63–75.

Finch, Janet. 1987. "The Vignette Technique in Survey Research." *Sociology* 21: 105–111.

Ford, Robert C., and Woodrow D. Richardson. 1994. "Ethical Decision Making: A Review of the Empirical Literature." *Journal of Business Ethics* 13: 205–221.

Frederickson, George H., and Jeremy David Walling. 2001. "Research and Knowledge in Administrative Ethics." In *Handbook of Administrative Ethics*, ed. Terry L. Cooper, 37–58. 2nd ed. New York and Basel: Marcel Dekker.

Frey, Bruno S. 1997. *Not Just for the Money: An Economic Theory of Personal Motivation*. Cheltenham, UK: Edward Elgar.

Frey, Bruno S., and Reto Jegen. 2001. "Motivational Interactions: Effects on Behaviour." *Annales d'Économie et de Statistique* 63/64 (July): 131–153. doi:10.2307/20076299.

Furnham, Adrian, and Tracy Ribchester. 1995. "Tolerance of Ambiguity: A Review of the Concept, Its Measurement and Applications." *Current Psychology* 14 (3): 179–199.

Gilman, Stuart. 1999. "Public Sector Ethics and Government Reinvention: Realigning Systems to Meet Organizational Change." *Public Integrity* 1: 1180–1198.

Giusta, Paolo. 2006. *Ethics Matters: Practical Micro-Ethics for Civil Servants of the European Union*. Luxembourg: Office for Official Publications of the European Communities.

Gortner, Harold F. 1991. *Ethics for Public Managers*. New York: Greenwood Press.

Greasley, Stephen, Johnston Lorraine, Gerry Stoker, and Gains Francesca. 2006. *The Components of an Ethical Environment: Final Research Report to the Standards Board of England*. Manchester. Available at: http://webarchive.nationalarchives.gov.uk/20120202153716/www.standardsforengland.gov.uk/Resources/Research/Researcharchive/filedownload,16132,en.pdf [Accessed March 30, 2012].

Greasley, Stephen, Gerry Stoker, and Francesca Gains. 2005. *The Components of an Ethical Environment: A Review of the Literature*. Manchester: Institute for Political and Economic Governance, University of Manchester.

Greenwood, Justin, and Joanna Dreger. 2013. "The Transparency Register: A European Vanguard of Strong Lobby Regulation?" *Interest Groups & Advocacy* 2: 139–162.

Greenwood, Justin, and Darren Halpin. 2007. "The European Commission and the Public Governance of Interest Groups in the European Union: Seeking a Niche between Accreditation and Laissez-Faire." *Perspectives on European Politics and Society* 8 (2): 189–210.

Grimmelikhuijsen, Stephan. 2009. "Do Transparent Government Agencies Strengthen Trust?" *Information Polity* 14 (3): 173–186.

Gulick, Luther. 1937. "Notes on the Theory of Organization." In *Papers on the Science of Administration*, ed. Luther Gulick and Lyndall Urwick, 1–46. New York: Institute of Public Administration, Columbia University.

Haidt, Jonathan. 2001. "The Emotional Dog and Its Rational Tail: A Social Intuitionist Approach to Moral Judgment." *Psychological Review* 108 (4) (October): 814–834.

Heres, Leonie, and Karin Lasthuizen. 2012. "What's the Difference? Ethical Leadership in Public, Hybrid and Private Sector Organizations." *Journal of Change Management* 12 (4): 441–466. doi:10.1080/14697017.2012.728768.

Héritier, Adrienne. 2003. "Composite Democracy in Europe: The Role of Transparency and Access to Information." *Journal of European Public Policy* 10 (5): 814–833.

Hine, D., and R. McMahon. 2004. *Ethics Management, Cultural Change, and the Ambiguities of European Commission Reform*. Oxford: Department of Politics and International Relations, University of Oxford. Available at: http://government.politics.ox.ac.uk/Projects/Papers/Hine-McMahon_Ethics_Management.pdf [Accessed January 22, 2008].

Hooghe, Liesbet. 2001. *The European Commission and the Integration of Europe: Images of Governance*. Cambridge: Cambridge University Press.

———. 2005. "Several Roads Lead to International Norms, but Few Via International Socialization: A Case Study of the European Commission." *International Organization* 59 (4): 861–898.

———. 2012. 'Images of Europe: How Commission Officials Conceive Their Institution's Role'. *JCMS: Journal of Common Market Studies* 50 (1): 87–111. doi:10.1111/j.1468-5965.2011.02210.x.

Huberts, Leo. 2014a. "Introduction." In *The Integrity of Governance: What Is It, What We Know, What Is Done and Where to Go*, ed. Leo Huberts, 20–35. Houndmills, Basingstoke, Hampshire: Palgrave Macmillan.

———. 2014b. "Placing Integrity of Governance in Context." In *The Integrity of Governance: What Is It, What We Know, What Is Done and Where to Go*, ed. Leo Huberts, 265–303. Houndmills, Basingstoke, Hampshire: Palgrave Macmillan.

Huberts, Leo, Frédérique Six, Mieke van Tankeren, Andre van Monfort, and Hester Paanakker. 2014. "What Is Done to Protect Integrity: Policies, Institutions and Systems." In *The Integrity of Governance: What Is It, What We Know, What Is Done and Where to Go*, ed. Leo Huberts, 227–264. Houndmills, Basingstoke, Hampshire: Palgrave Macmillan.

Huberts, Leo W.J.C., Jeroen Maesschalck, and Carole L. Jurkiewicz. 2008. "Global Perspectives on Good Governance Policies and Research." In *Ethics and Integrity of Governance: Perspectives Across Frontiers*, ed. Leo W.J.C. Huberts, Jeroen Maesschalck, and Carole L. Jurkiewicz, 239–264. Cheltenham and Northampton: Edward Elgar.

Huberts, Leo W.J.C., Muel Kaptein, and Karin Lasthuizen. 2007. "A Study of the Impact of Three Leadership Styles on Integrity Violations Committed by Police Officers." *Policing: An International Journal of Police Strategies & Management* 30 (4): 587–607. doi:10.1108/13639510710833884.

Hughes, Rhidian. 1998. "Considering the Vignette Technique and Its Application to a Study of Drug Injecting and HIV Risk and Safer Behaviour." *Sociology of Health & Illness* 20 (3): 381.

Intergroup on Integrity, Transparency, Corruption and Organised Crime (ITCO). 2015a. 'About ITCO.' Available at: http://itcointergroup.eu/about/ [Accessed October 14, 2015].

———. 2015b. 'ITCO Intergroup Pressures the Commission to Protect Whistleblowers.' Available at: http://itcointergroup.eu/sample-page/ [Accessed October 14, 2015].

Jenkins, Nicholas, Michael Bloor, Jan Fischer, Lee Berney, and Joanne Neale. 2010. "Putting It in Context: The Use of Vignettes in Qualitative Interviewing." *Qualitative Research* 10 (2): 175–198.

Joint Transparency Register Secretariat (JTRS). 2013. *Annual Report on the Operations of the Transparency Register 2013*. Brussels. Available at: http://ec.europa.eu/transparencyregister/public/staticPage/displayStaticPage.do?locale=en&reference=ANNUAL_REPORT [Accessed October 14, 2015].

———. 2015. *Transparency Register Statistics – 28 September 2015*. Brussels. Available at: http://ec.europa.eu/transparencyregister/public/consultation/statistics.do?locale=en&action=prepareView [Accessed October 14, 2015].

Jones, Thomas M. 1991. "Ethical Decision Making by Individuals in Organizations: An Issue-Contingent Model." *Academy of Management Review* 16 (2): 366–395.

Judge, David, and David Earnshaw. 2002. "The European Parliament and the Commission Crisis: A New Assertiveness?" *Governance* 15 (3): 345–374.

Juncker, Jean-Claude. 2014. 'A New Start for Europe: My Agenda for Jobs, Growth, Fairness and Democratic Change – Political Guidelines for the Next European Commission.' Available at: http://europa.eu/rapid/press-release_SPEECH-14-546_en.htm [Accessed October 14, 2015].

Kallas, Siim. 2007. 'Speech Delivered at the Staff Forum.' Available at: http://ec.europa.eu/archives/ commission_2004–2009/kallas/doc/20071012_staff_forum_en.pdf [Accessed March 30, 2012].

Kaptein, Muel, and Mark S. Schwartz. 2008. "The Effectiveness of Business Codes: A Critical Examination of Existing Studies and the Development of an Integrated Research Model." *Journal of Business Ethics* 77 (2): 111–127.

Kaptein, Muel, and Piet van Reenen. 2001. "Integrity Management of Police Organizations." *Policing: An International Journal of Police Strategies & Management* 24 (3): 281–300.

Kaptein, Muel, and Johan Wempe. 2002. *The Balanced Company: A Theory of Corporate Integrity*. Oxford: Oxford University Press.

Kassim, Hussein. 2004. "A Historic Accomplishment: The Prodi Commission and Administrative Reform." In *The Changing European Commission*, ed. D.G. Dimitrakopoulos, 33–62. Manchester: Manchester University Press.

———. 2008. " 'Mission Impossible', but Mission Accomplished: The Kinnock Reforms and the European Commission." *Journal of European Public Policy* 15 (5): 648–668.

Kassim, Hussein, Jon Peterson, Michael W. Bauer, Sara Connolly, Renaud Dehousse, Liesbet Hooghe, and Andrew Thompson. 2013. *The European Commission of the Twenty-First Century*. Oxford: Oxford University Press.

Kidder, Rushworth M. 2009. *How Good People Make Tough Choices: Resolving the Dilemmas of Ethical Living*. 2nd ed. New York, London, Toronto, Sydney: HarperCollins.

Klabbers, Jan. 2013. "Self-Control: International Organizations and the Quest for Accountability." In *The International Responsibility of the European Union: European and International Perspectives*, ed. Malcolm Evans and Panos Koutrakos, 75–100. Oxford and Portland, OR: Hart Publishing.

Kohler-Koch, Beate. 2010. "How to Put Matters Right? Assessing the Role of Civil Society in EU Accountability." *West European Politics* 33 (5): 1117–1141.

———. 2012. "Post-Maastricht Civil Society and Participatory Democracy." *Journal of European Integration* 34 (7): 809–824.

Kohler-Koch, Beate, and Christine Quittkat. 2013. *De-Mystification of Participatory Democracy: EU Governance and Civil Society*. Oxford: Oxford University Press.

Lasthuizen, Karin, Leo Huberts, and Leonie Heres. 2011. "How to Measure Integrity Violations." *Public Management Review* 13 (3): 383–408.

Lawton, Alan, and Alan Doig. 2006. 'Researching Ethics for Public Service Organizations: The View From Europe'. *Public Integrity* 8 (1): 11–33.

Lawton, Alan, and Michael Macaulay. 2009. "Ethics Management and Ethical Management." In *Ethics and Integrity in Public Administration: Concepts and Cases*, ed. Raymond W. Cox III, 107–120. Armonk and London: M.E. Sharpe.

Le Grand, Julian. 2003. *Motivation, Agency and Public Policy: Of Knights & Knaves, Pawns & Queens*. Oxford: Oxford University Press.

Levy, Roger P. 2004. "Between Rhetoric and Reality: Implementing Management Reform in the European Commission." *International Journal of Public Sector Management* 17 (2): 166–177.

———. 2006. "European Commission Overload and the Pathology of Management Reform: Garbage Can, Rationality and Risk Aversion." *Public Administration* 84 (2): 423–439.

Lewis, Carol W. 1991. *The Ethics Challenge in Public Service*. San Francisco, CA: Jossey-Bass.

Lewis, Carol W., and Stuart C. Gilman. 2005. "Normative and Institutional Currents and Commonalities: A Global Perspective for Public Managers." *Public Integrity* 7 (4): 331–343.

List, Dennis. 2004. 'Maximum Variation Sampling for Surveys and Consensus Groups.' Available at: www.audiencedialogue.org/maxvar.html [Accessed July 22, 2012].

Loe, Terry W., Linda Ferrell, and Phylis Mansfield. 2000. "A Review of Empirical Studies Assessing Ethical Decision-Making in Business." *Journal of Business Ethics* 25: 185–204.

Longstaff, Simon. 1994. "What Is Ethics Education and Training?" In *Ethics for the Public Sector: Education and Training*, ed. Noel Preston, 138–160. Sydney: The Federation Press.

Louis, Meryl Reis. 1980. "Surprise and Sense Making: What Newcomers Experience in Entering Unfamiliar Organizational Settings." *Administrative Science Quarterly* 25 (2) (June): 226–251.
Loyens, Kim. 2013. "Towards a Custom-Made Whistleblowing Policy: Using Grid-Group Cultural Theory to Match Policy Measures to Different Styles of Peer Reporting." *Journal of Business Ethics* 114 (2): 239–249.
McDonald, Maryon. 1997. "Identities in the European Commission." In *At the Heart of the Union: Studies of the European Commission*, ed. Neill Nugent, 49–70. Houndmills: Macmillan.
———. 2000. "Accountability, Anthropology and the European Commission." In *Audit Cultures: Anthropological Studies in Accountability, Ethics and the Academy*, ed. Marilyn Strathern, 106–134. London and New York: Routledge.
Maesschalck, Jeroen. 2004a. "The Impact of New Public Management Reforms on Public Servants' Ethics: Towards a Theory." *Public Administration* 82 (2): 465–489.
———. 2004b. 'Towards a Public Administration Theory on Public Servants' Ethics: A Comparative Study.' Doctoral dissertation, Leuven, Belgium: Faculteit Sociale Wetenschappen – Departement Politieke Wetenschappen, Katholieke Universiteit Leuven.
———. 2005. "Approaches to Ethics Management in the Public Sector: A Proposed Extension of the Compliance-Integrity Continuum." *Public Integrity* 7 (1): 21–41.
March, James G., and Johan P. Olsen. 1989. *Rediscovering Institutions: The Organizational Basis of Politics*. New York: Free Press.
———. 2006. "The Logic of Appropriateness." In *Oxford Handbook of Public Policy*, ed. Martin Rein and Robert E. Goodin, 689–708. Oxford: Oxford University Press.
March, James G., and Herbert Simon. 1993. *Organizations*. 2nd ed. Cambridge, MA: Blackwell Publishers.
Mazey, Sonia, and Jeremy J. Richardson. 1993. "Conclusion: A European Policy Style?" In *Lobbying in the European Community*, ed. Sonia Mazey and Jeremy Richardson, 246–258. Oxford: Oxford University Press.
———. 2006. "The Commission and the Lobby." In *The European Commission*, ed. David Spence and Geoffrey Edwards, 279–293. 3rd ed. London: John Harper Publishing.
Menzel, Donald C. 2001. "Ethics Management in Public Organizations: What, Why and How?" In *Handbook of Administrative Ethics*, ed. Terry L. Cooper, 355–366. 2nd ed. New York and Basel: Marcel Dekker.
———. 2005. "Research on Ethics and Integrity in Governance." *Public Integrity* 7 (2): 147–168.
———. 2007. *Ethics Management for Public Administrators: Building Organizations of Integrity*. Armonk, NY: M.E. Sharpe.
Metcalfe, Les. 2000. "Reforming the Commission: Will Organizational Efficiency Produce Effective Governance?" *JCMS: Journal of Common Market Studies* 38 (5): 817–841.
Miller, Vernon D., and Fredric M. Jablin. 1991. "Information Seeking During Organizational Entry: Influences, Tactics, and a Model of the Process." *Academy of Management Review* 16 (1): 92–120.
Moilanen, Timo, and Ari Salminen. 2007. 'Comparative Study on the Public Service Ethics of the EU Member States.' 1/2007. Research and Studies. Finish Ministry of Finance. Available at: www.vm.fi /julkaisut [Accessed August 1, 2008].
Morrison, Elizabeth Wolfe. 1993. "Newcomer Information Seeking: Exploring Types, Models, Sources, and Outcomes." *Academy of Management Journal* 36 (3): 557–589.
Murdoch, Zuzana, and Benny Geys. 2012. "Instrumental Calculation, Cognitive Role-Playing, or Both? Self-Perceptions of Seconded National Experts in the European

Commission." *Journal of European Public Policy* 19 (9): 1357–1376. doi:10.1080/1350 1763.2012.677186.

Năstase, Andreea. 2013. "Managing Ethics in the European Commission Services." *Public Management Review* 15 (1): 63–81.

Naurin, Daniel. 2007. *Deliberation Behind Closed Doors: Transparency and Lobbying in the European Union*. Colchester: ECPR Press.

Nedergaard, Peter, and Mads Dagnis Jensen. 2014. "The Anatomy of Intergroups – Network Governance in the Political Engine Room of the European Parliament." *Policy Studies* 35 (2): 192–209.

Nugent, Neill. 1997. "At the Heart of the Union." In *At the Heart of the Union: Studies of the European Commission*, ed. Neill Nugent, 1–26. Houndmills: Macmillan.

———. 2001. *The European Commission*. Houndmills, Basingstoke, Hampshire: Palgrave Macmillan.

———. 2010. *The Government and Politics of the European Union*. 7th ed. Houndmills, Basingstoke, Hampshire: Palgrave Macmillan.

OECD. 1996. *Ethics in the Public Service: Current Issues and Practice*. Public Management Occasional Papers, no 14. Paris: OECD, Public Management Service.

———. 1998. *Principles for Managing Ethics in the Public Service – OECD Recommendation*. PUMA Policy Brief, no 4. OECD, Public Management Service. Available at: www.oecd.org/gov/digital-government/1900037.pdf [Accessed June 13, 2016].

———. 2000. *Trust in Government: Ethics Measures in OECD Countries*. Paris: OECD Publishing.

———. May 4–5, 2009. *Towards a Sound Integrity Framework: Instruments, Processes, Structures, and Conditions for Implementation*. Paris: OECD Publishing. Available at: www.oecd.org/officialdocuments/publicdisplaydocumentpdf/?doclanguage=en&cote=GOV/PGC/GF(2009)1 [Accessed November 2, 2015].

———. "Conflict-of-Interest Disclosure by Top Decision Makers." In *Government at a Glance 2011*. OECD Publishing. Available at: http://dx.doi.org/10.1787/gov_glance-2011-45-en [Accessed January 13, 2015].

O'Fallon, Michael J., and Kenneth D. Butterfield. 2005. "A Review of the Empirical Ethical Decision-Making Literature: 1996–2003." *Journal of Business Ethics* 59: 375–413.

Ostroff, Cheri, and Steve W.J. Kozlowski. 1992. "Organizational Socialization as a Learning Process: The Role of Information Acquisition." *Personnel Psychology* 45 (4): 849–874.

Page, Edward C. 1997. *People Who Run Europe*. Oxford: Clarendon Press.

Paine, Lynn Sharp. 1994. "Managing for Organizational Integrity." *Harvard Business Review* 72 (2): 106–117.

Palidauskaite, Jolanta. 2005. "Codes of Ethics in Transitional Democracies." *Public Integrity* 8 (1): 34–48.

Palidauskaite, Jolanta, Aive Pevkur, and Iveta Reinholde. 2010. "A Comparative Approach to Civil Service Ethics in Estonia, Latvia and Lithuania." *Journal of Baltic Studies* 41 (1): 45–71.

Patton, Michael Quinn. 2002. *Qualitative Research and Evaluation Methods*. 3rd ed. Thousand Oaks, CA: Sage Publications.

Perry, James L., and Lois Recascino Wise. 1990. "The Motivational Bases of Public Service." *Public Administration Review* 50 (3): 367–373.

Peters, B. Guy. 2001. *The Politics of Bureaucracy*. 5th ed. London and New York: Routledge.

Peterson, John. 2008. "Enlargement, Reform and the European Commission: Weathering a Perfect Storm?" *Journal of European Public Policy* 15 (5): 761–780.

Pollitt, Christopher, and Geert Bouckaert. 2004. *Public Management Reform: A Comparative Analysis*. Oxford: Oxford University Press.
Pope, Jeremy. 2008. "The Third Phase in the Fight Against Corruption: Implementation and Comparative Administrative Ethics." *Public Integrity* 10 (1): 75–83.
PricewaterhouseCoopers Belgium & iForce. 2011. *Corruption and Conflict of Interests in the European Institutions: The Effectiveness of Whistleblowers*. Brussels. Available at: www.europarl.europa.eu/studies [Accessed February 20, 2012].
Pujas, Veronique, and Martin Rhodes. 1999. "A Clash of Cultures? Corruption and the Ethics of Administration in Western Europe." *Parliamentary Affairs* 10 (1): 688–703.
Quittkat, Christine. 2011. "The European Commission's Online Consultations: A Success Story?" *JCMS: Journal of Common Market Studies* 49 (3): 653–674.
RCC (Risk Communication Concepts). 2006. *Whistleblowing Rules: Best Practice: Assessment and Revision of Rules Existing in EU Institutions*. Brussels: European Parliament, Directorate-General Internal Policies, Directorate D – Budgetary Affairs.
Renold, Emma. 2002. "Using Vignettes in Qualitative Research." *Building Research Capacity*. No. 3: 3–5.
Rest, James R. 1986. *Moral Development: Advances in Research and Theory*. New York: Praeger.
Roberts, Robert. 2009. "The Rise of Compliance-Based Ethics Management." *Public Integrity* 11 (3): 261–277.
Rohr, John A. 1978. *Ethics for Bureaucrats: An Essay on Law and Values*. New York and Basel: Marcel Dekker.
———. 1998. *Public Service, Ethics and Constitutional Practice*. Lawrence, KS: University Press of Kansas.
Rubin, Allen, and Earl Babbie. 2009. *Essential Research Methods for Social Work*. 2nd ed. Belmont, CA: Brooks/Cole, Cengage Learning.
Ryan, Richard M., and Edward L. Deci. 2000. "Self-Determination Theory and the Facilitation of Intrinsic Motivation, Social Development, and Well-Being." *American Psychologist* 55 (1): 68–78.
Saks, Alan M., and Blake E. Ashforth. 1997. "Organizational Socialization: Making Sense of the Past and Present as a Prologue for the Future." *Journal of Vocational Behaviour* 51: 234–269.
Sbargia, Alberta M. 1992. "Thinking about the European Future: The Uses of Comparison." In *Euro-Politics: Institutions and Policymaking in the 'New' European Community*, ed. Alberta M. Sbargia, 257–292. Washington, DC: Brookings.
Scharpf, Fritz W. 1988. "The Joint-Decision Trap: Lessons from German Federalism and European Integration." *Public Administration* 66 (3): 239–278.
Schmidt, Vivien A. 2013. "Democracy and Legitimacy in the European Union Revisited: Input, Output and 'Throughput'." *Political Studies* 61 (1): 2–22.
Schoenberg, Nancy E., and Hege Ravdal. 2000. "Using Vignettes in Awareness and Attitudinal Research." *International Journal of Social Research Methodology* 3 (1): 63–74.
Schön-Quinlivan, Emmanuelle. 2008. "Implementing Organizational Change – The Case of the Kinnock Reforms." *Journal of European Public Policy* 15 (5): 726–742.
———. 2011. *Reforming the European Commission*. Houndmills, Basingstoke, Hampshire, NY: Palgrave Macmillan.
Šefčovič, Maroš. 2013. 'Ethics and the European Commission.' Available at: http://europa.eu/rapid/press-release_SPEECH-13-201_en.htm [Accessed October 14, 2015].
———. 2014. 'Lobbying in Brussels – *Transparence Oblige*: Scope and Prospects of the Transparency Register.' Available at: http://europa.eu/rapid/press-release_SPEECH-14-480_en.htm [Accessed October 14, 2015].

Shore, Cris. 2000. *Building Europe: The Cultural Politics of European Integration*. London: Routledge.
———. 2005. "Culture and Corruption in the EU: Reflections of Fraud, Nepotism and Cronyism in the European Commission." In *Corruption: Anthropological Perspectives*, ed. Dieter Haller and Cris Shore, 131–155. London: Pluto Press.
———. 2007. "European Integration in Anthropological Perspective: Studying the 'Culture' of the EU Civil Service." In *Observing Government Elites: Up Close and Personal*, ed. R.A.W. Rhodes, Paul't Hart, and Mirko Noordegraaf, 180–206. Houndmills, Basingstoke, Hampshire: Palgrave Macmillan.
Singer, Peter. 1991. "Introduction." In *A Companion to Ethics*, ed. Peter Singer, v–vii. Cambridge, MA: Blackwell Publishers.
Six, Frédérique. 2013. 'Trust in Regulatory Relations'. *Public Management Review* 15 (2): 163–85. doi:10.1080/14719037.2012.727461.
Six, Frédérique, and Alan Lawton. 2013. "Towards a Theory of Integrity Systems: A Configurational Approach." *International Review of Administrative Sciences* 79 (4): 639–658.
Smismans, Stijn. 2006. *Civil Society and Legitimate European Governance*. Cheltenham and Northampton: Edward Elgar.
Smith, Robert W. 2003. "Corporate Ethics Officers and Government Ethics Administrators." *Administration & Society* 34 (1): 632–652.
———. 2004. "A Comparison of the Ethics Infrastructure in China and the United States." *Public Integrity* 6 (4): 299–318.
Spence, David. 2006. "The Directorates General and the Services: Structures, Functions and Procedures." In *The European Commission*, ed. David Spence and Geoffrey Edwards, 128–155. 3rd ed. London: John Harper Publishing.
Spence, David, and Anne Stevens. 2006. "Staff and Personnel Policy in the Commission." In *The European Commission*, ed. David Spence and Geoffrey Edwards, 173–208. 3rd ed. London: John Harper Publishing.
Stevens, Anne, and Handley Stevens. 2001. *Brussels Bureaucrats?: The Administration of the European Union*. New York: Palgrave.
Stewart, Debra W., and Norman A. Sprinthall. 1991. "Strengthening Ethical Judgment in Public Administration." In *Ethical Frontiers in Public Management*, ed. J.S. Bowman, 243–260. San Francisco, CA: Jossey-Bass.
———. 1993. "The Impact of Demographic, Professional and Organizational Variables and Domain on the Moral Reasoning of Public Administrators." In *Ethics and Public Administration*, ed. H. George Frederickson, 205–219. Armonk, NY: M.E. Sharpe.
Stewart, Debra W., Norman A. Sprinthall, and Jackie D. Kern. 2002. "Moral Reasoning in the Context of Reform: A Study of Russian Officials." *Public Administration Review* 62 (3): 282–297.
Stewart, Debra W., Norman A. Sprinthall, and Renata Siemienska. 1997. "Ethical Reasoning in a Time of Revolution: A Study of Local Officials in Poland." *Public Administration Review* 57 (5): 445–453.
Suvarierol, Semin. 2008. "Beyond the Myth of Nationality: Analysing Networks Within the European Commission." *West European Politics* 31 (4): 701–724.
Suvarierol, Semin, Madalina Busuioc, and Martijn Groenleer. 2013. "Working for Europe? Socialization in the European Commission and Agencies of the European Union." *Public Administration* 91 (4): 908–927.
Tenbrunsel, Ann E., and Kristin Smith-Crowe. 2008. "Ethical Decision Making: Where We've Been and Where We're Going." *The Academy of Management Annals* 2 (1): 545–607.

Tenbrunsel, Ann E., Kristin Smith-Crowe, and Elizabeth E. Umphress. 2003. "Building Houses on Rocks: The Role of the Ethical Infrastructure in Organizations." *Social Justice Research* 16 (3): 285–307.

Thomson, Robert. 2008. "National Actors in International Organizations: The Case of the European Commission." *Comparative Political Studies* 41 (2) (February 1): 169–192.

TNS Opinion & Social. 2014. 'Special Eurobarometer 397 — Corruption.' European Commission, Directorate-General for Home Affairs. Available at: http://ec.europa.eu/public_opinion/index_en.htm [Accessed October 14, 2015].

Transparency International (TI). 2015a. 'What Is Transparency International?' Available at: www.transparency.org/about/ [Accessed October 14, 2015].

———. 2015b. 'What Is Corruption?' Available at: www.transparency.org/what-is-corruption#define [Accessed October 14, 2015].

Transparency International EU Office (TI-EU). 2014. *The European Union Integrity System*. Brussels. Available at: www.transparencyinternational.eu/wp-content/uploads/2014/04/EU_Integrity_System_Report.pdf [Accessed October 14, 2015].

Treviño, Linda K. 1986. "Ethical Decision Making in Organizations: A Person-Situation Interactionist Model." *Academy of Management Review* 11 (3): 601–617.

Treviño, Linda K., Laura Pincus Hartman, and Michael Brown. 2000. "Moral Person and Moral Manager: How Executives Develop a Reputation for Ethical Leadership." *California Management Review* 42 (4): 128–142.

Treviño, Linda K., and Gary R. Weaver. 2003. *Managing Ethics in Business Organizations: Social Scientific Perspectives*. Stanford: Stanford University Press.

Treviño, Linda K., Gary R. Weaver, and Scott J. Reynolds. 2006. "Behavioural Ethics in Organizations: A Review." *Journal of Management* 32 (6): 951–990.

Trondal, Jarle. 2006. "Governing at the Frontier of the European Commission: The Case of Seconded National Officials." *West European Politics* 29 (1): 147–160.

———. 2007. "The Public Administration Turn in Integration Research." *Journal of European Public Policy* 14 (6): 960–972.

Trondal, Jarle, Martin Marcussen, Torbjorn Larsson, and Frode Veggeland. 2010. *Unpacking International Organizations: The Dynamics of Compound Bureaucracies*. Manchester, NY: Manchester University Press.

Trondal, Jarle, and B. Guy Peters. 2013. "The Rise of the European Administrative Space: Lessons Learned." *Journal of European Public Policy* 20 (2): 295–307.

Trondal, Jarle, Caspar Van Den Berg, and Semin Suvarierol. 2008. "The Compound Machinery of Government: The Case of Seconded Officials in the European Commission." *Governance* 21 (2): 253–274.

Van Buitenen, Paul. 2000. *Blowing the Whistle: Fraud in the European Commission*. London: Politicos Publishing.

Van de Walle, Steven. 2008. "Perceptions of Corruption as Distrust? Cause and Effect in Attitudes toward Government." In *Ethics and Integrity of Governance: Perspectives Across Frontiers*, ed. Leo W.J.C. Huberts, Jeroen Maesschalck, and Carole L. Jurkiewicz, 215–237. Cheltenham and Northampton: Edward Elgar.

Van de Walle, Steven, and Geert Bouckaert. 2007. "Perceptions of Productivity and Performance in Europe and the United States." *International Journal of Public Administration* 30 (11): 1123–1140.

van Montfort, André, Laura Beck, and Anneke Twijnstra. 2013. "Can Integrity Be Taught in Public Organizations?" *Public Integrity* 15 (2): 117–132.

Van Wart, Montgomery. 2003. "Codes of Ethics as Living Documents: The Case of the American Society for Public Administration." *Public Integrity* 5 (4): 331–346.

Vassalos, Yiorgos. 2010. "Expert Groups – Letting the Corporate Interests Set the Agenda?" In *Bursting the Brussels Bubble: The Battle to Expose Corporate Lobbying at the Heart of the EU*, 76–86. Brussels: Alliance for Lobbying Transparency and Ethics Regulation (ALTER-EU). Available at: www.alter-eu.org/sites/default/files/documents/bursting-the-brussels-bubble.pdf [Accessed August 20, 2012].

Victor, Bart, and John B. Cullen. 1987. "A Theory and Measure of Ethical Climate in Organizations." In *Corporate Social Performance and Policy*, ed. William. C. Frederick, 51–71. Greenwich, CT: JAI Press.

———. 1988. "The Organizational Bases of Ethical Work Climates." *Administrative Science Quarterly* 33 (1): 101–125.

Wallace, William. 1983. 'Less Than a Federation. More Than a Regime: The Community as a Political System'. In *Policy-Making in the European Community*, edited by Helen Wallace and William Wallace, 2nd ed., 403–436. Chicester: John Wiley & Sons.

Wark, Gillian R., and Dennis L. Krebs. 2000. "The Construction of Moral Dilemmas in Everyday Life." *Journal of Moral Education* 29 (1): 5–21.

Weaver, Gary R., and Linda Klebe Treviño. 1999. "Compliance and Value-Oriented Ethics Programs: Influences on Employees' Attitudes and Behaviour." *Business Ethics Quarterly* 9 (2): 315–335.

Weaver, Gary R., Linda Klebe Treviño, and Bradley Agle. 2005. "'Somebody I Look Up To:': Ethical Role Models in Organizations." *Organizational Dynamics* 34 (4): 313–330.

Weiss, Robert S. 1994. *Learning from Strangers: The Art and Method of Qualitative Interview Studies*. New York: The Free Press.

West, Jonathan P., and Evan M. Berman. 2003. "Audit Committees and Accountability in Local Government: A National Survey." *International Journal of Public Administration* 26: 329–362.

———. 2004. "Ethics Training in U.S. Cities: Content, Pedagogy, and Impact." *Public Integrity* 6 (3): 189–206.

Wille, Anchrit. 2007. "Senior Officials in a Reforming European Commission: Transforming the Top?" In *Management Reforms in International Organizations*, ed. Michael W. Bauer and Christoph Knill, 37–50. Baden: Nomos.

———. 2013. *The Normalization of the European Commission: Politics and Bureaucracy in the EU Executive*. Oxford: Oxford University Press.

Williamson, David. 1991. Redcliffe-Maud Memorial Lecture, 10 October 1991.

Wittmer, Dennis P. 2001. "Ethical Decision-Making." In *Handbook of Administrative Ethics*, ed. Terry L. Cooper, 481–508. 2nd ed. New York and Basel: Marcel Dekker.

———. 2005. "Developing a Behavioural Model for Ethical Decision Making in Organizations: Conceptual and Empirical Research." In *Ethics in Public Management*, ed. George H. Frederickson and Richard K. Ghere, 49–69. Armonk, NY: M.E. Sharpe.

Wonka, Arndt. 2008. "Decision-Making Dynamics in the European Commission: Partisan, National or Sectoral?" *Journal of European Public Policy* 15 (8): 1145–1163.

Yin, Robert K. 2003. *Case Study Research: Design and Methods*. 3rd ed. Thousand Oaks, CA: Sage Publications.

Zey-Ferrell, Mary, and O.C. Ferrell. 1982. "Role-Set Configuration and Opportunity as Predictors of Unethical Behaviour in Organizations." *Human Relations* 35 (7): 587–604.

Index

Page numbers in italic format indicate figures and tables.

administrative ethics 8, 13, 125
Alliance for Lobbying Transparency and Ethics Regulation (ALTER-EU) 54, 76, 139
anti-corruption activists 52, 58, 59, 76
anti-trust issues 107, 109
Appointing Authority (AA) 42, 46, 48, 69
audit systems 2, 44, 59

Barroso Commission 1, 48, 53, 138
Brussels sphere 52, 77
Budgetary Control Committee 56, 73

Charlie McCreevy case 53
circumspection, ethical standards and 18
civil society organizations 54, 139, 140
"clash of cultures" issue 29, 30
code of conduct: in DG COMP 65; ethics infrastructure and 23–4; for interest representatives 44, 76; introduction to 4; Parliament's role in 56; revision of 43
Code of Good Administrative Behaviour 16, 43, 57, 59, 74
College of Commissioners 136, 137
Committee of Independent Experts (CIE) 1, 52
commonalities and divergence, public ethics and 100–11
common line issues 10, 15, 27, 80, 100
competence, ethical standards and 18
compliance-integrity continuum 39–41, 50–1, 60, 131
conflicts of interests *21*, 49, 69–71, 88, 141
convergence towards public image 10, 110, 113, 128
corruption, worldwide 3–5
corruption scandals 2, 4, 10, 131, 135

decision making process 18–20, 40, 99, 110
democratic legitimacy 2, 8, 137, 140–1
dignity of the service, ethical standards and 18
Directorate General for Competition (DG COMP): codes of conduct in 65; conclusion about 128; dialogue with stakeholders and 106; functions of 33; introduction to 28, 32; investigative prerogatives of 107–8; providing guidance to staff of 63; regulatory framework of 108–9
Directorate-General for Trade (DG TRADE) 53–4, 74–6
Directorate-Generals (DGs) 32, *33*, 36
discretion and confidentiality, ethical standards and 17
divergence: commonalities and 100–1; nationality issues 102–5; organizational position and 105–10; possible factors for 102; *see also* public ethics

Edith Cresson case 52
employment contracts 30, 31, 34, 102
ethical behaviour: conclusion about 126, 128; ethical dilemmas and 18, 20; introduction to 1, 6; as a learned behaviour 23; nationality issues 102
ethical decision-making 19, 20, 40
ethical dilemmas: public ethics and 18–20; talking about 118–23; types of 67–9; vignettes related to 83–100
ethical leadership 24, 46, 123
ethical reasoning 20, 80, 82, 83, 113
ethics: as common sense 115–18, 122–3, 133–4; conclusion about 110–11;

discussion on 118–22, 135; "hot spots" 67–77, 82; individual positions on 83–100; interpretation of 64; "low road" and "high road" 40–1, 59–60, 66, 131–2; as a political liability 55–9; scandals related to 52–5; views towards 85–8, 91–2, 94–9, 116–17, 127–8; on the work floor 100–10; *see also* internal communication

Ethics Communication: agenda set by 59; awareness activities by 121, 122; conclusion about 134–5; delivery of change and 49–59; electronic approval system and 46, 48; elements of 45–6; ethics correspondents and 46–9; Ethics Website and 46, 48; outcomes of 57, 62; as a reform package 45

ethics correspondents 40, 46–9, 51, 64, 71–3

Ethics Day 45, 47, 48, 50

ethics infrastructure/system: code of conduct and 23–4; concept of 22, 125; defined 20; introduction to 5, 7, 9; "more values, no more rules" agenda 46, 58; organizational socialization and 22, 26; purpose of 20; rule-based 42–4; trust-based 44–7

ethics management: compliance-integrity continuum and 40–1, 50–1, 60, 131; corruption worldwide and 3–5; defined 5; development of 41–9; diversification of 51; hard-line approach to 10, 44, 58, 78, 130, 131; impact of 122–4; introduction to 39–40; limits of 129–34; in public organizations 20–2; research approach 11–13; *see also* public ethics

ethics policies/reforms: conclusion about 59–60, 129, 130, 140–1; democratic legitimacy and 2, 8, 137, 140–1; ethics training and 50; European Commission after 134–7; European institutions and 44, 48, 49; gifts and hospitality policy and 46, 48, 51; influence of 115, 121, 128; introduction to 2; limited usefulness of 115; as a part of transformation process 8; *see also Ethics Communication*

ethics training and education: by ethics correspondents 64; ethics policy and 50; events dedicated to 115, 116; highlight of 65

EU budget 1, 27, *33*, 54

European Anti-Fraud Office (OLAF) 43, 53, 65, 66, 72

European civil service: ethics management in 41–9; structure of 28–9; tenure issues 30, 31; *see also* public ethics

European Commission: administrative levels of 6, 24–5; after ethics reforms 134–7; bad publicity about 52; budgetary matters for 56; control and trust mechanisms in 132; Directorate-Generals of 32, *33*, 36; functions of 27–8; gaining access to 34–5; as a guardian of treaties 27, 30; introduction to 1; loyalty to 97, 99, 100, 110, 130; multinational staff 10; organizational positions within 105–10; policy development by 27–8; prestige of working for 29; public image of 63–7, 113, 114, 127; structure of 28–9; whistleblowing issues 73; *see also* ethical dilemmas; internal communication

European Commission officials: categories of 28–9; common line issues 10, 15, 27, 80, 100; employment contract of 30, 31; ethical judgement issues 105; ethics guidelines for 75; "gray" gift situation for 19; motivation issues 31, 101, 120, 122, 135; nationality issues 11, 12, 29–32, 34, 36; organizational position of 30; organizational socialization and 26–35; professional background 31; recruitment of 34–6; risk avoidance by 101, 104; sample of 32–4; selection of 29–32; *see also* ethical dilemmas; ethics; vignettes

European Commission services: compliance-integrity continuum and 40–1; ethical standards in 17–18; ethics management in 41–9; post-employment issues in 54

European institutions: ethics reforms and 44, 48, 49; introduction to 7, 8, 9; policy initiatives and 27

European integration 2, 13, 15, 25, 27

European Ombudsman 54–5, 76, 137, 141

European Parliament: amendments by 58; budgetary matters for 56; conclusion about 130, 136–7; ethics scandals and 53, 55; Juncker Commission and 139–40; Santer resignation as a victory for 55–6; whistleblowing issues and 56–7

European Transparency Initiative (ETI) 1, 44–5, 47, 54, 59, 76

Eurostat affair 52–3

financial management 27, 43, 44, 58, 136

Index

freedom of expression: exercise of 86; limits of 69–71; vs. organizational loyalty 83, 84, 88; positions on *85*
Fritz-Harald Wenig case 53, 75–6

gifts and hospitality policy: ethics reforms and 46, 48, 51; guidelines for 75, 77; vignettes related to 93–100, 114–15
Guidelines on Whistleblowing 57, 72–3, 134
Gunther Verheugen case 53

human resources management 42, 43, 48, 59

independence, ethical standards and 17
individual freedom of expression *see* freedom of expression
integrity, ethical standards and 17
integrity instruments 9, *21*, 44
interest representatives *see* lobbyists
Intergroup on Integrity, Transparency, Corruption and Organized Crime 139, 141
internal communication: about post-employment issues 70; conclusion about 77–8, 127; ethics in 63–77; features in 66–7; introduction to 62–3
internal decision-making 99, 110
Investigation and Disciplinary Office (IDOC) 43, 65–6, 71–2
investigative journalism 51, 52, 54, 77

John Dalli case 53
Juncker Commission 2, 137–40

Kallas packages 44–9, 63, 126
Kinnock reforms: conclusion about 126; introduction to 1, 2, 7, 8; rule-based ethics system 42–4

lawfulness, ethical standards and 17
leaders as ethical role models 24, 46, 123
lobbyists: concern for influence exerted by 54; dealing with 58, 75; disclosing information to 97, *98*, 106; positions on meeting *95*; undercover journalists posing as 53; vignettes related to 93–100
loyalty, ethical standards and 17

Marta Andreasen case 73–4
Member States: introduction to 3, 7, 9; national culture hypothesis and 104; policy implementation in 27–8
money management *see* financial management

nationality issues: conclusion about 128; divergence and 102–5; officials-related 11, 12, 29–32, 34, 36; strict/flexible positions and *103*, 104, 110
non-governmental organizations (NGOs) 54–5, 72, 76, 137

objectivity and impartiality, ethical standards and 17
official communication 113–15, 123
organizational integrity 5, 20, 125
organizational loyalty 83, 84, 88, 100, 101
organizational position: conclusion about 126, 128, 132; divergence and 105–10; of officials 30
organizational socialization: as acquiring role knowledge 25–6; Commission's officials and 26–35; conclusion about 125–6; defined 11, 26; learning sources related to 22–6, 123
Organization for Economic Co-operation and Development (OECD) 3, 9–10, 20–2, 40–1
outside activities 18, 48, 69–71, 77

Paul van Buitenen case 73–4
post-employment issues 3, *21*, 54, 56, 70
Practical Guide on Staff Ethics and Conduct 63, 64, 74
private interests 53, 54, 74–7
Prodi Commission 1, 54, 59
professional background of officials 31, 32, 34, 36, 126
public appearances 70, 71, 86, 114
public ethics: commonalities and divergence and 100–11; conclusion about 141; defined 15; ethical dilemmas and 18–20; framework for addressing 15–16, 18–22; individual positions on 83–100; introduction to 7; parameters of 16, 35, 125; *see also* ethics
public officials *see* European Commission officials
public organizations 3, 9, 20–2
public scandals 2, 60, 130, 135, 141
public scrutiny 17, 52–5, 60, 132
"public service motivation" (PSM) 31
Public Service Principles for the EU Civil Service 16, 57, 64

respect and courtesy, ethical standards and 18
responsibility, ethical standards and 18

"revolving door" phenomenon 53, 54, 58, 70, 84
rules-based ethics system 40, 42–4

Santer Commission 1, 10, 42, 73
Santer resignation 7, 52, 55, 130, 135
social learning 11, 22, 36, 66, 125
social media 48, 71
Staff Regulations: amendments to 1; Article 17 of 70, 75, 94; revision of 47, 49; Title 2 of 42; whistleblowing provisions in 72
Statement of Principles of Professional Ethics 46, 63

Transparency International (TI) 5, 30, 54, 136, 139
Transparency Register 74, 76, 138–9
trust-based ethics system 44–7

unethical behaviour 15, 19

value internalization 26
values-based approach 10, 40, 131, 132, 135

vignettes: challenges of 81; commonalities and divergence and 100–1; general observations on 81; introduction to 80; officials within the organization 88–93, 106; organization and individual 83–8; organization and outside world 93–100, 114–15; purpose of 81; stages of 84, 89, 93–4, 97; strict/flexible positions related to *103*, 104, 110; use of 82–3

watchdog groups *see* anti-corruption activists; non-governmental organizations (NGOs)
whistleblowers/whistleblowing: cases related to 73–4; Commission's experience with 73; description of 72; guidelines for 57, 72–3, 134; policy framework for 43; positions on *90*; protection of 56, 57, 72, 127; public image and 114; vignettes related to 88–91, 106
work floor: on the ethics 100–10, 128; views from 113–15
wrongdoing: IDOC and 65–6; observing and reporting 3, 20; vignettes related to 88–91, 93